W9-BUO-184

Robyn Montana Turner, Ph.D.
Program Author

Sara A. Chapman, M.Ed.
Contributing Author

James M. Clarke, M.Ed.
Contributing Author

Editorial Offices: Glenview, Illinois • Parsippany, New Jersey • New York, New York

Sales Offices: Boston, Massachusetts • Duluth, Georgia • Glenview, Illinois • Coppell, Texas • Sacramento, California • Mesa, Arizona

ISBN: 0-328-08036-5
California ISBN: 0-328-26015-0

7 8 9 10 V063 09 08 07 06

Program *Consultants*

Christopher Adejumo, Ph.D.
Associate Professor
Visual Art Studies
University of Texas
Austin, Texas

Doug Blandy, Ph.D.
Professor and Director
Arts and Administration Program
Institute for Community Arts and Studies
University of Oregon
Eugene, Oregon

Rebecca Brooks, Ph.D.
Professor
Department of Art and Art History
University of Texas
Austin, Texas

Georgia Collins, Ph.D.
Professor Emeritus
College of Fine Arts
University of Kentucky
Lexington, Kentucky

Deborah Cooper, M.Ed.
Coordinating Director of Arts Education
Curriculum and Instruction
Charlotte-Mecklenburg Schools
Charlotte, North Carolina

Sandra M. Epps, Ph.D.
Multicultural Art Education Consultant
New York, New York

Mary Jo Gardere
Multi-Arts Specialist
Eladio Martinez Learning Center
Dallas, Texas

Carlos G. Gómez, M.F.A.
Professor of Fine Art
University of Texas at Brownsville and Texas Southmost College
Brownsville, Texas

Kristina Lamour, M.F.A.
Assistant Professor
The Art Institute of Boston at Lesley University
Boston, Massachusetts

Melinda M. Mayer, Ph.D.
Assistant Professor
School of Visual Arts
University of North Texas
Denton, Texas

Reviewers

Studio Reviewers

Judy Abbott, *Art Educator*
Allison Elementary School
Austin Independent School District
Austin, Texas

Lin Altman, *Art Educator*
Cedar Creek Elementary School
Eanes Independent School District
Austin, Texas

Geral T. Butler, *Art Educator (Retired)*
Heritage High School
Lynchburg City Schools
Lynchburg, Virginia

Dale Case, *Elementary Principal*
Fox Meadow Elementary School
Nettleton School District
Jonesboro, Arkansas

Deborah McLouth, *Art Educator*
Zavala Elementary School
Austin Independent School District
Austin, Texas

Patricia Newman, *Art Educator*
Saint Francis Xavier School
Archdiocese of Chicago
La Grange, Illinois

Nancy Sass, *Art Educator*
Cambridge Elementary School
Alamo Heights Independent School District
San Antonio, Texas

Sue Spiva Telle, *Art Educator*
Woodridge Elementary School
Alamo Heights Independent School District
San Antonio, Texas

Cari Washburn, *Art Educator*
Great Oaks Elementary School
Round Rock Independent School District
Round Rock, Texas

Critic Readers

Celeste Anderson
Roosevelt Elementary School
Nampa, Idaho

Mary Jo Birkholz
Wilson Elementary School
Janesville, Wisconsin

Mary Jane Cahalan
Mitzi Bond Elementary School
El Paso, Texas

Cindy Collar
Cloverleaf Elementary School
Cartersville, Georgia

Yvonne Days
St. Louis Public Schools
St. Louis, Missouri

Shirley Dickey
Creative Art Magnet School
Houston, Texas

Ray Durkee
Charlotte Performing Arts Center
Punta Gorda, Florida

Sue Flores-Minick
Bryker Woods Elementary
Austin, Texas

Denise Jennings
Fulton County Schools
Atlanta, Georgia

Alicia Lewis
Stevens Elementary School
Houston, Texas

James Miller
Margo Elementary School
Weslaco, Texas

Marta Olson
Seattle Public Schools
Seattle, Washington

Judy Preble
Florence Avenue School
Irvington, New Jersey

Tonya Roberson
Oleson Elementary School
Houston, Texas

Andrew Southwick
Edgewood Independent School District
San Antonio, Texas

Nita Ulaszek
Audelia Creek Elementary School
Dallas, Texas

Tessie Varthas
Office of Creative and Public Art
Philadelphia, Pennsylvania

Penelope Venola
Spurgeon Intermediate School
Santa Ana, California

Elizabeth Willett
Art Specialist
Fort Worth, Texas

Contents

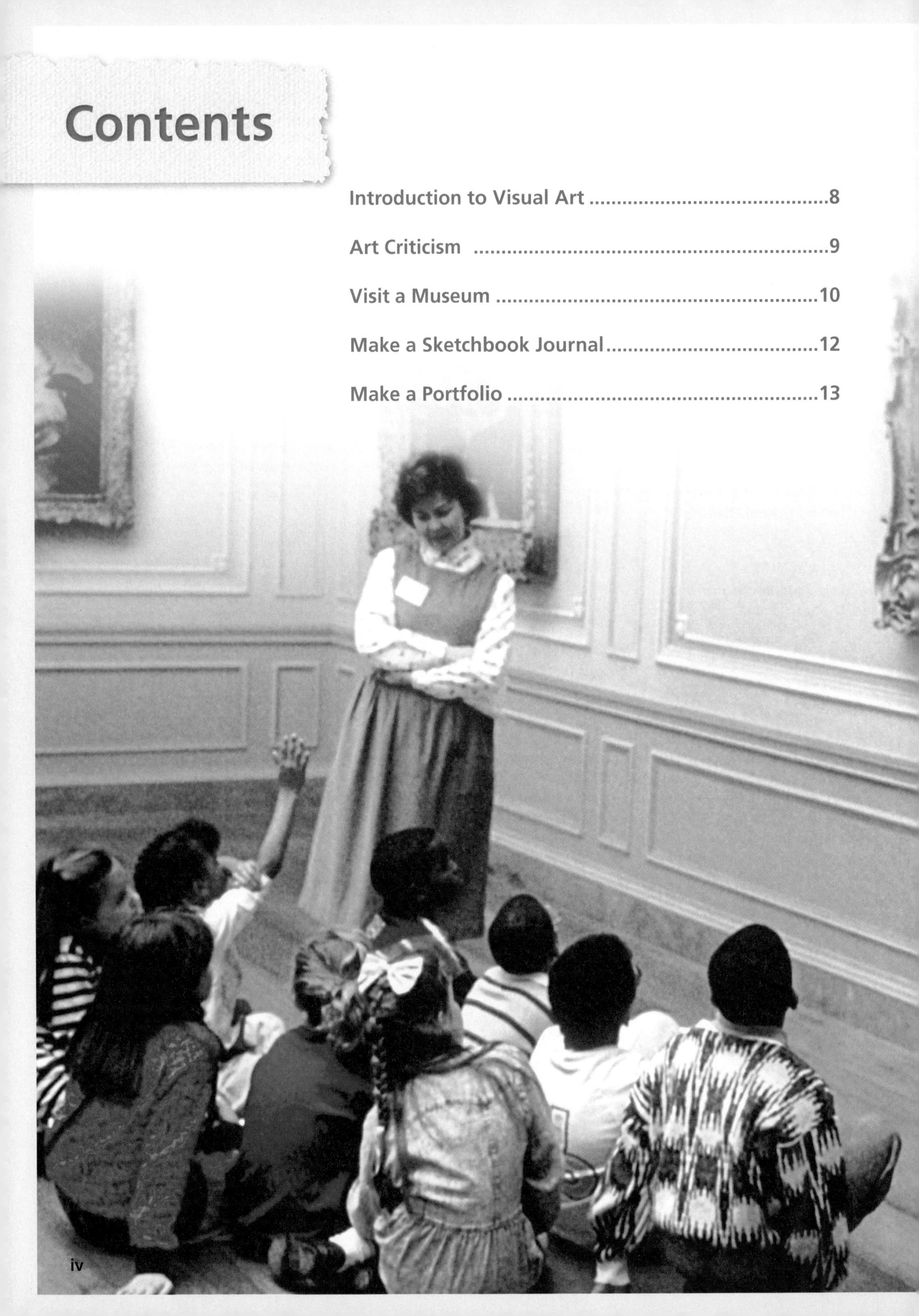

Unit 1

The Elements of Art 14

Dale Chihuly. *Isola di San Giacomo in Palude Chandelier,* 1996.

Artist unknown, Greek. *Krater,* ca. 750–700 B.C.

Unit 2

The Principles of Design..................64

Henri Matisse. *Self-Portrait,* 1900.

Artist unknown, Tolima culture.
Pectoral, ca. A.D. 600–800.

Unit 3

Media and Methods 106

David Hockney. *Stephen Spender, Mas St. Jerome II,* 1985.

Artist unknown, Nkanu culture. *Figure (drummer),* date unknown.

Unit 4

A World of Art and Artists............160

Architect unknown. *The so-called Castle, the pyramid of the Tulum ceremonial center, and the surrounding temples,* 12th–15th century.

Unit 5

Subjects and Styles 214

Georges Braque. *The Table,* 1928.

David Strickland. *Case Alien,* 1991.

Unit 6

Expression and Meaning 264

Harri Koskinen, designer.
Block Lamp, 1996.

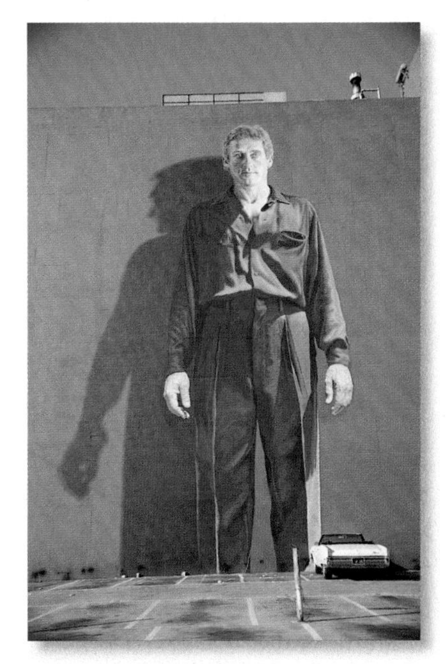

Kent Twitchell. *Edward Ruscha Monument,* 1978–1987.

John Yancey. *East Austin Mural,* 2003.

Introduction to Visual Art

Suppose someone asked you to define visual art. Many people throughout time have offered various definitions. As you read this book, jot down some notes to help shape your own meaning of visual art. Here are some ideas to get you started.

Visual art is a way to express ideas, thoughts, and feelings, using a variety of materials. Paintings, sculptures, huge bridges, and landmark buildings are all ways in which artists express themselves visually.

Some images are designed to convey a specific message. You see, read, and bring meaning to such items in your visual culture every day. Decorated T-shirts, posters, cereal boxes, logos, signs and symbols are only part of your **visual culture.**

Observing these and other objects in your environment will help you discover, understand, and appreciate visual art. Your observations may also inspire your own works of art!

Antonio Gaudí, architect. *Church of the Sagrada Familia,* 1882–1926. Barcelona, Spain

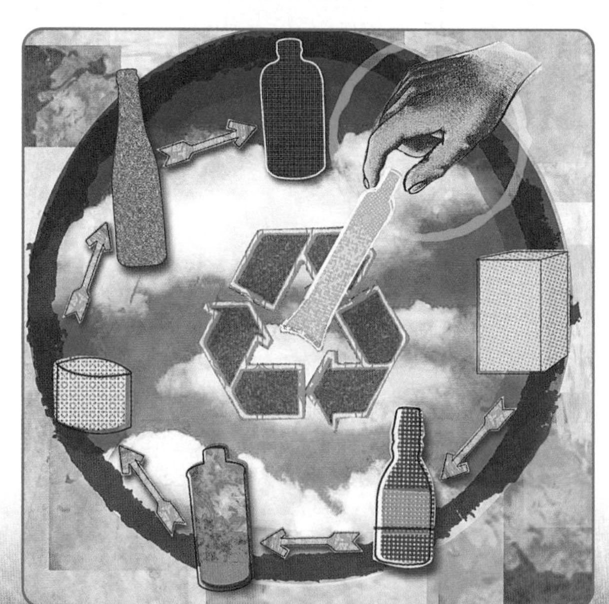

Art Criticism

Viewing and understanding your own or someone else's artwork is an exercise in problem solving. In this book you are asked to look at artworks with a careful eye. Four steps, known as an **art criticism** process, help you think carefully about the artworks.

Examine the artwork on this page as you read about the four levels of art criticism and answer the questions.

Describe asks you to research information about the artist and observe the artwork carefully.

- What was happening in the artist's life when the artwork was created?
- What is happening in the artwork?
- Name some types of lines and shapes you see in it.

Glenna Goodacre. *Vietnam Women's Memorial,* 1993. Bronze cast, height 92 inches. National Mall, Washington, D.C.

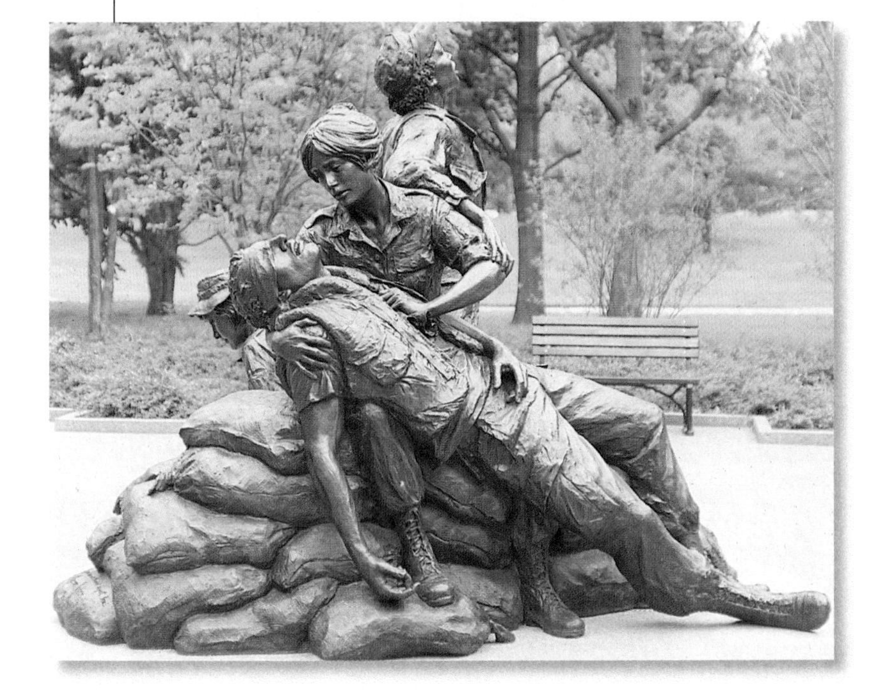

Analyze is a problem-solving process. The puzzle in this step is to figure out how the lines, shapes, and other parts of the artwork work together.

- Point to repeated shapes.
- Which shapes do you notice first?
- How is this artwork balanced?

Interpret is the way you use information to help you figure out what the artist intended.

- What mood does the sculpture show?
- Tell about what the artist was saying.
- What symbols do you see, and what do they mean?

Judge is your opportunity to decide if you think the artwork is a success. Your judgment is based on your discoveries in the first three steps.

- What are its qualities?
- Where in your community would you place this sculpture?
- How would you change it?

Visit a Museum

Art museums are buildings designed to protect and exhibit artworks. Art museums exhibit many types of artworks from many cultures. They serve as a resource that helps people learn about different art styles throughout art history. Observing these artworks gives visitors an opportunity to share each artist's experience.

The structures and grounds of some art museums are themselves works of art. The Getty Museum in Los Angeles, California, is perched high on a bluff overlooking the Pacific Ocean. It exhibits artworks from ancient and modern cultures. The National Gallery of Art in Washington, D.C., features a six-acre outdoor sculpture garden as part of its collection.

The National Gallery of Art began its collection in 1937 with gifts from art collector Andrew W. Mellon.

Artists throughout the history of art have used different materials to express their thoughts and ideas. Art museums provide an opportunity for you to observe these artistic expressions and respond to them in your own way.

The Getty Museum and its grounds are themselves spectacular works of art.

There are many different careers at an art museum. Some employees work behind the scenes to design and set up exhibits, take care of the artwork, and provide research and education. Most museum workers are employed by the museum. Others volunteer their time.

A **docent** greets museum visitors and guides them through the museum's exhibits. Her or his job is to provide information and answer questions about the artworks, artists, and the museum.

A **curator** selects the artworks for an exhibition and decides where they should be displayed. Curators may travel the world looking for artworks to acquire for a museum's permanent collection. They also borrow artworks from other museums' collections to create temporary exhibitions. These traveling exhibits add interest and variety to the museum's permanent collection of artworks.

A **conservator** studies ways to protect artworks from damage. Conservators work to clean, preserve, and protect artworks so that future generations can enjoy them.

Museum Etiquette

When visiting an art museum, remember to:

- **Obey all posted signs.**
- **Talk softly so that you do not disturb others. Loud voices carry in museum galleries.**
- **Never touch an artwork. Stay at least an arm's length away from artwork.**
- **Do not walk in front of someone who is viewing an artwork.**
- **Do not bring food or drink near the artworks.**
- **Do not take photographs. Flash photography can damage works of art.**
- **Do not carry backpacks or book bags. Bulky objects can swing and bump into works of art.**

Make a Sketchbook Journal

Artists fill the blank pages of their sketchbooks with pictures and words that reflect their observations, ideas, and experiences. It is the place where artists experiment, make changes, and practice techniques. It is also the perfect place to take notes and plan art projects.

Follow these steps to make your own Sketchbook Journal.

Materials

- ✓ cardboard (two 10" × 13" sheets)
- ✓ construction paper
- ✓ drawing paper (9" × 12" sheets)
- ✓ fabric (two 12" × 15" pieces)
- ✓ hammer and nail ⚠S
- ✓ scissors, tape, glue ⚠S
- ✓ raffia, yarn, or twine

1 **Use scissors to score one of the pieces of cardboard one inch from the left edge to make a front cover that will fold.**

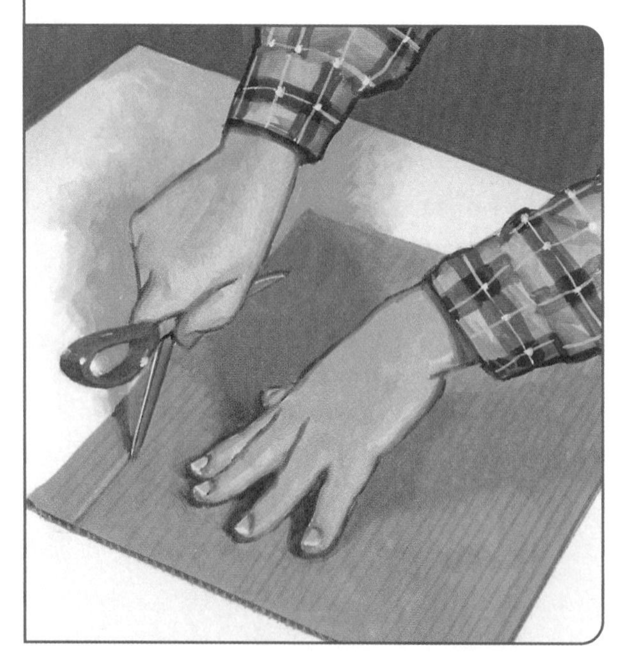

2 **Cut two pieces of fabric one inch larger than your cardboard. Pull the fabric tight and wrap it around the cardboard. Tape the edges to the backside. Glue construction paper over the taped edges to cover them.**

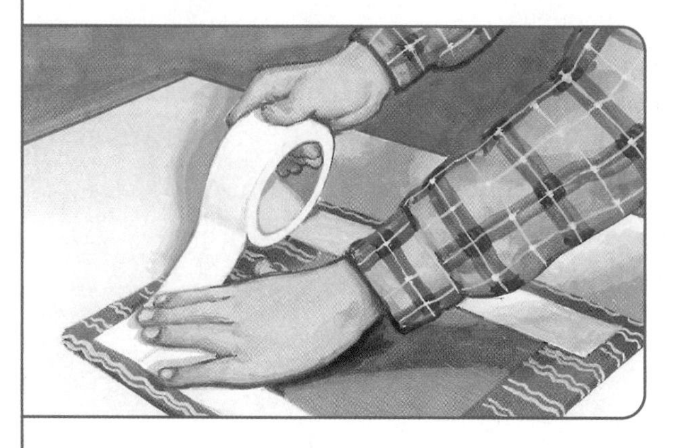

3 **Use a hammer and nail to punch holes in a zigzag pattern along the spine of the sketchbook. Use your cover as a guide to punch holes through a stack of drawing paper.**

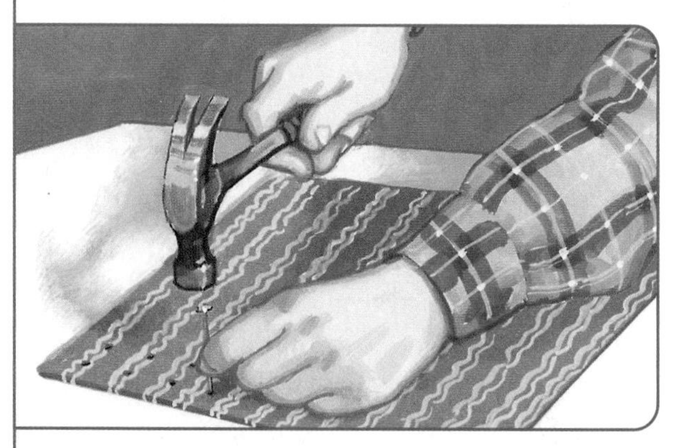

4 **Weave raffia, yarn, or twine through holes to bind the pages and cover together.**

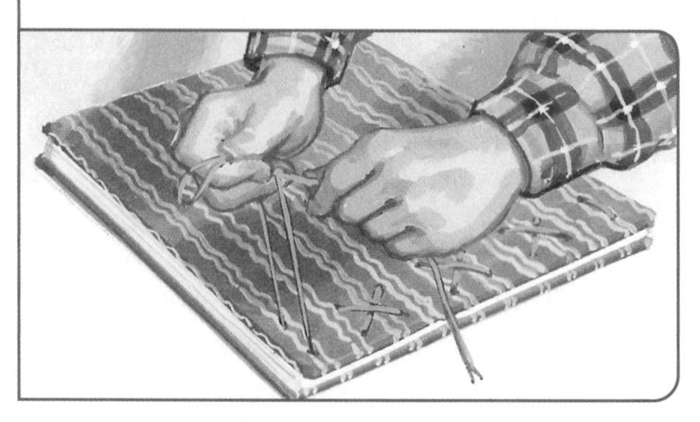

Make a Portfolio

Many artists keep their artworks in a portfolio. This allows them to protect and transport the artworks. A portfolio also allows artists to review and critique their artistic progress and techniques.

Follow these steps to make your own portfolio.

Materials

- ✓ posterboard
- ✓ tape
- ✓ scissors ⚠
- ✓ yarn or twine
- ✓ stapler
- ✓ markers or oil pastels

1 **Staple or tape two sheets of posterboard along three sides.**

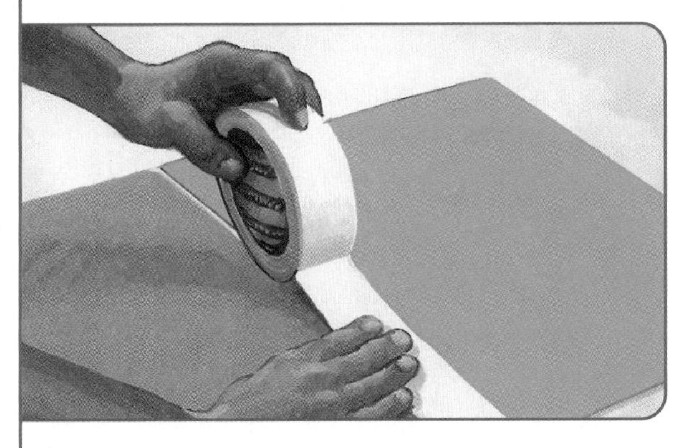

2 **Cut a six-inch piece of posterboard the width of the open side. Tape the piece to the back of the open side, fold over the top, and crease it to create a flap.**

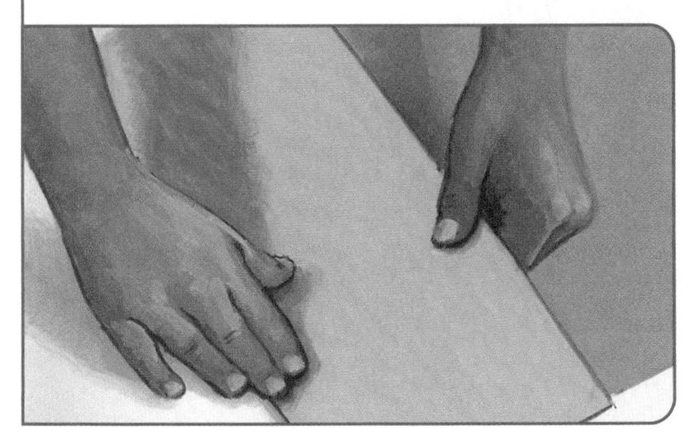

3 **Staple a five-inch piece of yarn or twine to the flap as a wraparound tie closure.**

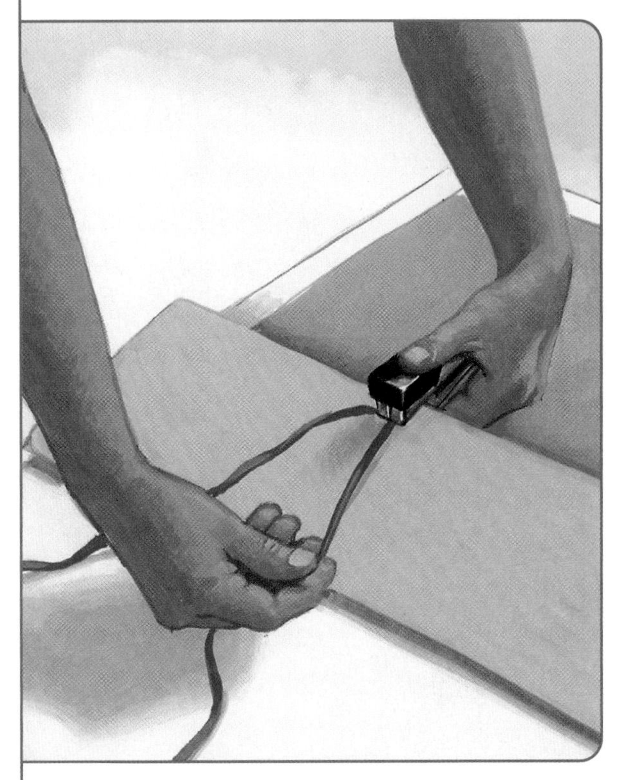

4 **Design your portfolio using markers, oil pastels, or a collage technique. Use your imagination! Remember to write your name on your portfolio.**

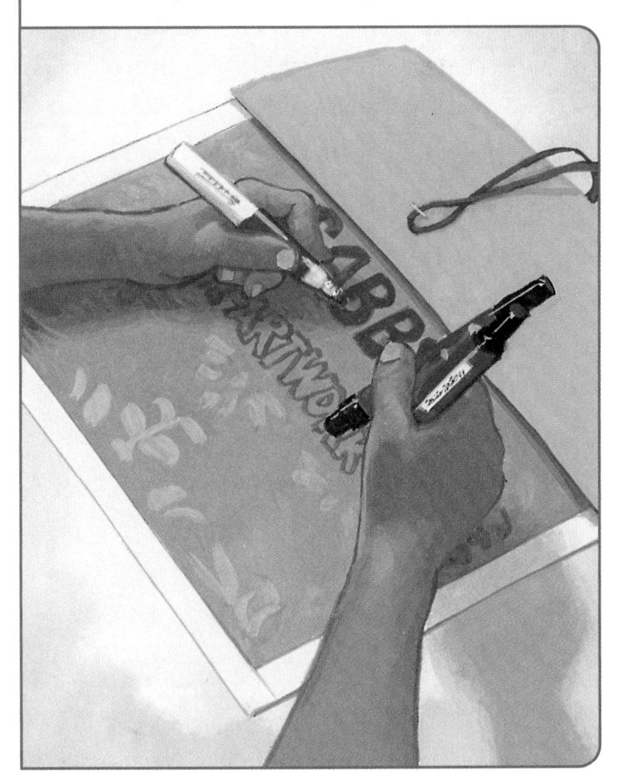

Vincent van Gogh. (Detail) *Enclosed Field with Rising Sun*, 1889. Oil on canvas, 27 2/3 by 35 1/3 inches. Private collection.

Unit 1

The Elements of Art

Artworks are all around you. You may see them as designs in nature, such as a ripple in a puddle or stripes on a zebra. They can also be created by people, as in an artist's design, known as a composition. Artists plan their artworks to help them communicate their ideas and feelings.

The composition on the opposite page shows how artist Vincent van Gogh (1853–1890) felt about the sun rising over this field. Van Gogh used the **elements of art** — **line**, **shape**, **form**, **space**, **value**, **color**, and **texture** —to create this painting. Artists use these elements of art the way writers use words. They are the building blocks used to construct ideas and convey feelings in artworks.

This unit will help you discover how artists throughout time have used the elements of art. You will also learn to use them to express your own thoughts, feelings, and imagination.

About *the Artist*

Van Gogh painted this vibrant sunrise while living in southern France. Read more about Van Gogh and his style on page 36. Discover his early artworks by visiting the Van Gogh Museum at http://www.vangoghmuseum.nl/.

Vincent van Gogh. *Self-Portrait with Straw Hat,* 1887.

Lesson 1

Line

A **line** is the path of a point moving through space. You can make a line in the dirt with a stick, or on a canvas with a brush. Artists use different types of lines to convey different information. While creating an artwork, artists pay close attention to **line quality** —the special character of any line. Lines can be thick or thin, smooth or rough, continuous or broken.

Types of Lines

Vertical lines run up and down, like a flagpole or a giant redwood tree. They can appear strong and powerful.

Horizontal lines run from side to side, like the horizon where the ocean meets the sky. They often appear peaceful and calm.

Diagonal lines slant, as though they are leaning. They suggest movement and excitement.

Zigzag lines are slanted lines that move in different directions and come together at sharp angles. They can show confusion or excitement.

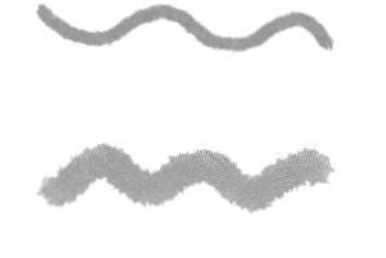

Curved lines change direction without sharp angles, like a twisting path across a field. They move in a graceful way.

Lines can be found in nature.

What types of lines do you see in this human-made object?

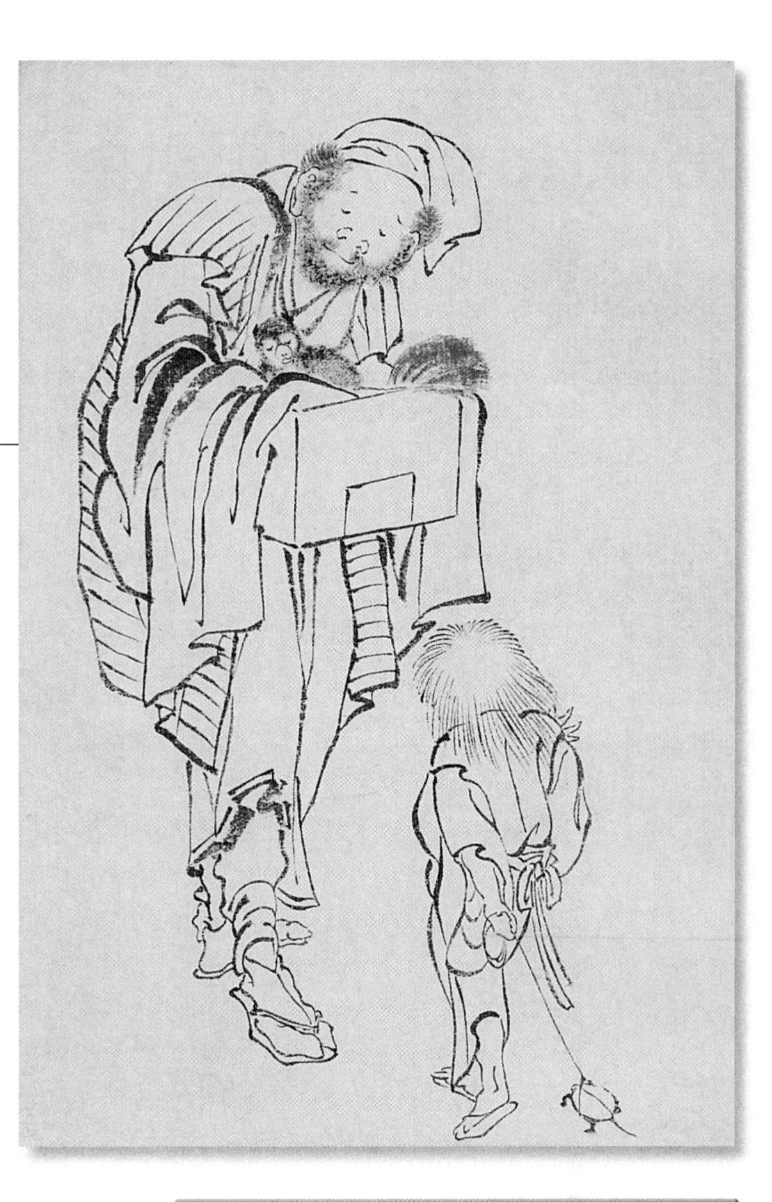

Katsushika Hokusai. *Man and Boy,* Edo period (1658–1868). Ink on paper, 12 11/16 by 8 11/16 inches. Freer Gallery of Art. Courtesy of the Freer Gallery of Art, Smithsonian Institution, Washington, D.C. 04.232.

Lines and Expression

Japanese artist Katsushika Hokusai (1760–1849) used realism, humor, and movement in his scenes from everyday life. This drawing shows an encounter between a man and a young boy. How would you describe the types of lines in this drawing?

The artist used curved lines of various widths to suggest clothing. Hokusai also used the lines of the box and the posture of the child to draw your eye to the monkey. How did the artist use lines to suggest hair or fur?

Sketchbook Journal

Identify different types of lines in your classroom. Divide a page into eight equal spaces to make a Technique Sheet. Draw different types of lines in each space. Experiment with various drawing tools, such as crayons, pens, or markers. Label each line with the type of tool you used.

Studio 1 Setup
Contour *Drawings*

Henri Matisse. *Girl with Gold Necklace*, 1944. Ink on paper, 20 1/4 by 15 1/8 inches. The University of Arizona Museum of Art, Tuscon. Gift of Edward J. Gallagher, Jr. (ACC# 55.7.7).

How did the artist use line quality to reflect the subject?

Artists observe the **contours,** or edges, of an object as they draw. They make contour drawings by slowly moving their drawing tool over the paper as they closely observe the contours of the object.

In this drawing, French artist Henri Matisse (1869–1954) drew the contours of a woman deep in thought. Look for these details:

- Thin, delicate lines show details and bold lines show contrast.
- Curved lines suggest the shape of the woman's necklace and the folds of her clothing.
- The position of the woman's hands and head give the impression that she is at rest and thinking.

Actual and Implied Lines

Most of the lines Matisse used in this drawing are **actual lines,** real lines that can actually be seen. Matisse also used **implied lines,** which are imagined rather than seen. The placement of other lines, shapes, and colors helps you imagine implied lines. Where do you see an implied line in the woman's features?

Technique Tip

One Tool, Many Qualities

The same drawing tool can make lines of many different qualities. Hold the tool lightly to make a faint line. Press the tool firmly to make a heavy line. Use the point or the edge of the tool to make a thin line. Tip the tool to one side to make a thicker line.

Studio 1

Create a Contour Drawing

Use what you have learned about lines to make a contour drawing.

Materials

- ✓ 12" × 18" white drawing paper
- ✓ masking tape
- ✓ drawing tools, such as pens, markers, crayons, oil pastels, or charcoal
- ✓ an object with interesting lines to draw, such as a shoe, plastic bottle, stapler, or trash can

1 **Tape your drawing paper to your desk. Look at the contours of the object as you practice with your drawing tool in the air.**

2 **Draw all the lines—inside and outside. Keep your eyes on the contours of the object and do not lift your drawing tool from the paper.**

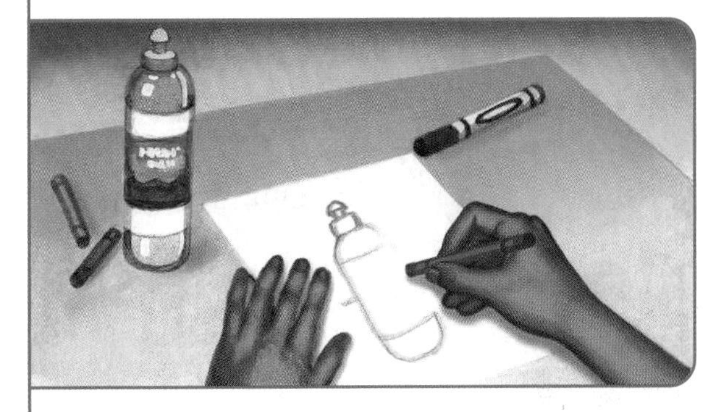

3 **Detach and rotate your drawing paper, and draw a different object with another drawing tool. Repeat and overlap your contour drawings.**

Review and Reflect

- What types of lines did you use? Which qualities do they show?
- How does contour drawing affect the arrangement of your lines?
- What feeling does your drawing convey? How does it convey that feeling?
- What is most effective about your drawing? Explain.

Lesson 2

Shape

How are a tablecloth, a sheet of paper, and the shadow cast by a basketball alike? As an artist, you might say that each one is a shape. A **shape** is a flat, two-dimensional area with height and width. It might have an edge, or an outline, around it. Or you might know it by its area, like the shape of a shadow. Artists think of shape as being a flat area created when actual or implied lines meet to surround a space.

Types of Shapes

Shapes can be either geometric or organic. **Geometric shapes** are precise, mathematical shapes. The basic and most common geometric shapes are the circle, square, and triangle. All other shapes, such as the oval and rectangle, are variations of these basic shapes. Most geometric shapes can be drawn with a ruler.

Organic shapes, also called "free-form," are irregular and uneven. Organic shapes are often found in nature. They form natural curves or zigzags. The shapes of a leaf, a flower, and a cloud are organic.

As you create sketches of shapes, think about the other elements that define them. Are the lines actual or implied? Does color help you see them? Then ask yourself how the shapes—geometric and organic—enhance your composition.

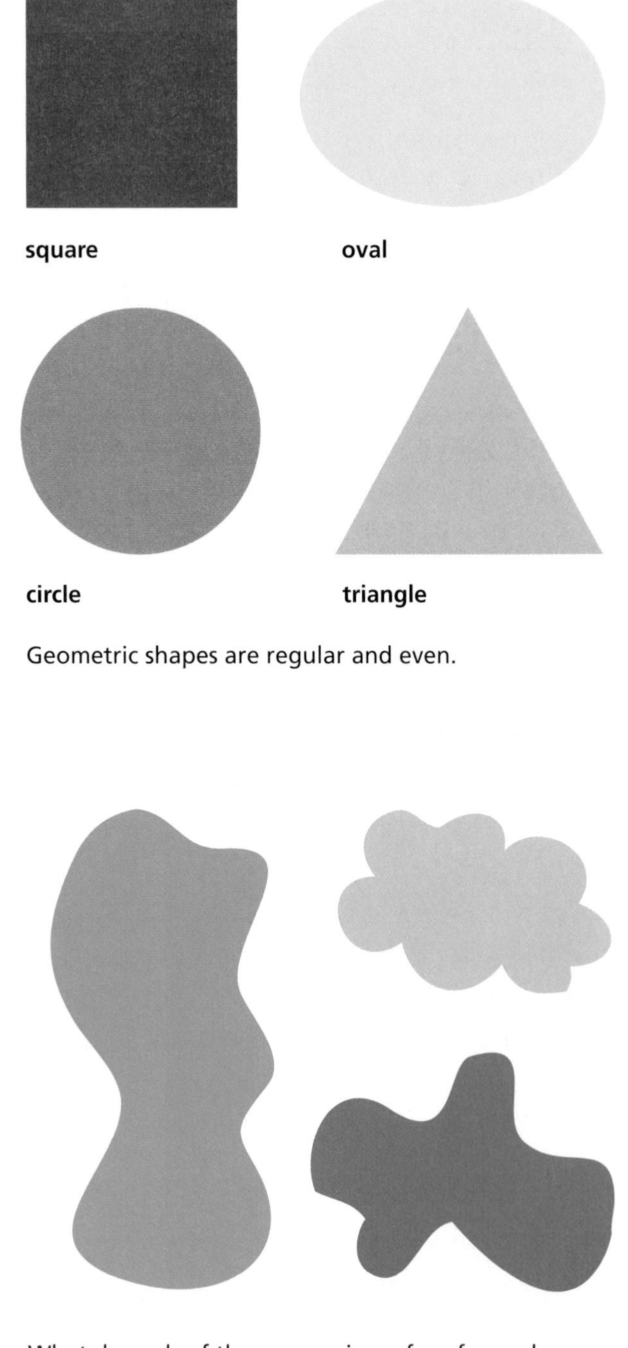

Geometric shapes are regular and even.

What do each of these organic, or free-form, shapes remind you of?

John Storrs. *Genesis,* 1932. Oil on board, 32 by 25 1/8 inches. Courtesy of SBC Communications Inc.

Shapes in a Composition

American-born artist John Bradley Storrs (1885–1956) used a variety of geometric and organic shapes when he composed this artwork. Look at the credit line to the left of the artwork. What does the title *Genesis* tell you?

Now read the credit line to discover the materials Storrs used to create this painting. Notice the types of shapes he used and how they are arranged in the composition. What colors and types of lines did he use? Where have you seen similar shapes?

Sketchbook Journal

Make a viewfinder by cutting a rectangle from a larger piece of paper. Use your viewfinder to frame a variety of shapes around you. In your Sketchbook Journal, make some thumbnail sketches of the shapes. Make notes next to each sketch about why these shapes are interesting to you.

Use a viewfinder to frame a view.

Studio 2 Setup

Shapes *in Places and Events*

Grandma Moses. *Moving Day on the Farm,* 1951. Oil on pressed wood, 17 by 22 inches. © 1951, (renewed 1979) Grandma Moses Properties Co., New York.

Where do you notice organic and geometric shapes in this painting?

Artists use the elements of line and shape to create compositions that show places and events. What event did Grandma Moses capture in this painting, using line and shape? Notice how she used actual and implied lines to show the scene. Use your viewfinder to see a **detail,** or small part of the artwork. Look for these features:

- Geometric shapes are used to show human-made objects, such as wheels, wagons, buildings, and boxes.
- Organic shapes reflect features of nature, such as the hills, lake, trees, and animals.
- Colorful shapes make the scene appear lively and energetic.

Shapes and Movement

Grandma Moses used a variety of shapes and lines to show movement. The shape of the cows shows that they are walking. How does the shape of each person give you clues about their activities?

Technique Tip

Arrangement

The effect of your design depends on its arrangement. Before you glue the shapes into place, notice how the shapes fill your composition. Try rearranging shapes for a more pleasing effect. Once you are satisfied with the overall design, glue your shapes into place.

Studio 2

Create with Shapes

Use what you have learned about shapes to compose a scene about a place that is important to you.

Materials

- ✓ 12" × 18" white drawing paper
- ✓ colored construction paper
- ✓ wallpaper samples
- ✓ scissors ⚠S
- ✓ glue or gluestick

1 **Make a sketch of your important place on the 12" by 18" paper. Include only the basic lines and shapes, without details.**

2 **Cut shapes from the paper and wallpaper samples. Choose colors and patterns that express your feelings about the scene.**

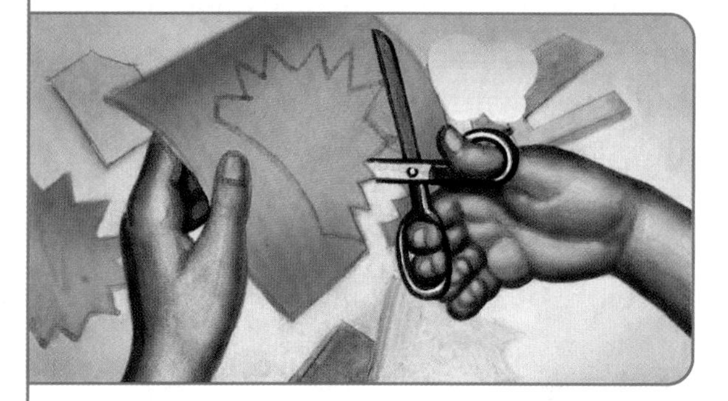

3 **Arrange the shapes on the 12" × 18" paper. Trim or move the shapes and add others until you are satisfied with the results. Glue your shapes into place.**

Review and Reflect

- What geometric and organic shapes did you use in your artwork?
- How would your artwork be different if you removed all of the organic shapes?
- What feelings about your important place did you want to convey?
- How well does your artwork convey your feelings about your place? Explain.

Lesson 3

Form

A **form** is an object with three dimensions: height, width, and depth. A basketball is a form. Like a flat circle, it has height and width, but it also has depth. Some forms, like a basketball, are empty. Other forms, like a rock, are full. To fully understand a form, you can examine it from the front, sides, and back. Sometimes you can even examine the interior of a form, as you might explore the inside of a building.

Types of Forms

Basic **geometric forms** are the sphere, cube, and pyramid. Their contours resemble a circle, square, and triangle, respectively. All other geometric forms, such as the cylinder and cone, are variations of these basic forms. Skyscrapers, barrels, and hot-air balloons are geometric forms. Notice some geometric forms around you.

Like organic shapes, **organic forms** have irregular and uneven edges. They are often found in nature, and are sometimes called "free-forms." Unlike organic shapes, however, organic forms also have depth. Apples, trees, and animals are organic forms. Find some organic forms in this sculpture and on page 25.

Dale Chihuly. *Isola di San Giacomo in Palude Chandelier,* 1996. Blown-glass, 9 by 7 feet. Venice, Italy. © Chihuly Studio. Photo by Russell Johnson.

What geometric and organic forms do you see in this sculpture?

Isabel De Obaldía. *Sebastian's Beast,* 1997. Kiln cast glass, 6 3/4 by 17 by 6 inches. Courtesy of Mary-Anne Martin/Fine Art, New York.

Explore a Form

American–born artist Isabel De Obaldía (1957–) made this three-dimensional form out of glass. She does not strive for decorative and detailed effects in her glass forms. Notice how she used a simple form and a single color to emphasize the power and force of this "beast."

Would you describe the form of De Obaldía's sculpture as organic or geometric? How does this form compare to the sculpture by Dale Chihuly (1941–) on the previous page?

Sketchbook Journal

Identify several geometric and organic forms around you. Use modeling clay to make a model of each form. Make a contour drawing of each clay model in your Sketchbook Journal. Make notes about the relationship between your contour drawings and your clay models.

Studio 3 Setup
Forms *in Clay*

The parts of a form—height, width, and depth—can be viewed in artworks such as pottery. In this ceramic vase, the artist created form by using a variation of two basic shapes: a cylinder and an oval. Look for these details:

- The upper portion of the vase is an oval with an opening at the top.
- The lower portion of the vase is a cylinder that widens slightly toward the bottom.

What forms do you see in this vase?

Artist unknown, Greek. *Krater,* ca. 750–700 B.C. Terracotta, height 42 5/8 inches. Geometric, attributed to the Hirshfeld Workshop. Side A. The Metropolitan Museum of Art, New York.

Greek Forms

This vase was made during the Geometric period of ancient Greek art. This period began about 900 B.C. Vases in the geometric style show painted horizontal bands. The bands usually cover the entire surface of the vase and are divided by rows of lines. The areas between the lines are filled with shapes.

Vases like this one were often used as grave markers for wealthy citizens. What clues tell you that this vase was created during the Geometric period? Artists of this period often included shapes of people and animals in their vase designs. What might these figures represent? Think of ways that you can use shapes and lines in the forms you make.

Technique Tip

A Light Touch

Prepare several coils of clay so they are ready to use when needed. Make a coil, or rope, of clay by rolling the clay back and forth between your palms and a work surface covered by a piece of canvas cloth. Start rolling in the middle, then move out to the edges to make the coil even in thickness. Keep rolling until the coil is the desired size.

Studio 3

Create Clay Forms

Use what you have learned about forms to design a coiled clay pot.

Materials

- ✓ potter's clay (to be fired by teacher)
- ✓ canvas cloth
- ✓ clean foam meat tray
- ✓ scoring tool
- ✓ clay slip

1 **In the center of your tray, flatten a ball of clay to form a slab for the base. Score the edges of the base.**

2 **Make a coil of clay and score the edge of the coil. Apply slip to the scored areas of the base and coil. Wind the coil onto the base to begin making a form.**

3 **Stack additional coils to create a clay form. Score and apply slip each time before you press them into place.**

Review and Reflect

- What geometric and organic forms did you use in the design of your clay pot?
- How did you arrange the forms to create an overall design?
- What is the mood or feeling of your clay pot design?
- Would you make any changes to the form of your pot? Explain.

Lesson 4

Space

Space means many things to many people. To a writer, it refers to the blank area between words on a page. To an astronomer, it means the vast universe that surrounds Earth. To an artist, **space** means the area in and around an object. In the language of art, space can describe empty or full areas, areas that are far away or nearby, and areas that are huge or small.

Artists show two kinds of space, positive and negative. **Positive space** is the area occupied by an object. The area around the object, which defines the object's edges, is called **negative space.** The form of your body, for example, is positive space. The empty area around you is negative space.

In the two-dimensional illustration below, the black triangle is the positive space. The white background around the triangle is the negative space.

Find the positive and negative spaces in this blanket.

Artist unknown, Navajo, Arizona. *Blanket: The American Flag,* ca. 1960. Tapestry-woven wool, 30 1/8 by 31 1/4 inches. From the Girard Foundation Collection, in the Museum of International Folk Art, a unit of the Museum of New Mexico, Santa Fe, NM.

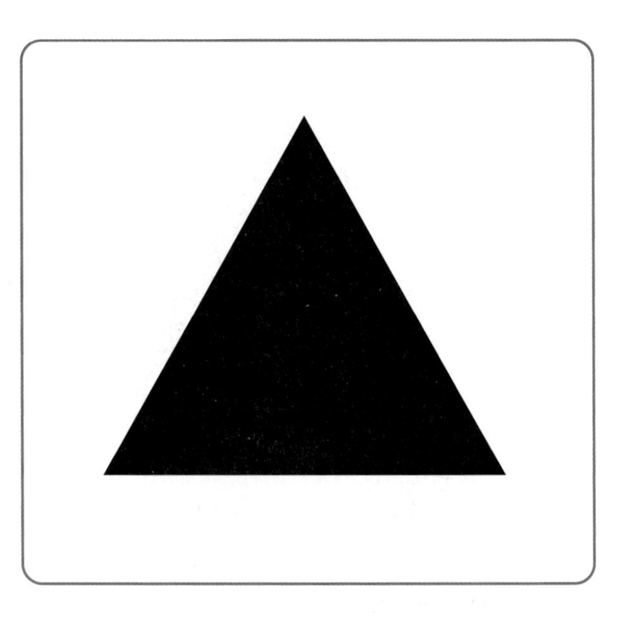

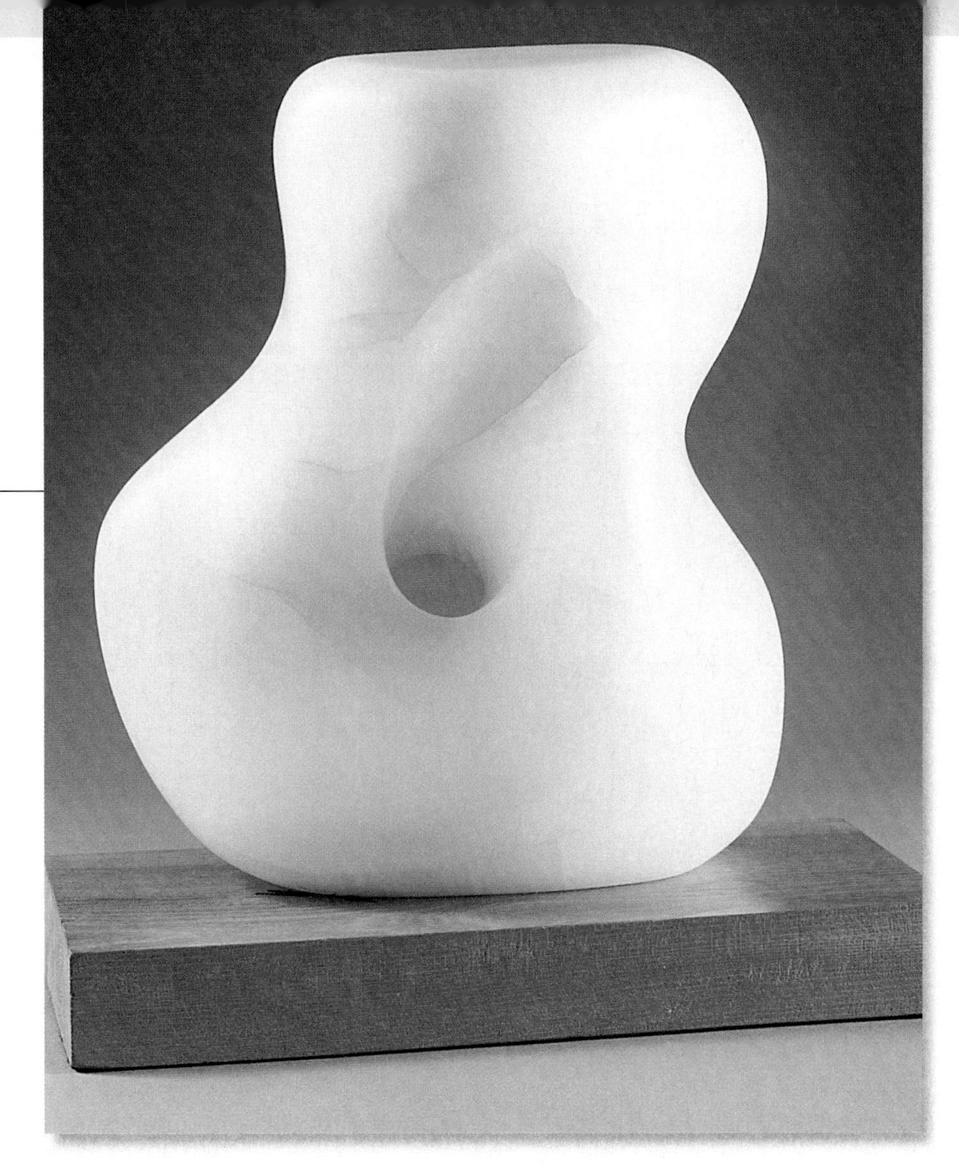

Barbara Hepworth.
Merryn, 1962. Alabaster, 13 by 11 1/2 by 8 1/4 inches. The National Museum of Women in the Arts. Gift of Wallace and Wilhelmina Holladay.

Space Creates Interest

In this Barbara Hepworth (1903–1975) sculpture, the carved stone itself is the positive space. Notice how the artist created negative space by placing a hole in the center of the sculpture.

Hepworth often uses holes in her sculptures to draw the viewer's interest. What form is this sculpture? How would you describe the positive and negative space in this artwork?

Imagine moving around Hepworth's three-dimensional sculpture. Think about how the sculpture would look when viewed from different angles.

Sketchbook Journal

Divide a Sketchbook Journal page into eight equal spaces to create a Technique Sheet. In each box, draw a variety of simple objects, such as cups, jugs, or bottles. Label the positive space by shading it gray and the negative space by leaving it white. Record any notes you might have about space.

Studio 4 Setup
Shapes *in Space*

Joan Miró. *Painting,* 1933. Oil on canvas, 68 1/2 by 77 1/4 inches. The Museum of Modern Art, NY.

What forms the negative space in the painting?

Spanish artist Joan Miró (1893–1983) experimented with positive and negative space to add interest to his playful works of art. Notice these details in Miró's *Painting* above:

- A variety of organic shapes provides the positive space, while the multicolored background is the negative space.
- Some of the shapes are full or solid, but other shapes are empty and show only the contour of a shape. They appear empty because the background colors are visible in their centers.

Background Space

When talking about two-dimensional art, people usually refer to the artwork's background as negative space. In Miró's painting, the background surrounding the full or solid shapes creates the negative space. Empty shapes that allow you to see the background are also part of the negative space.

Technique Tip

Shapely Shapes

Fold a small piece of paper in half. Cut out a shape, starting and ending at the fold. Unfold both pieces of paper. The shape you cut out is a positive space. The hole left in the sheet of paper is a negative space with the same shape.

Studio 4

Change Space with Shapes

Use what you have learned about positive and negative space to create a paper artwork.

Materials

- ✓ two sheets of different colored paper
- ✓ one sheet of white paper
- ✓ scissors ⚠S
- ✓ glue

1 **Cut a variety of shapes out of the two sheets of colored paper. Cut shapes out of the middle of your shapes.**

2 **Arrange the shapes on the white sheet of paper. Move them or flip them over to experiment with different arrangements.**

3 **When you find an arrangement that pleases you, glue the shapes to the white sheet of paper.**

Review and Reflect

- Where is the negative space in your artwork? Where is the positive space?
- Describe the relationships between the shapes and spaces in your artwork.
- What do your shapes and spaces remind you of?
- Which part of your artwork is the most interesting? Why?

Lesson 5

Space and Distance

Artists use a variety of techniques to create the illusion of deep space, or depth, in a two-dimensional artwork. A painting may be on a flat canvas, yet it seems as though some objects are close and others are far away. To create this illusion of depth, artists show close objects larger with clearer details. Close objects sometimes cover the objects behind them. Objects in the distance are smaller and less detailed, even fuzzy.

African-American artist Dr. John Biggers (1924–2001) made full use of the techniques that create the illusion of depth in his painting *25th Precinct, 3rd Ward.* Look at the painting by John Biggers to identify the following techniques:

- Biggers made the people in the **foreground** appear closer to the viewer by painting them larger and placing them toward the bottom of the artwork.
- Biggers made the houses in the **background** appear farther away by making them smaller and placing them toward the top of the artwork.
- Some of the houses are smaller than those in front, yet larger than those in the background. These houses are in the **middle ground,** between the foreground and background.
- To enhance the illusion of depth, Biggers painted nearer objects **overlapping** those that are farther away.

Dr. John Biggers. *25th Precinct, 3rd Ward, Houston,* 1984. Mixed media, 42 by 50 inches. Photograph courtesy of Earlie Hudnall.

The figures in the foreground overlap the houses in the background.

How does this illustration show space and distance?

Pierre-Auguste Renoir. *Le Moulin de la Galette,* 1876. Oil on canvas, 68 by 51 inches. Musée d'Orsay, Paris.

Perspective and Size

French Impressionist Pierre-Auguste Renoir (1841–1919) used color, light, and softened detail in this painting. Impressionist artists used variations of light and color to draw or paint their views of everyday life. They often showed outdoor scenes like this one. Notice how the artist used position and size to give the viewer a sense of space and distance. The people and objects in the foreground appear larger, closer to the viewer, and have more detail. What did the artist include in the middle ground? How did he show that some objects are in the background?

Artists usually apply more than one technique for showing space. How might you show space and distance?

Sketchbook Journal

Divide a Sketchbook Journal page into four equal spaces to create a Technique Sheet. In each space, sketch a variety of objects with some in the foreground, some in the background, and some in the middle ground. Use details, size, and overlapping to create the illusion of depth.

Studio 5 Setup

Perspective *Drawings*

Artists use **linear perspective** to create depth by positioning lines so they meet at a point in the distance, eye-level to the viewer. In *A Game of Hand Sumo in the New Yoshiwara,* notice how lines of linear perspective create depth:

Furuyama Moromasa. *A Game of Hand Sumo in the New Yoshiwara,* ca. 1740. Woodblock print, 13 by 18 1/2 inches. The Metropolitan Museum of Art, Frederick C. Hewitt Fund, 1911. (JP655)

The artist of this print used the techniques of perspective to show space and distance.

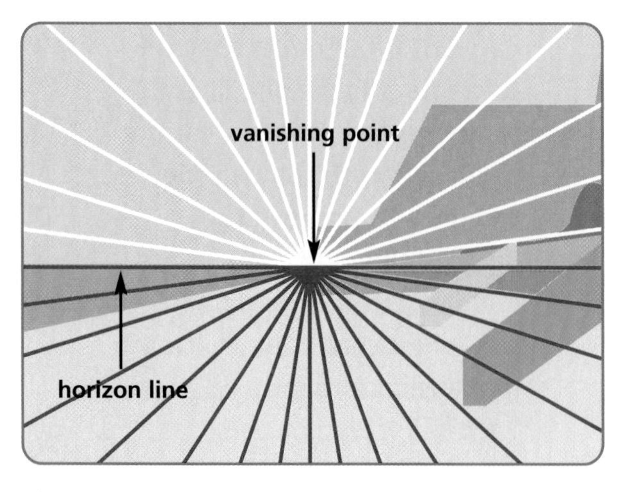

This diagram shows how lines create linear perspective.

- The diagram shows a **horizon line** where earth and sky meet. In Moromasa's print, the horizon line is behind the back wall. Notice how the lines of the ceiling and floor get closer together as they near the horizon line.
- The guidelines set a place on the horizon line as a **vanishing point** where all the lines of perspective come together or converge. Notice how the pillars and side walls appear shorter and narrower as they move back toward the vanishing point.

Atmospheric Perspective

Atmospheric perspective can create the illusion of air and space. In this technique, the artist uses soft colors and large portions of white to show faraway objects and air. Close-up objects are brighter, have darker colors, and show more details, as in Renoir's painting on page 33.

Technique Tip

Setting Lines of Perspective

With a ruler, draw a horizon line across a sheet of drawing paper. Mark a vanishing point on the horizon line. Draw diagonal lines from the paper's four corners to the vanishing point. In a drawing of a hallway, the diagonal lines below the horizon line are where the floor meets the walls. The diagonal lines above the horizon line are where the walls meet the ceiling.

Studio 5

Draw with Perspective

Use what you have learned about perspective to draw a school hallway.

Materials

- ✓ 9" × 12" white drawing paper
- ✓ pencil
- ✓ ruler
- ✓ drawing board
- ✓ colored pencils

1 **Stand in a hallway and observe where the ceiling, floor, and walls meet to form lines of perspective.**

2 **Use linear perspective to draw the hallway on white drawing paper with a pencil and ruler.**

3 **Use colored pencils to draw a geometric form three times. Decrease the size of the forms to create depth.**

Review and Reflect

- How did you create the illusion of depth in your drawing?
- Explain how linear perspective helped you arrange the lines in your drawing.
- How would you explain the meaning of the illusion of depth to a friend who is younger than you?
- Do you like using perspective techniques? Explain.

Meet *the Artist*

Vincent van Gogh

Vincent van Gogh hoped to be a successful artist, but he died desperately poor and virtually unknown. Of his more than eight hundred paintings and seven hundred drawings, only one sold during his lifetime. Only after his death did people appreciate his style of painting. In 1990, Van Gogh's *Portrait of Dr. Gachet* sold at a world record price for an artwork at that time—$82.5 million!

Vincent van Gogh. *Self-Portrait with Straw Hat.* Paris. Summer 1887. Oil on canvas, 15 3/4 by 12 2/3 inches. F469, JH 1310. Amsterdam, Rijksmuseum Vincent van Gogh, Vincent van Gogh Foundation.

Van Gogh painted at least twenty self-portraits, experimenting with style and color.

". . . There are certain pictures I have painted that will be liked one day." —VINCENT VAN GOGH

The Early Years

"How can I be useful, of what service can I be? There is something inside me, what can it be?" These words by Vincent van Gogh reflect his early struggle to find what he wanted to do in life. At age sixteen, Van Gogh went to work for an art dealer. But he wanted to serve people, so he became a minister for a short while before deciding to dedicate himself to his work as an artist.

A Style of His Own

Van Gogh moved to Paris in 1886. Influenced by Impressionist artists, he began painting with vivid colors and bold brushstrokes. In 1888, he moved to Arles where he completed more than 200 paintings. One of these, *The Red Vineyard,* was his only painting sold during his lifetime. Van Gogh suffered a series of mental breakdowns while in Arles, which led to his cutting off his left earlobe. He admitted himself to a mental hospital where he continued using heavy brushstrokes in an impasto style. **Impasto** painting is using paint that is thick, leaving texture that can be seen and touched when the paint is dry. In June of 1890, he painted *Portrait of Dr. Gachet.* Van Gogh died one month later with his brother, Theo, at his side.

Talk About It

- **Van Gogh once wrote, "I dream my painting, and then I paint my dream." How is this reflected in his artworks?**
- **What effect do you think moving to Paris had on Van Gogh's artwork?**

The Life of Van Gogh

1850

1853 Vincent van Gogh born March 30 in Zundert, Netherlands

1860

Camille Pissarro

1870

1874 Pissarro and other French artists develop the Impressionist style of painting

1876 Van Gogh becomes a preacher

1880 Van Gogh becomes an artist by profession

1880

1885 Van Gogh completes *The Potato Eaters*

1886 Van Gogh moves to Paris and studies Impressionism

asylum at Saint-Rémy, France

1889 Van Gogh admits himself to an asylum where he paints *Starry Night*

1890 Van Gogh paints *Portrait of Dr. Gachet;* Van Gogh dies near Paris

1890

Look *and Compare*

An Artist's Style

Many artists develop their own special style. Vincent van Gogh painted *Road Menders at Saint-Rémy* while he lived in France. This painting is a good example of the Dutch artist's style of painting. Notice how he used heavy strokes of paint to convey a certain mood. The vertical lines and heavy, gnarled shapes of the trees give a sense of power to the painting.

Art and Culture

Artworks hold many clues about the culture in which they are created if the viewer looks closely at the people and objects portrayed. By knowing when an artwork was made, the viewer can get a sense of what life was like at that time. Look at the credit line for Van Gogh's *Road Menders at Saint-Rémy* to find out when it was painted. Now look at the people and the objects in the painting. What do they tell you about France at that time? Consider how this scene is different from what you might see in France today.

Look at the elements of art Van Gogh used. What effect does line have in this painting? What time of year do you think it is? Explain.

A Different Point of View

Look at the credit line beneath *The Turning Road, L'Estaque,* by French artist André Derain (1880–1954). How many years after Van Gogh painted *Road Menders at Saint-Rémy* did Derain paint this artwork? Compare the people and objects that you see in Derain's painting with those in Van Gogh's.

Notice Derain's use of the elements of art. How is his style different from that of Van Gogh?

Vincent van Gogh. *Road Menders at Saint-Rémy,* 1889. Oil on canvas, 28 3/4 by 36 1/4 inches. The Phillips Collection, Washington, D.C.

André Derain. *The Turning Road, L'Estaque,* 1906. Oil on canvas, 51 by 76 3/4 inches. The Museum of Fine Arts, Houston, The John A. and Audrey Jones Beck Collection.

Compare & Contrast

- **What elements of art do the two paintings share? What makes them different?**
- **Each artwork shows people in their environments. What similarities and differences do you notice in each artist's depiction of the people?**

Lesson 6

Value

Value refers to the lightness or darkness of a color. With the absence of color, value can be shown in stepped shades of gray. Artists use different values to give flat, two-dimensional shapes a three-dimensional appearance. In this abstract charcoal drawing, American artist Georgia O'Keeffe (1887–1986) used a range of values to create interest and depth. Even though the surface is flat, O'Keeffe's use of value gives the shapes the illusion of being three-dimensional.

Georgia O'Keeffe. *Drawing XIII,* 1915. Charcoal on paper, 24 1/2 by 19 inches. The Metropolitan Museum of Art. Alfred Stieglitz Collection, 1950. (50.236.2).

Techniques for Achieving Value

The illustration shows a value scale, the range of values between white and black. Try matching the different values in this scale with those in O'Keeffe's artwork. Notice how she used almost every value on the scale, including light, medium, and dark, in her drawing.

Abrupt changes in value create **contrast,** the effect showing the difference between light and dark values. Artists use contrast to make darker areas recede and lighter areas project.

To create contrast and gradual changes in light to dark values in an artwork, artists use **shading.** Shading helps make objects and shapes in an artwork appear more three-dimensional by giving them the illusion of depth and form.

A value scale shows the degrees of value between black and white.

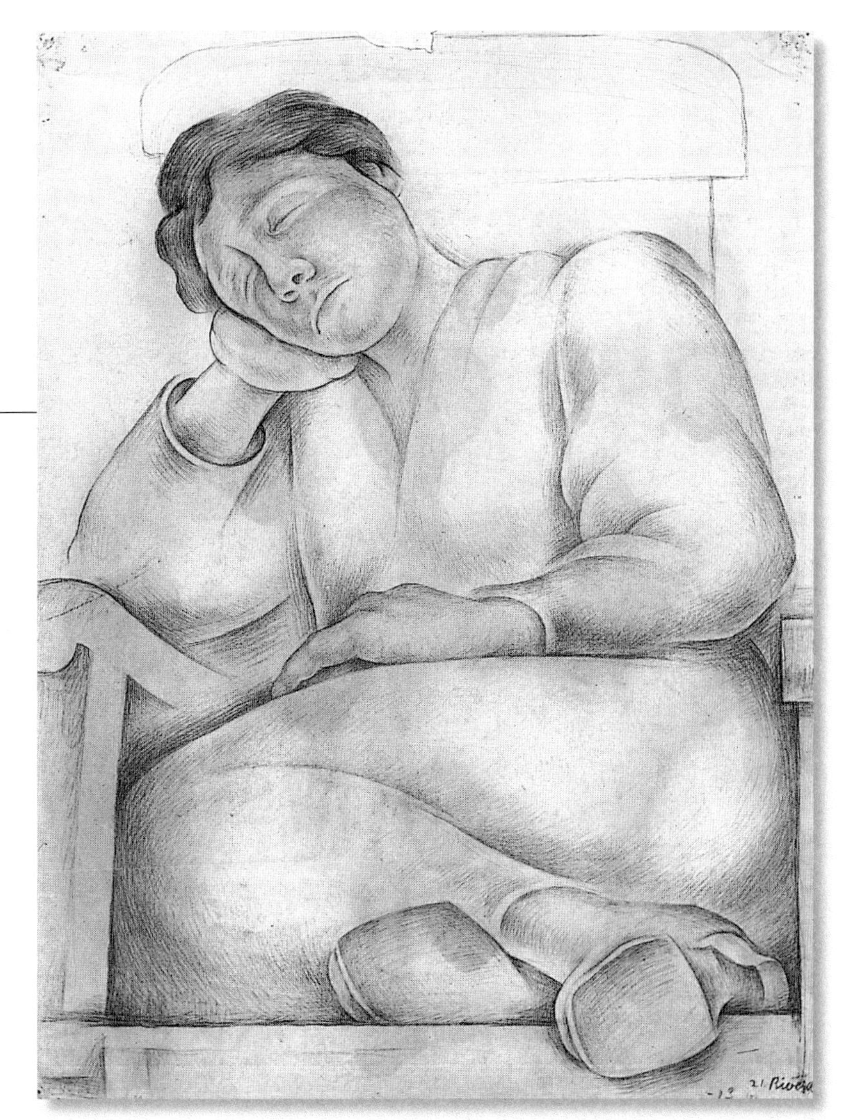

Diego Rivera. *Study of a Sleeping Woman,* 1921. Black crayon on off-white laid paper, 24 1/2 inches by 18 1/3 inches. Courtesy of the Fogg Art Museum, Harvard University.

The soft, subtle values in this drawing add to its mood.

Value and Mood

Artist Diego Rivera (1886–1957) lived and worked in Mexico for most of his life. He created bold, dramatic artworks that reflected the people and culture of Mexico. How did he use value and shading to show contrast in this drawing?

The artist used different values that blend softly with one another to show the woman's form, giving her a three-dimensional appearance. Notice also how Rivera's use of value in the lines, shapes, and spaces help establish the mood or feeling of the drawing. What mood might the artist have intended? Why do you think so?

Sketchbook Journal

Draw a two-inch by four-inch rectangle in your Sketchbook Journal. Divide the rectangle into eight equal spaces. Use these spaces to create a value scale that shows gradual shading. Leave the first space white and show a gradual increase in shading. The last space will be black.

Studio 6 Setup

Value *Drawings*

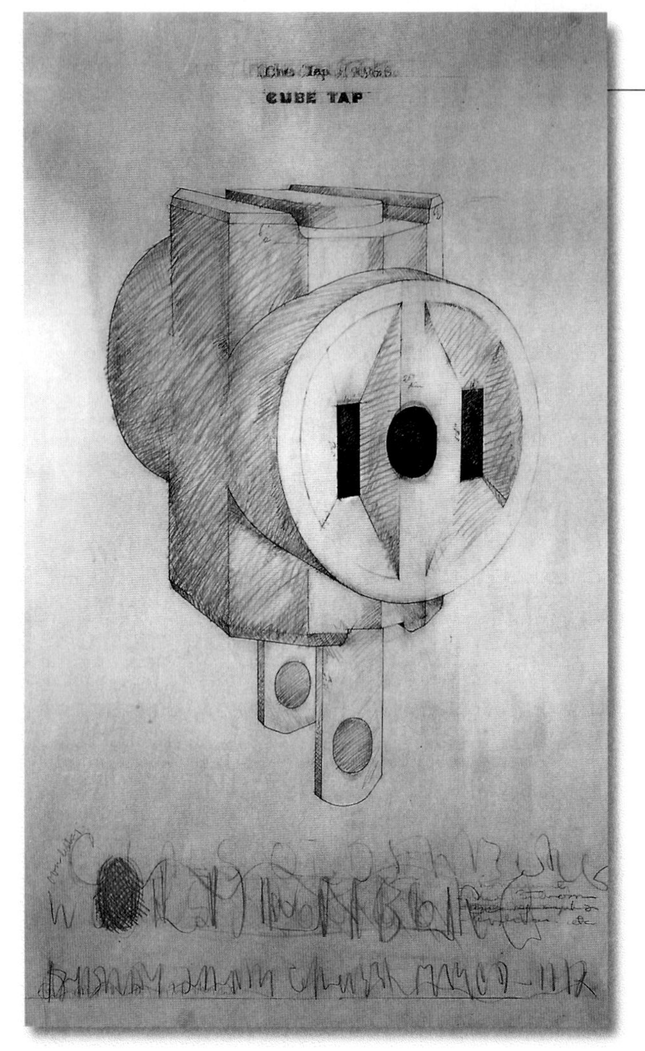

Claes Oldenburg. *Cube Tap (Plug),* 1968. Pencil on white woven paper. The Art Institute of Chicago, Chicago, IL.

How did the artist use shading and contrast to create depth?

Artists use value to give the illusion of depth to two-dimensional artworks. Dark values seem to recede. Swedish American artist Claes Oldenburg (1929–) used values to make the object in this artwork appear three-dimensional. Look for these details:

- Oldenburg applied the darkest value for the plug openings, creating negative space and the appearance of holes.
- Lighter values on the circular front of the object make it appear that light is shining on this side of the object.
- The artist used darker values on the sides and top, where less light shines. This creates the illusion of depth.

Value and Perspective

Using different values in artworks can make two-dimensional objects appear three-dimensional. Oldenburg also used perspective to show depth and dimension. The diagonal lines seem to move away from the viewer, creating a sense of depth.

Technique Tip

Pencil Values

Try using the side of a pencil lead, rather than its tip, to create graded values. Press lightly and evenly to create lighter values. Build up layers of pencil color to create darker values. Smudge with your finger to smooth out any lines made by the pencil and create even shading.

Studio 6

Create a Value Drawing

Use what you have learned about value to create drawings of objects as they might appear at different times of day.

Materials

- ✓ pencil or charcoal
- ✓ 12" × 18" white drawing paper
- ✓ soft eraser
- ✓ an object to draw, such as a ball, a can, or a vase
- ✓ lamp or other bright light

1 **Choose an object to draw and place it on your desk or table.**

2 **Place the lamp or other light on one side of the object. Use value to draw the effects of the light shining on your object.**

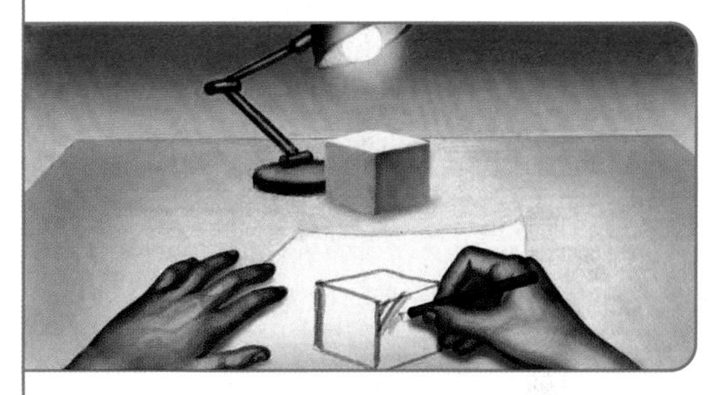

3 **Move the light and draw the object again. Repeat this step one more time. Then record notes about the effects of light and value on the object.**

Review and Reflect

- What value techniques did you use in your drawing?
- What mood does the changing position of light create in your drawing?
- How did your knowledge of value help you make your drawing appear three-dimensional?
- Which techniques for showing value do you prefer? Why?

Lesson 7

Color

In the 1660s, Sir Isaac Newton passed a beam of sunlight from an opening in a darkened room into a prism, a device that separates light into a spectrum of colors. Newton proved with this experiment that light is a combination of the seven colors of the rainbow. His discovery helped artists better understand **color,** the visual quality of objects caused by the amount of light they reflect or absorb. **Hue** is another word for color.

Kinds of Colors

Primary colors are yellow, red, and blue. Just as *primary* means "basic or first," these hues cannot be mixed from other colors. Primary colors, along with black and white, can help you mix any color you might imagine.

Secondary colors are orange, violet, and green. They are made by mixing two primary colors. Study the color wheel below to see how primary colors can be mixed to make secondary colors.

Intermediate colors are mixed from a primary and a secondary color next to each other on a color wheel. Find examples of each of these colors on the color wheel.

Color Wheel

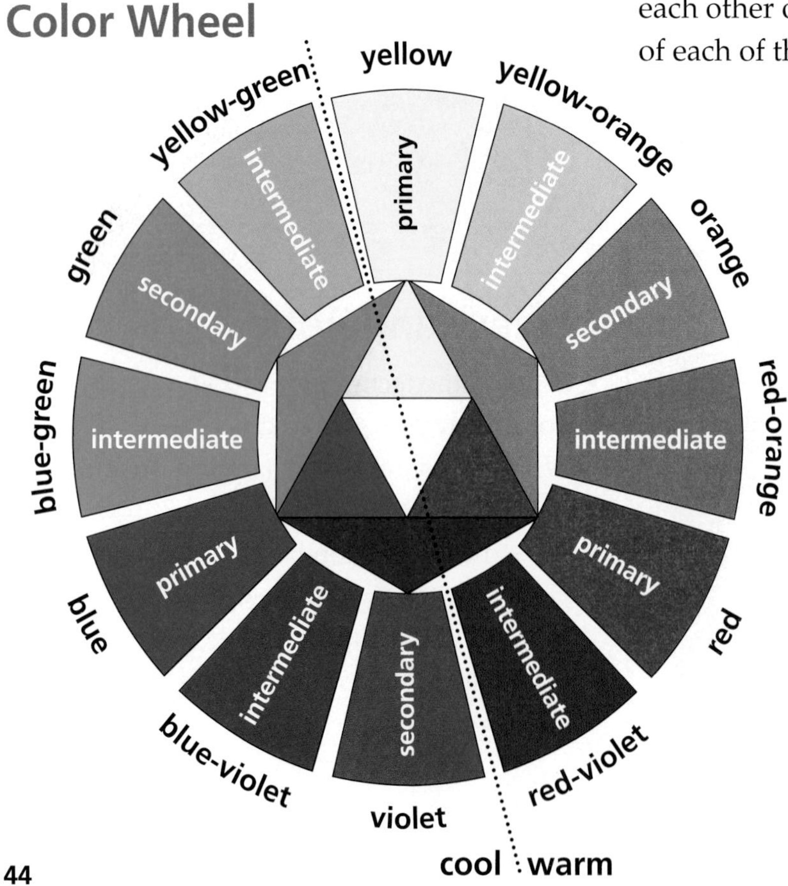

Sonia Delaunay. *Electric Prisms,* 1915. Oil on canvas. Musée d'Art Moderne, Paris, France.

Colors and Shapes

Russian artist Sonia Terk Delaunay (1885–1979) developed a personal style of painting highlighted by the arrangement of colorful shapes. This painting is composed of color, shape, and implied lines. Notice how the shapes of dark and light colors draw your eye to certain parts of the painting. Find primary, secondary, and intermediate colors in the painting. Why do you think the artist titled the painting *Electric Prisms?*

The artist used color to suggest lines and shapes. How did she use color to create implied lines? Notice how the colors change where they overlap other colors.

Research

Discover more about the art of Sonia Delaunay by visiting the New York Museum of Modern Art at http://www.moma.org. Type the artist's last name in the Search box for links to the colorful artworks by Delaunay and her husband, Robert Delaunay. Compare their styles and compositions, and find out how each artist used color to create a certain mood in their artworks.

Studio 7 Setup

Colors *and Feelings*

Janet Fish. *Yellow Pad,* 1997. Oil on canvas, 36 by 50 inches. The Columbus Museum, Columbus, GA. © Janet Fish/Licensed by VAGA, New York, NY. Photo by Beth Phillips, courtesy DC Moore Gallery, NY.

What mood is created by the colors in each of these artworks?

Sandy Skoglund. *The Green House,* 1990. Photo cibachrome, 52 1/4 by 64 inches. © Sandy Skoglund.

Artists know that colors can create a certain **mood,** or feeling in their artworks. In these artworks, the artists chose a combination of colors that emphasize the mood they wanted to convey. Look for these details:

- In *Yellow Pad,* American artist Janet Fish (1938–) used **warm colors** —reds, yellows, and oranges—to create a sunny, lively mood.
- In *The Green House,* American artist Sandy Skoglund (1946–) created a different mood by using **cool colors,** which include greens, blues, and violets. The blue dogs and green room suggest a feeling of calm.

Color and Contrast

The cool colors in Skoglund's artwork set the overall mood, while small amounts of warm color add contrast and interest. Notice how the warm flesh tones of the people stand out against the cool green and blue. In the same way, Fish included small amounts of cool colors to add contrast and interest to her painting of warm colors.

Technique Tip

Mixing Colors

Experiment with mixing colors by first combining two primary colors to make a secondary color. To mix intermediate colors, combine a secondary with a primary color next to each other on the color wheel. Write the "recipe" you use so you can mix more of the same color.

Studio 7

Paint with Warm and Cool Colors

Use what you have learned about color to mix hues on a color wheel. Then paint a scene using warm or cool colors.

Materials

- ✓ two sheets of 8 1/2 " × 11" white drawing paper
- ✓ containers of water
- ✓ mixing trays
- ✓ red, blue, yellow, and white tempera paint
- ✓ paintbrushes

1 **Mix tempera paints to paint a color wheel. Once the paint dries, label the primary, secondary, and intermediate colors.**

2 **Sketch a scene that makes you feel happy or sad. Choose warm or cool colors to reflect the mood your scene will show.**

3 **Mix the warm or cool colors you have selected, and paint your drawing.**

Review and Reflect

- Which primary, secondary, and intermediate colors did you use in your artwork?
- How did you arrange the colors to create certain effects in your artwork?
- How would you describe the mood of your artwork?
- What changes would you make to your artwork, if any? Why?

Lesson 8

Color and Colorists

Swiss-born Paul Klee (1879–1940) was known as a colorist. He used color with great skill to create shapes and forms in his artworks. Klee incorporated the properties, or attributes, of colors in his artworks, including hue, value, tints, shades, and intensity.

Properties of Color

Value refers to the lightness or darkness of a hue. A **tint** is a lighter color value made by adding a hue to white. Mixing black with a hue creates a **shade,** a darker color value.

The color wheel on page 44 shows bright, strong hues of high intensity. **Intensity** is the brightness or dullness of a hue. These high-intensity hues are sometimes referred to as "pure" color. The intensity of a hue can be muted by mixing it with its complement, the color directly across from it on the color wheel. You can get a lower intensity of red, for example, by adding small amounts of green.

Artists adjust the intensity of their colors for purposes such as changing the mood of a composition, creating the hues of a specific season, or providing contrast between bright and dull objects.

Paul Klee. *Color Shapes,* 1914. Watercolor, 4 by 5 1/2 inches. Barnes Foundation, Merion, Pennsylvania.

Klee applied tints and shades of color to create shapes.

Beverly Buchanan. *St. Simons,* 1989. Oil pastel on paper, 38 by 50 inches. © 1989 Beverly Buchanan. Courtesy Bernice Steinbaum Gallery, Miami. Photograph by Gamma One Conversions, New York.

Color and Expression

American artist Beverly Buchanan (1940–) uses the properties of color to create vitality and interest in her artworks. Notice the intensity of the different hues in *St. Simons.* Look at the red structure in the artwork. The artist changed the intensity and value of the red to add depth to the structure. How did the artist show the light shining on the structure?

Buchanan combined bright colors with a variety of lines to create the shapes of the houses. This combination of elements of art helps give the drawing a sense of energy and excitement. How is this different from Klee's painting?

Visual Culture

Advertisers use certain colors to sell products. Observe the breakfast food aisle in a local grocery store. Look at the entire aisle and determine which color is dominant. Then look at three different boxes of a similar product. Decide which of the three you would most likely buy based on the boxes. What effect did the colors have in your decision?

Studio 8 Setup
Color *Schemes*

Pablo Picasso. *Two Acrobats with a Dog,* 1905. Gouache on cardboard, 41 1/2 by 29 1/2 inches. Museum of Modern Art, NY.

Artists plan ways to combine colors to achieve special effects. **Color schemes,** plans for combining colors in a work of art, affect the way the viewer feels about an artwork.

- **Monochromatic** means "one color." This color scheme uses tints and shades of the same hue, and can be used to unify an artwork.
- The hues in an **analogous** color scheme are side by side on a color wheel and share a hue. Analogous color schemes can include both warm and cool colors.
- **Complementary** color schemes feature colors directly across from each other on a color wheel. Artists use complementary colors to achieve bold, jarring effects.
- **Neutral** color schemes use black, white, and tints and shades of gray. Many artists include brown, too. Neutral color schemes can reflect a calm, quiet mood.

What color scheme did Spanish artist Pablo Picasso (1881–1973) use in this artwork? How did he add interest?

How does the color scheme in this artwork complement the facial expressions of the acrobats?

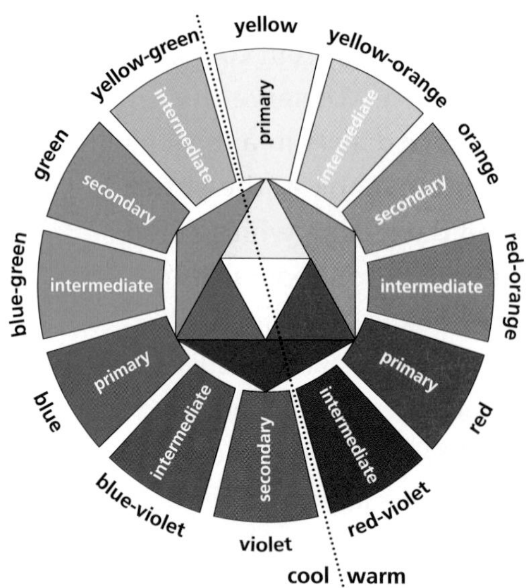

Technique Tip

Careful Color Mixing

To mix small amounts of tempera paint, you can use a paintbrush. When mixing larger amounts of tempera paint, use a spoon or a craft stick and a cup. Using a paintbrush to mix large amounts of paint can embed paint deep into the bristles, making it difficult to clean.

Studio 8

Paint in Complementary Colors

Use what you have learned about complementary colors to make a painting of a favorite outfit.

Materials

- ✓ pencil
- ✓ practice paper
- ✓ tempera paints
- ✓ 12" × 18" paper

1 **Use the pencil and 12" × 18" paper to sketch yourself wearing a favorite real or imagined outfit.**

2 **Use the practice paper to experiment with different hues by painting dabs of various complementary colors next to each other.**

3 **Choose a set of complementary colors and paint your sketch.**

Review and Reflect

- Describe the outfit you chose to paint.
- How did you decide what colors to use in your painting?
- How do the colors you chose reflect how you feel about the outfit?
- Does your choice of complementary colors result in an outfit that "goes together"? Why or why not?

Lesson 9

Texture

The horse's coat is as shiny as gold. His hands are sandpaper.

Writers use similes and metaphors like these to describe **texture,** the way something feels to the touch or looks to the eye. Words like *rough, silky, shiny,* and *dull* help writers describe the texture of an object. Visual artists *show* texture to accomplish the same goal.

Types of Texture

Artists know that texture can be sensed by touch and by sight. They work one or both types of texture into their compositions to help viewers understand surfaces.

Tactile texture, often called actual texture, is the way a surface would feel if you could touch it. In *Buffalo,* the artist provides tactile texture by making the buffalo from a variety of recycled materials. Look for rough, smooth, or soft textures you might feel if you could touch the materials in this artwork.

Visual texture, sometimes called simulated texture, is the way a surface appears through the sense of vision. Notice the visual texture in the eye detail of *Buffalo.* The artist placed a clear plastic spoon in the buffalo's eye to create the illusion of a shiny texture.

Holly Hughes. *Buffalo,* 1992. Found object mixed media, 78 by 54 inches. Capitol Building, New Mexico.

Look at the tactile texture in this artwork.

Holly Hughes. (Detail) *Buffalo*, 1992.

Notice the visual texture in this detail of *Buffalo.*

Audrey Flack. *Energy Apples,* 1980. Oil over acrylic on canvas, 47 3/4 by 48 1/4 inches. Courtesy Louis K. Meisel Gallery, New York. Photo by Stephen Lopez.

Texture and Color

The painting *Energy Apples* by American artist Audrey Flack (1931–) shows how visual texture can make a two-dimensional painting appear more realistic. How did the artist use color and value to add visual texture to this artwork?

Notice how the artist used white and light tints to give the illusion of highlights on several surfaces. The highlights on the apple create a visual texture that makes the apple look shiny. Flack also created contrast through her use of both shiny and dull textures on the paint tray, giving the tray the appearance of shiny metal. What other objects appear shiny?

Sketchbook Journal

Closely observe the variety of textures in your surroundings. Make sketches of some of these textures in your Sketchbook Journal. Next to each sketch, indicate where you observed the texture. Use similes and metaphors to describe the textures you sketched.

Studio 9 Setup
Painted *Texture*

James Wyeth. *Portrait of Pig,* 1970. Oil on canvas, 51 1/2 by 83 1/4 inches. Collection of the Brandywine River Museum, Gift of Betsy James Wyeth. ©1998 James Wyeth.

How would you describe the visual texture in this artwork?

American artist James Wyeth (1946–) used visual texture to add interest to this portrait of a pig. Wyeth used brushstrokes and colors to create the illusion of texture. You can imagine how it might feel to touch a real pig or straw. Look for these details:

- Thin, wispy brushstrokes in a light tint give the illusion of hair on the pig. Thicker, heavier brushstrokes make the straw look coarse and scratchy.
- Wyeth used subtle changes in color values to give depth to the pig's rounded form. It appears as if the viewer can feel the shape of the pig.

Visual Textures

Wyeth used the elements of value, color, line, and shape to add visual texture to this painting. The textures help to show the physical characteristics of the pig and the straw. Look closely at the wrinkles on the snout of the pig. What words would you use to describe how the snout might feel? Think of ways that you can use the elements of art to show texture in your artwork.

Technique Tip

Texture and Rubbings

One way to capture the texture of a flat surface is to make a rubbing. Begin by placing a thin sheet of paper over a textured surface. Then rub the side of an unwrapped crayon over the paper.

Studio 9

Create a Scene to Show Texture

Use what you have learned about tactile and visual texture to compose an outdoor scene.

Materials

- ✓ unwrapped crayons
- ✓ 12" × 18" newsprint
- ✓ 12" × 18" black or white construction paper
- ✓ scissors
- ✓ glue

1 **Make several rubbings of tactile textures by placing newsprint over a variety of flat, heavily textured surfaces.**

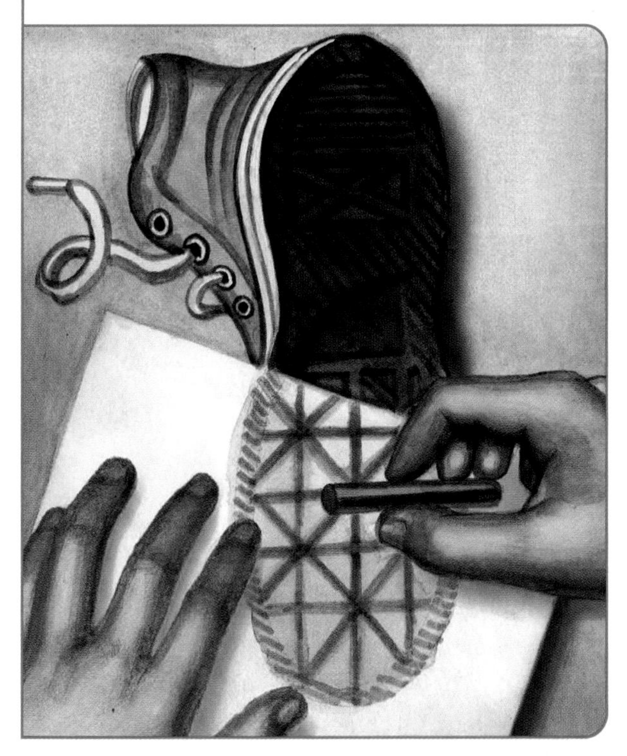

2 **Cut shapes out of your rubbings. Arrange and glue them to the construction paper in a way that suggests an outdoor scene.**

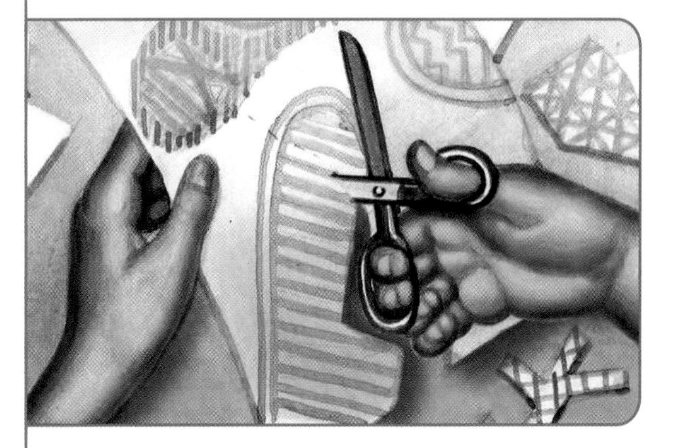

3 **Use a crayon to emphasize textured areas. Add details to show foreground, middle ground, and background.**

Review and Reflect

- Describe the textures you chose.
- Which texture do you notice first in your artwork? Why?
- Tell about the objects the textures represent.
- How well do the textures depict your outdoor scene? Explain.

Artist *at Work*

Art You Can Use

Artists are not limited to creating artworks that simply hang on the wall or sit in a corner. Georgia artist Barbara Brozik, for example, makes art you can sit on. "I think of my work as a painting or sculpture which is functional," Brozik says. "You can really use it. Sit on it. Write on it. Set things on it . . . enjoy it."

Deco Chair

Brozik designs and builds furniture that shows her playful, colorful style. *Deco Chair,* like much of her artwork, is a one-of-a-kind design that she built by hand. Think about how this chair compares with furniture made by machines. Brozik's furniture is decorative as well as functional.

Beneath the glossy surface of *Deco Chair,* a thin layer of gold- and silver-leaf shimmers against a royal burgundy hue. Look closely at the textures the artist achieved with brushstrokes.

This chair is built on a wood base, which the artist made by cutting and gluing parts together. Brozik and other furniture artists apply skill and detail to their designs.

Barbara Brozik. *Deco Chair,* 1997. Acrylic on wood, carved, and gold- and silver-leafed, 42 by 18 by 18 inches.

An Artist of Many Talents

Brozik was born in Minnesota and moved to Atlanta in 1967. Her early artworks include silkscreen prints and handmade paper sculptures. She has created torn paper collages and large painted wall weavings. She has also done paintings on canvas and paper.

Brozik's one-of-a-kind furniture sculptures often include animal patterns and images from nature. Geometric shapes and forms can often be found in her artworks. Each item of furniture has its own design, form, and pattern. Yet when her furniture is placed in a room, all the pieces appear to belong together.

Like other artists, Brozik sometimes takes commissions, or is hired, to make a specific artwork. Brozik also displays her furniture in shops and galleries where buyers might see them.

Barbara Brozik is inspired by childhood memories of her mother's antique furniture collection.

Portfolio *Project*

Paint a Colorful Landscape

Maurice de Vlaminck. *Olive Trees,* 1905–1906. Oil on canvas, 20 2/3 by 25 1/3 inches. Fundacion Coleccion Thyssen-Bornemisza, Madrid, Spain.

Plan

French painter Maurice de Vlaminck (1876–1958) used generous amounts of paint in his *Olive Trees.* Notice how de Vlaminck used short, thick brushstrokes of black, blue, and red to paint the field. Now look at the texture of the paint that the artist used on the trunk and branches of the olive tree. De Vlaminck applied the paint in thick, heavy layers that left visible ridges. This impasto technique created a highly textured surface that conveys motion and energy.

- What colors do you see in the landscape? Where do you see warm colors? Where do you find cool colors?
- In what area is de Vlaminck's use of the impasto technique most noticeable? What effect does this technique have on the mood of the landscape?
- What kind of mood would you like to create in a landscape? How could you use the elements of art to achieve this mood?

Sketchbook Journal

Pick an object that will appear in your landscape and practice drawing it. Try placing the object in different places on the page, such as close and far away. Try drawing the object by using only geometric shapes. Try using different colors, keeping in mind the impact of color in a landscape painting.

Materials

- ✓ 11" × 17" white drawing paper or watercolor paper
- ✓ white drawing paper
- ✓ tempera and watercolor
- ✓ palette for mixing paints
- ✓ small natural sponges
- ✓ container with water for rinsing
- ✓ paintbrushes

Create

1 **Choose an analogous color scheme that will convey a mood. Test the tints and shades you will use.**

2 **Decide where your horizon line will be. Paint the sky with one color of watercolor and paint the ground with another color.**

3 **When the paint dries, use the darkest shades of your color scheme to paint tree trunks with tempera in front of the horizon line; overlap to show distance.**

4 **Use small sponges dipped in tints and shades of tempera to create the foliage of the trees. Apply the lighter colors first.**

Reflect

- Describe the elements of art you used in your artwork.
- How did you create a feeling of space?
- What mood does your color scheme convey?
- What medium did you most enjoy using? Why?

Unit 1 *Review*

Vocabulary Review

A Match each art term below with its definition.

line	value
diagonal	intensity
geometric shape	monochromatic
organic shape	texture
shape	negative space
vertical line	middle ground

1. a two-dimensional area with height and width
2. the path of movement made by a point
3. a shape such as a circle, a triangle, or a square
4. a slanted edge or line
5. a line that runs up and down
6. the lightness and darkness of a color
7. the brightness or dullness of a color
8. a color scheme that uses different values of a single hue
9. a shape often found in nature that is irregular and uneven
10. the empty space around an object
11. the space between the foreground and the background
12. a reference to how things feel or appear

Artists and Their Art

B Each artwork listed in the box appears in this unit. Use the titles to finish the sentences.

Enclosed Field with Rising Sun
Girl with Gold Necklace
Merryn
Le Moulin de la Galette
Study of a Sleeping Woman
Color Shapes
Buffalo
A Game of Hand Sumo in the New Yoshiwara
Sebastian's Beast

1. Diego Rivera used value to make the figure in ___ appear full and round.
2. Pierre-Auguste Renoir uses atmospheric perspective to create distance in ___.
3. ___ by Holly Hughes is an example of tactile texture.
4. Paul Klee used tints and shades to create ___.
5. Impasto is the technique Van Gogh used in ___.
6. ___ by Henri Matisse is an example of a contour drawing.
7. Barbara Hepworth created___, which shows positive and negative space.
8. ___ demonstrates how Furuyama Moromasa used linear perspective.
9. In ___, Isabel De Obaldía created an organic shape from glass.

Respond to Art

C **Look at the painting *Red Balloon* by Paul Klee. In a class discussion or on a sheet of paper, match each art term below with examples from the painting.**

Paul Klee. *Red Balloon,* 1922. Oil on canvas, 25 1/2 by 19 1/2 inches. Solomon R. Guggenheim Museum, NY.

Art Terms

1. geometric shape
2. warm colors
3. cool colors
4. diagonal line
5. horizontal line
6. texture
7. tint
8. positive space

Unit 1 *Review*

Write About Art

Persuasive Paragraphs

D **Look back at the artworks you saw in this unit. Choose one that especially appealed to you. Consider how the elements of art are used in this artwork. Write one or two paragraphs to persuade others why the artist's use of the elements of art make the artwork appealing. Copy the chart below and use it to organize your thoughts before writing.**

Conclusion

Elements of Art

1. line
2. shape
3. form
4. space
5. value
6. color
7. texture

Your Studio Work

E **Answer these questions in your Sketchbook Journal or on a separate sheet of paper.**

1. How did you generate ideas for your artworks? What medium did you most enjoy working with? Why?
2. Which elements of art did you most enjoy using? Which did you find less enjoyable? Explain.
3. How did the elements of art help you convey a mood or feeling in your artworks? Explain.
4. Which element of art in this unit would you best be able to explain to someone else? How would you describe the way artists use this element of art to another person?

Put It All Together

Paul Cézanne. *The Artist's Father,* 1866. Oil on canvas, 78 1/8 by 47 inches. National Gallery of Art, Washington, D.C.

F **Discuss or write about Cézanne's painting *The Artist's Father,* using the four steps below for viewing artwork critically.**

1. **Describe** What is the subject of this artwork? Identify each of the objects that the artist painted. What colors did the artist use and where did he use them?
2. **Analyze** What kind of shapes did Cézanne use primarily? What technique did he use to show space and distance in this artwork? How did Cézanne show texture in the painting?
3. **Interpret** What mood is the artist expressing in this painting? How did he use color to create that mood? What other elements of art contribute to the mood?
4. **Judge** French painter Paul Cézanne (1839–1906) painted several oil portraits of his father between 1865–1871. This portrait was painted early in Cézanne's career. How do you think this painting reflects how Cézanne felt about his father?

Paul Cézanne. *Self-Portrait,* ca. 1890. Oil on canvas. Private collection.

Though critics often shunned his Post-Impressionist artworks, Cézanne once said,

"With an apple, I will astonish Paris."

—PAUL CÉZANNE

Henri Matisse. *Interior with Egyptian Curtain,* 1948. Oil on canvas, 45 3/4 by 35 1/8 inches. The Phillips Collection, Washington, D.C.

Unit 2

The Principles of Design

French artist Henri Matisse (1869–1954) used the elements of art to lead your eye through *Interior with Egyptian Curtain.* Color and shape may draw your eye to the curtain. Line and value may lead your eye to the palm tree or to the fruit bowl.

Artists arrange the elements of art. They use the **principles of design: balance, emphasis, proportion, pattern, rhythm, unity,** and **variety.**

The elements of art are to artists as words are to writers. The principles of design are like sentences and paragraphs. They help artists organize the elements of art to express their thoughts and feelings.

In this unit you will read about how artists use the principles of design to combine the elements of art. You also will discover how to use these principles to express thoughts and feelings in your own artworks.

Henri Matisse. *Self-Portrait,* 1900.

About *the Artist*

He lived through two world wars and was often bedridden by illness. But **Henri Matisse** never stopped making joyous, colorful artworks. Learn more about the life of Matisse and his artworks on page 82.

Lesson 1

Balance

Balance in an artwork means that the elements of art are arranged according to their "visual weight." No one part of a balanced artwork overpowers another. Artists arrange elements in three types of balance: symmetrical, asymmetrical, and radial.

Types of Balance

An artwork has **symmetrical balance,** or formal balance, when one half matches the other half. Divide *Pectoral* down the middle. The left side is almost a mirror image of the right.

An artwork with two sides that do not look the same has **asymmetrical balance,** or informal balance. Both sides have similar visual weight. For example, a large tree on one side of a drawing can be balanced with three bright red apples on the other.

When lines or shapes spread in a regular pattern from a center point, the artwork shows **radial balance.** Bicycle wheels and dartboards have radial balance.

Dawid Stanislawa. *Big Star,* ca. 1962. Cut paper, diameter 11 3/4 inches. The Museum of International Folk Art, Santa Fe, NM.

Which two types of balance are shown in this paper-cut?

Artist unknown, Tolima culture. *Pectoral,* ca. A.D. 600–800. Gold, height 9 inches.

Why is this gold sculpture an example of symmetrical balance?

Winslow Homer. *Breezing Up,* 1873–1876. Oil on canvas, 24 1/8 by 38 1/8 inches. National Gallery of Art, Washington, D.C.

How does this painting show asymmetrical balance?

Balance and Shape

American artist Winslow Homer (1836–1910) captured the movement of wind and water on a blustery day in *Breezing Up.* The diagonal lines created by the masts and the shapes of the boys and the boat add to the sense of movement.

Homer composed the painting to draw your eye first to the boat on the left. He made this boat large and detailed so it seems closer to the viewer.

On the right, Homer painted a ship smaller so it would seem farther away. He painted heavy, dark clouds over the ship. This provides the small ship with enough visual weight to balance the large boat.

Sketchbook Journal

Look around you at objects that have different shapes. Identify the type of balance each shape has. Draw some of these shapes in your Sketchbook Journal. Include at least two examples of each type of balance. Label each object you draw with the type of balance it has.

Studio 1 Setup

Visual *Balance*

American artist Alma Woodsey Thomas (1891–1978) was seventy-nine years of age when she painted *The Eclipse.* She used color and shape to create balance. Look for these details that show techniques for showing balance:

- The widening rings of color show radial balance. The rings radiate from the large black circle.
- The rings are symmetrical, but the artwork itself is asymmetrical. The radiating rings are placed slightly to the right of center.

Artists use color in a variety of ways to create balance. They can balance warm colors with cool colors. They can also use different tints and shades of the same color to create balance. Where do you notice the artist's use of tints and shades in this painting?

Another way artists create balance is by placing warm bright colors opposite large areas of a dull, dark color. Notice how the bright yellow on the left side of the painting balances the large black circle on the right.

Consider how you can achieve visual balance in your artworks. You might choose to use bold lines balanced by bright colors. You might decide to show two similar shapes of different colors. You might even want to balance a geometric form on one side of a sculpture with an organic form on the other side. In what other ways could you use the elements of art to show visual balance?

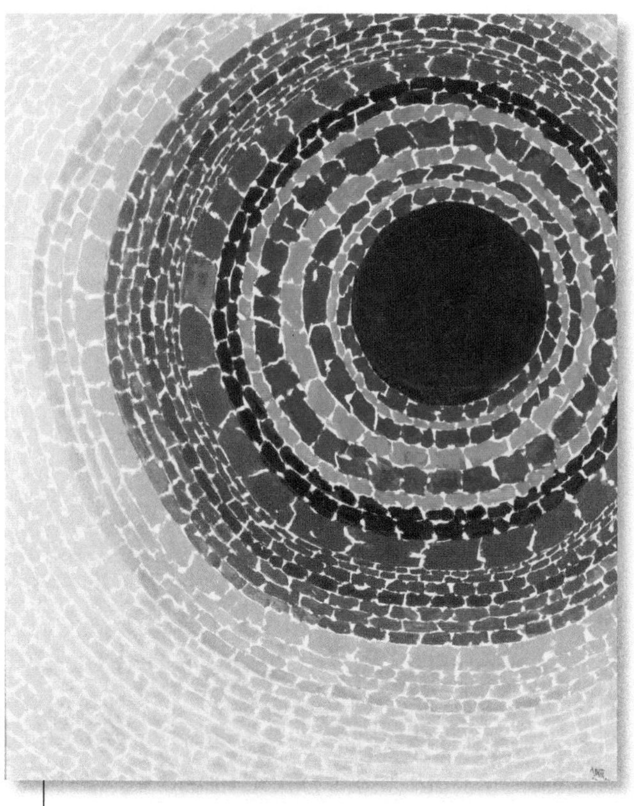

Alma Woodsey Thomas. *The Eclipse,* 1970. Acrylic on canvas, 62 by 49 3/4 inches. Smithsonian American Art Museum, Washington, D.C.

How did the artist achieve balance in this artwork?

Technique Tip

Choose the Right Tool

It is a good idea for artists to collect many different widths of markers, pencils, and paintbrushes. To make a heavy line with a thin marker, you have to go over the line again and again. With a thicker marker, you can draw one heavy line and move on.

Studio 1

Draw to Show Balance

Use what you have learned about balance to create a balanced artwork with common objects.

Materials

- ✓ 12" × 18" drawing paper
- ✓ common object, such as a pencil, crayon, or fork
- ✓ colored pencils or markers

1 **Fold a sheet of paper into three equal sections. Choose a common object to draw, such as a pencil, crayon, or fork.**

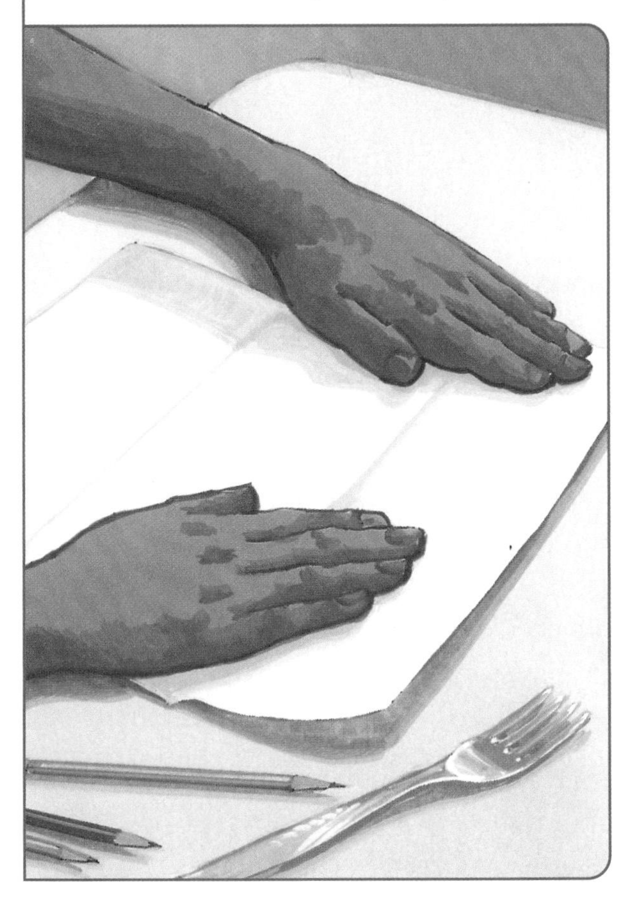

2 **Use each section to show the three types of balance. Using contour lines, draw the same object several times and in varying sizes to fill each space.**

3 **Use colored pencils or markers to add color to emphasize each type of balance.**

Review and Reflect

- Describe how each of your drawings shows different types of balance.
- How does color and size of the object you drew affect the balance in each drawing?
- What feelings are created by each drawing?
- Why is it important to show balance?

Lesson 2

Emphasis

Leonora Carrington.
Red Cow, 1989.
Oil on canvas, 24 by 36 inches. Private collection.

The artist used color and size to make the cow the focal point of this painting.

When speaking, you can stress important points in many ways. You can repeat what you said. You can raise your voice. You can use hand gestures. Similarly, artists control the things that stand out in their artworks by using emphasis. As a principle of design, **emphasis** means the sense of importance the artist gives to a part of an artwork.

Ways to Show Emphasis

One way artists show emphasis is by making one element or object the strongest or most important. This is called **dominance.** The dominant element or object can be an unusual color, shape, or brushstroke. Or it can be an interesting placement of a form or shape.

Another way artists show emphasis is by creating a **focal point,** or center of interest. This can be as easy as placing the object in the center of the artwork. Or the artist can make an object larger or brighter than other objects. Artists also can direct attention to an object using lines or shapes.

A third way artists show emphasis is by using **contrast,** a difference between two unlike things. Artists can create contrast by placing tints next to shades. Or they can change a color's intensity, its brightness or dullness.

Gabriele Münter. *Girl with Doll,* 1908–1909. Oil on cardboard, 27 1/2 by 19 inches. Milwaukee Art Museum, Milwaukee, WI. Gift of Mrs. Harry Lynde Bradley.

Emphasis and Color

German artist Gabriele Münter (1877–1962) used bold colors and simplified forms to show emphasis in *Girl with Doll.* Notice how the girl's red dress helps draw the viewer's eye. The blue background color makes the girl's red dress seem to stand out.

The girl, the chair, and the doll are outlined with heavy black lines. Münter placed the girl and the doll in the center to make them the focal point. How does the doll's blue dress create emphasis?

Think about the message you want to convey as you plan to create emphasis in your artworks.

Visual Culture

Look for advertisements in magazines, newspapers, and on billboards. Ads try to catch your attention and convince you to buy a product. How do the ads use emphasis to grab your attention? Glue a few ads in your Sketchbook Journal. Note how each ad uses dominance, focal point, or contrast.

Studio 2 Setup

Emphasis *and Contrast*

Nicolas Tarkhoff. *Black Cat on a Window Railing.* Watercolor. Private collection.

How did the artist create emphasis in this painting of a cat?

Russian artist Nicolas Tarkhoff (1871–1930) captured the position of a curious cat. He used many techniques to create emphasis. Look for these details:

- Tarkhoff made the cat the focal point by placing it at the center of the painting.
- He added emphasis by framing the cat in the window.
- The cat's body position creates additional emphasis. The cat appears focused on an object not visible in the painting, perhaps a bird outside the window.
- The position of the chairs in the foreground and the diagonal lines of the windowpanes help lead the viewer's eye to the cat.

The Effect of Contrast

Often an artist will make the focal point an intense color to attract the viewer's eye. In this painting, Tarkhoff chose instead to use muted hues, placing the black cat against the light tints of the outdoor background. How does this help emphasize the cat?

Technique Tip

Lines for Emphasis

Experiment with thin and thick lines to create emphasis. With a fine-tip marker, sketch a scene. Include a dominant object as the focal point. Now, outline the dominant object with a wide-tip marker. Notice how the thicker lines add even more emphasis to the dominant object.

Studio 2

Draw with Emphasis

Use what you have learned about dominance, focal points, and contrast to create a drawing that shows emphasis.

Materials

- ✓ drawing from Sketchbook Journal (optional)
- ✓ pencil
- ✓ 12" × 18" white drawing paper
- ✓ black markers with tips of different widths
- ✓ crayons or oil pastels

1 Select a drawing from your Sketchbook Journal or create a new drawing. Select an object in the drawing to emphasize.

2 Redraw the design on another sheet of paper. Show dominance by making the selected object larger and more detailed.

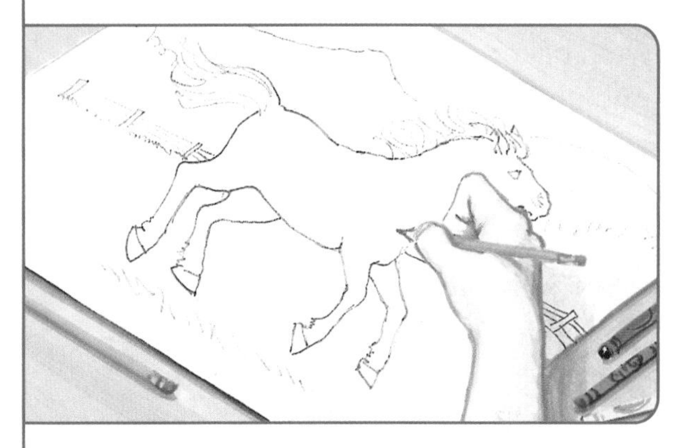

3 Outline the object or its details with black markers to add emphasis. Add color to create contrast in the emphasized area.

Review and Reflect

- What is the focal point of your drawing?
- How did you use dominance and contrast to help you create emphasis?
- How do you feel about the subject of your artwork? Why?
- What kind of story would you tell about your drawing?

Lesson 3

Proportion

When bakers make cookies, they pay attention to the proportions of the ingredients. Too much flour makes the cookies hard. Too much liquid makes them runny. Like bakers, artists pay attention to proportion in their artworks. To an artist, **proportion** refers to how the parts of an artwork relate to each other and to the whole. They often show proportion through the size or placement of an object in their composition.

Size Relationships

Artists think of the human body as being of **standard proportions.** So you might say that everything else in the world relates in proportion to your own body. However, artists often choose not to use standard proportions. They can change an object's expected size to add interest.

Monumental objects have larger-than-life proportions. These objects are much larger than expected. They can create a sense of awe in the viewer.

Miniature objects are smaller than expected. A miniature object can seem small and fragile.

Artists also show emphasis by using **exaggerated** or distorted proportions. This can make an object seem more important than it really is.

Artist unknown. *Olmec Head,* 1200–900 B.C. Volcanic stone, approximately 9 by 7 by 6 feet. Museum of Anthropology of Xalapa, Veracruz, Mexico.

This monumental sculpture is much larger than your own head. In fact, it is bigger than your whole body!

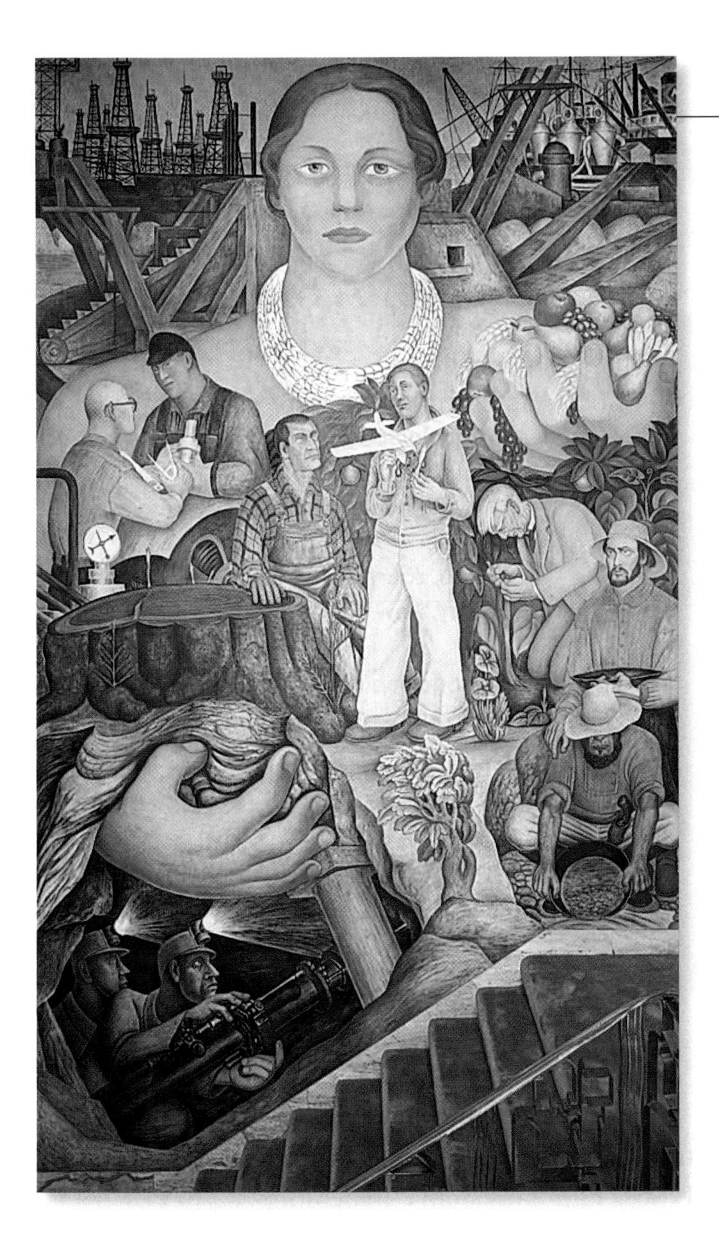

Diego Rivera. (Detail) *The Riches of California,* 1931. Fresco, approximately 22 by 13 feet. The City Club of San Francisco, San Francisco, CA.

How did Rivera show space and depth in this painting?

Proportion and Emphasis

Diego Rivera (1886–1957) lived and worked as an artist in Mexico. He also created artworks for cities in the United States. Rivera showed proportion and emphasis in many of his **murals.** These large works of art are painted directly onto a wall or ceiling. Many of his murals have political themes. Find the title of Rivera's mural on this page and study this detail of the mural. Notice the industries and products the artist included.

The woman is the focal point of the painting. Her huge hands hold the riches of California. What type of proportion did Rivera use to show the woman? Why do you think Rivera painted the woman in this way? Notice how he used overlapping and techniques of perspective. These give the illusion of space and depth to the painting. Look closely to notice objects placed in the foreground, middle ground, and background.

Rivera considered the placement of each figure and object as he planned the mural. This helps lead the viewer's eye around the artwork. Notice also how Rivera made the figures of equal proportions. This gives the impression that each industry is equally important to California. Think about how you can use proportion to create emphasis as you plan your artworks.

Research

Diego Rivera's mural at City College of San Francisco represents many cultures. You can study the mural in great detail by visiting www.riveramural.org. Learn how Rivera came to paint the mural and what it means. Then use the site to discover letters and photographs related to the mural. Find out how the college is working to preserve this work of art.

Lesson 4

Pattern

Pattern is a repeated use of an element, such as lines, shapes, or colors, in a regular way. Rugs, wallpaper, and clothes often have patterns. Even books on a shelf may form a pattern. Identify lines, shapes, or colors around you that make patterns. You can create patterns to add interest to an artwork's **design,** or its creative and methodical organization. Your design might also use spaces, forms, and textures to make a pattern.

Which elements of art form a pattern on this snake?

Pattern in Nature

Artists can make patterns that are precise and geometric, but patterns in nature tend to be less exact. Look at the photographs on this page.

Patterns in nature include organic shapes. Lines are rarely straight. Notice the pattern on the scales of this snake. Are the shapes all the same? Are the lines straight?

When objects repeat in nature, they tend to vary in shape and size. Look at the pattern created by the shell of a nautilus, a snail-like creature. The shell is divided into chambers. These repeated chambers grow larger as they spiral toward the outer edge.

Nature shows that patterns can be formed even when the elements of art vary. Taking inspiration from this, many artists make patterns the same way.

Patterns are formed even when repeated shapes vary in size.

Studio 4

Show Pattern in Clothing

Do research about clothing from other cultures. Use what you have learned about pattern to show pattern in your own design for clothing.

Materials

- ✓ pencil
- ✓ Sketchbook Journal or sketch paper
- ✓ 12" × 18" white drawing paper
- ✓ colored construction paper
- ✓ scissors ⚠
- ✓ glue or glue stick
- ✓ markers

1 **Make sketches of some patterns you found in your research.**

2 **Draw a design for clothing that shows your best pattern sketches.**

3 **Cut and glue shapes from construction paper to show the pattern. Use markers to add interesting lines.**

Review and Reflect

- Describe the patterns you designed.
- How do the materials you used help show off the pattern designs in your outfit?
- What cultural meanings do you think these patterns hold?
- Where might you wear an outfit made from your design?

Meet *the Artist*

Henri Matisse

Henri Matisse was born in France on New Year's Eve, 1869. He got a late start as a visual artist. But the artist and his art made an impact on the way artworks are created and viewed. He worked with color and its expressive qualities throughout his career. His paper cutout artworks are often known for their childlike qualities. Today, Matisse's colorful works of art continue to lead viewers into his visions of beauty and joy.

Henri Matisse. *Self-Portrait,* ca. 1900. Oil on canvas, 25 1/4 by 17 3/4 inches. Private collection.

"What I dream of is an art of balance, of purity and serenity . . . ."

—HENRI MATISSE

Matisse wanted to give viewers of his artworks the calmness that he felt as he painted.

An Artist Emerges

Matisse showed little interest in art for the first twenty years of his life. He was preparing for a law career when he began to attend drawing classes. Then, at twenty-one, a serious illness confined him to bed. His mother gave him a box of oil paints to pass the time. Before long, Matisse enrolled in art school.

Though he started late, Matisse wasted little time. "I plunged head down into work on the principle I had heard, all my young life, expressed by the words 'Hurry up!'" he said.

'The Wild Beasts'

Matisse became the leader of a group of painters who used vivid colors to express emotions. Shocked critics called the group *les fauves,* or "the wild beasts." The style became known as Fauvism.

During both world wars, Matisse stayed in France and produced lively, colorful works of art. After World War II, he designed a chapel that was completed in his early eighties. When his health no longer allowed him to paint, Matisse again created a revolution in art with his huge colored-paper cutouts.

Although his life was shadowed by war and illness, Matisse never stopped working. And he never lost his faith in the power of art.

Talk About It

Matisse believed that drawing was like making an expressive gesture. The difference between them is that the drawing is permanent. How is Matisse's painting on page 64 an example of his belief?

The Life of Henri Matisse

1865

1869 Matisse born on December 31

Matisse in his studio

1890 Starts painting while recovering from appendicitis

1890

1905 Paints *Woman with a Hat;* is labeled a 'Wild Beast'

1906 Meets Pablo Picasso

1915

1917 Moves to Nice, France

1940

Matisse creating paper cutouts

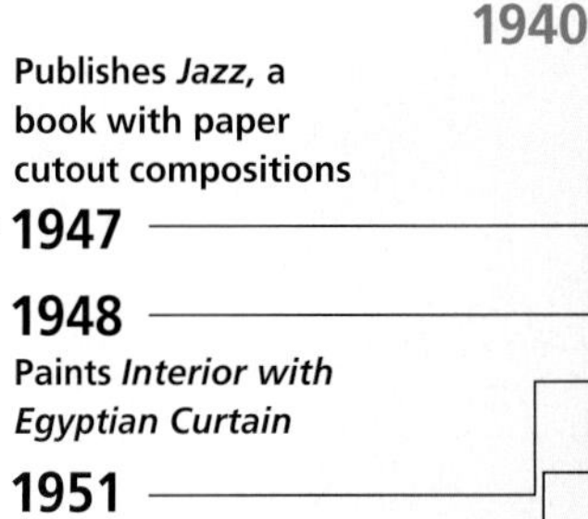

1947 Publishes *Jazz,* a book with paper cutout compositions

1948 Paints *Interior with Egyptian Curtain*

1951 Completes the design for the Chapel of the Rosary

1954 Matisse dies in France on November 3

1965

Look *and Compare*

The Art of the Everyday

Henri Matisse often painted scenes from everyday life. In *Pianist and Checker Players,* Matisse captured a moment in the life of a French family. Notice the bright, colorful patterns on the floor and walls. Patterns also draw your eye to the checker players. Notice the stripes on their shirts. Find the patterns in the tablecloth and the game board.

Art and History

Artworks can show what life was like at different times in history. Some artworks show important events. Others show how ordinary people lived.

Look at *Pianist and Checker Players.* This painting shows that before video games and television, people entertained themselves with musical instruments and board games.

In Another Time

In *The Chess Game,* Italian artist Sofonisba Anguissola (ca. 1532–1625) showed two girls playing chess. A third girl and a woman watch. Find the dates when the two paintings were made. How many years were there between them?

These artworks are from different times, but both show board games that are still popular. The paintings also show how people dressed in different eras. How are the clothing and hairstyles of the girls in *The Chess Game* different from those of the woman in *Pianist and Checker Players,* and those of today?

Henri Matisse. *Pianist and Checker Players,* 1924. Oil on canvas, 29 by 36 3/8 inches. Collection of Mr. and Mrs. Paul Mellon. Photograph © 1996 Board of Trustees, National Gallery of Art, Washington, D.C. © 1998 Succession H. Matisse, Paris/Artists Rights Society (ARS), New York.

Sofonisba Anguissola. *The Chess Game,* 1555. Oil on canvas, 28 3/4 by 38 3/4 inches. Museum Narodowe W. Poznaniu, Poznan, Poland.

Compare & Contrast

- **Compare the principles of balance, emphasis, proportion, and pattern in the two paintings. How are they the same? How are they different?**
- **How do the patterns in each painting affect the emotional quality?**

Lesson 5

Rhythm

Artists repeat visual elements in an artwork to create **rhythm,** a sense of real or visual motion. When you are dancing, the rhythm of the music can lead you all over the dance floor. Similarly, artists use rhythm to lead your eye around the composition. Rhythm also can make an object in an artwork appear to be moving. Rhythm can be steady and repetitive, or it can be varied and chaotic.

Artists use three types of rhythm to give their artworks energy.

Repeating the same element, such as a shape, over and over creates a **regular rhythm.** Like the steady ticking of a clock, regular rhythm has one beat.

Repeating two or more elements in a regular pattern creates an **alternating rhythm.** A heartbeat is an example of an alternating rhythm.

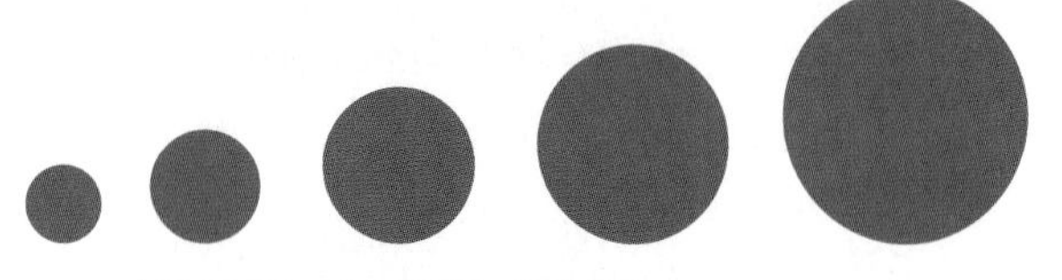

A **progressive rhythm** is built on regular changes in a repeated element. It is like a drumbeat that gets louder and louder. The element can go from small to large or from light to dark.

Carlos Almaraz. *Two of a Kind,* 1986. Oil on canvas, 83 1/2 by 69 1/2 inches. Los Angeles County Museum of Art, Los Angeles, CA.

What repeated element gives a sense of movement to this painting?

Andy Warhol. *Letter to the World—The Kick,* 1986. Serigraph, 35 1/2 by 35 5/8 inches. Courtesy of SBC Communications, Inc.

Rhythm and Motion

Letter to the World—The Kick, by American artist Andy Warhol (1928–1987), is a serigraph. Serigraphs are also called silk-screens. Warhol created this artwork by applying different colors of ink one at a time through screens made of silk. Study the pattern of the lines in the dancer's skirt. Notice how they go from bottom to top in a regular, yet somewhat free and jazzy rhythm.

Even though the woman's skirt hides her legs, you can tell that she is kicking back and up. How do the positions of her body and clothing suggest a kick?

Sketchbook Journal

Divide a Sketchbook Journal page into three equal boxes to create a Technique Sheet. Think about different types of music that you like. Consider how you can show the rhythm of the music with line, color, shape, and pattern. Draw and label the rhythm of a different song in each box.

Studio 5 Setup

The Rhythm *of Op Art*

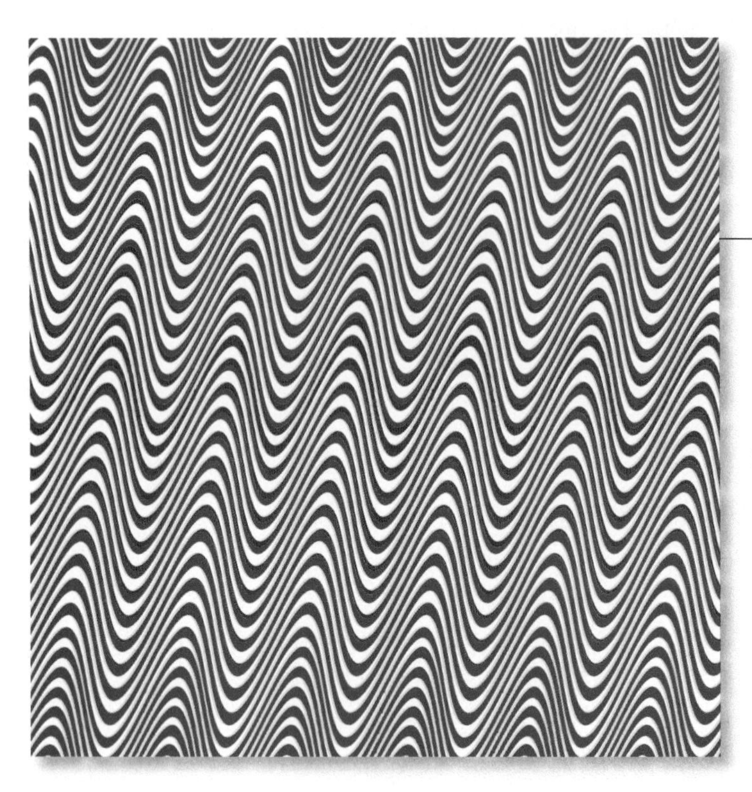

How does viewing this artwork make you feel?

Stare at the work on this page for about fifteen seconds. Do you feel dizzy or slightly uncomfortable? If so, you are feeling exactly what the artist intended. This artwork is an example of **Op Art.** The term, short for "optical art," originated in the 1960s to describe artworks that create optical illusions. Look for these details:

- The design includes a series of evenly spaced lines. Each line narrows and widens to make the two-dimensional surface seem warped.
- At the top of the artwork, the lines are blue and white. Toward the middle, the lines change to red, then back to blue toward the bottom. This alternating color creates a pulsating rhythm. The lines seem to move.

Optical Illusions

Op Art fools the eye into thinking it sees something that is not there. The wavy, horizontal lines in this artwork are set close together. This creates an illusion of yellowish, diagonal stripes. Do the diagonal stripes form actual or implied lines?

Technique Tip

Computer Op Art

Most computer programs allow you to define a line, copy it, and paste it numerous times. You can then move it without having to erase anything. These programs also allow you to save a version so you can experiment on a copy.

Studio 5

Create Op Art

Use what you have learned about rhythm to create an Op Art design.

Materials

- ✓ pencil
- ✓ graph paper
- ✓ 12" × 18" white drawing paper
- ✓ fine-tip markers
- ✓ ruler

1 **On the graph paper, draw a number of rhythmic lines of various widths. Use the graph paper grids to space the lines evenly.**

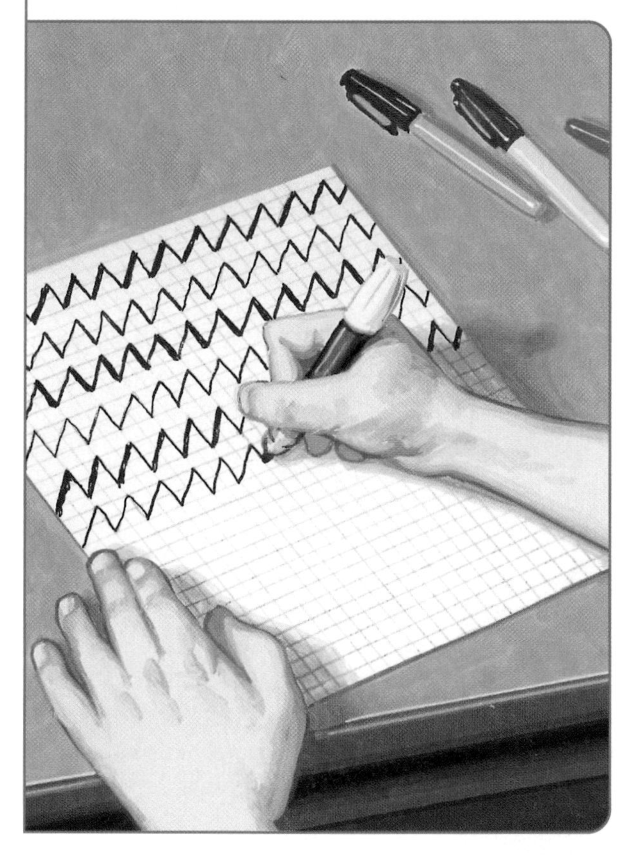

2 **Experiment with optical illusion by varying the width of individual lines or making some lines closer together than others.**

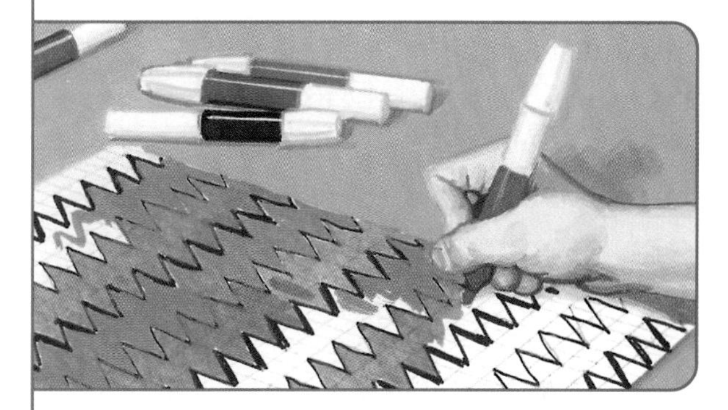

3 **Cut out parts of the graph paper that have good optical illusions. Arrange them as Op Art and glue them to the white paper.**

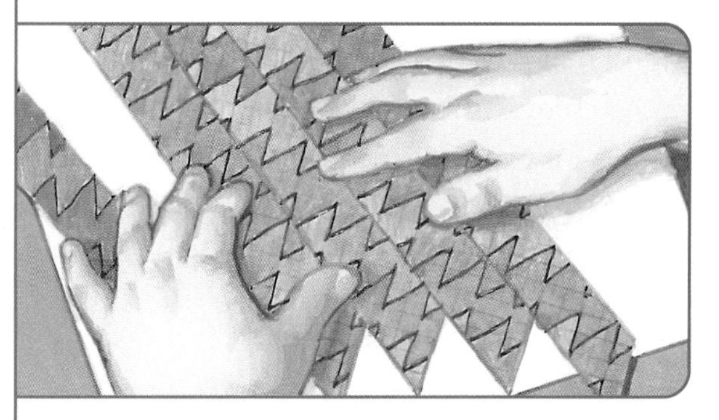

Review and Reflect

- What types of lines and rhythm did you use?
- How did you create an optical illusion?
- What sensations does your optical illusion cause when you stare at it?
- Did arranging sections of the graph paper design increase the optical effect of your composition? Why or why not?

Lesson 6

Unity

Most people enjoy being part of a group, but also like to stand out as individuals. Artists feel the same sort of thing when they arrange an artwork. They plan for the parts to look as if they belong together. At the same time, they make some elements stand out to add interest to their artworks. When the elements of art and the principles of design in an artwork belong together, artists say the work has **unity.**

Unity in Composition

Composition refers to how the elements of art and the principles of design are arranged in a work of art. Artists have many ways to achieve unity in their compositions. A painter, for example, might:

- Repeat a color, shape, pattern, or line
- Use one dominant color or shape
- Use related colors, such as in an analogous color scheme
- Arrange one shape, such as a triangle, with similar lines, such as zigzags
- Arrange the elements to create a feeling of order

Sometimes an artist will choose a theme or central idea for an artwork. Then, the artist composes the artwork with shapes or other elements which support the theme or idea.

Jaune Quick-to-See Smith. *Family Tree*, 1986. Pastel on paper, 30 by 22 inches. Private collection. © Jaune Quick-to-See Smith.

The repeating triangles and the zigzag lines create unity in this artwork. What else does the artist repeat?

Wang Yani. *Little Monkeys and Mummy,* 1980. Ink and pigment on paper, 15 by 21 inches. © Wang Shiqiang. Courtesy of Byron Preiss Visual Publications, Inc./New China Pictures.

Unity and Expression

Chinese artist Wang Yani (1975–) created this playful painting when she was only five years old! She spent a lot of time observing monkeys, and then painted them from memory. How do the postures of the monkeys create unity?

Wang also used color and brushstrokes to create unity. She used many different values of brown and soft, fuzzy brushstrokes to show the bodies of the monkeys. Notice that the largest monkey is the focal point. It faces the viewer while the other monkeys are painted in profile. What other elements of art create unity in this artwork?

Sketchbook Journal

Use colored pencils to draw an outdoor scene in your Sketchbook Journal. Use at least two techniques that help create unity. Write a brief description of its theme and describe how they helped create unity. Make notes about other elements you can use to create unity.

Studio 6 Setup

Unity *and Theme*

Melissa Miller. *Flood*, 1983. Oil on linen, 59 by 95 inches. Collection, Museum of Fine Arts, Houston, TX. Photograph by Bill Kennedy.

How do color and line unify this painting?

American artist Melissa Miller (1951–) made certain everything in *Flood* supports her theme of animals struggling with nature. Look for these details:

- Miller created unity with different values of orange. The tigers, bird, waves, and sky all have shades and tints of orange.
- Curved lines give the painting the energy and feeling of a storm. Look for curves in the tiger stripes, the waves, and the clouds.

Unity and Mood

Miller used the elements of art and the principles of design to create a unified mood in this stormy scene. Everything works to give the viewer a feeling of the danger the animals face from the flood. However, one tiger glances at a patch of blue sky. How does this affect the painting's mood?

Technique Tip

Unity, Mood, and Color

As you plan a composition, take extra time to make sure your colors match the mood you want to set. Paint several different color schemes on a sheet of paper and study them closely. What moods do each of the color schemes bring to mind? Which would best match the mood of your artwork?

Studio 6

Create a Unified Design

Use what you have learned about unity to draw a scene of you and your family or friends at a picnic or outdoor game.

Materials

- ✓ 12" × 18" white drawing paper
- ✓ oil pastels or crayons

1 **Choose an activity that you and your family or friends enjoy. Decide what elements will help unify your drawing.**

2 **Use these elements to draw your scene. Look for ways to repeat some elements to show unity.**

3 **Use crayons or pastels to add color and further create unity among the parts of your composition.**

Review and Reflect

- Which techniques did you use to show unity?
- How do the elements and objects in your composition work together?
- How does your composition reflect your feelings about the activity?
- Which unifying technique worked best for you? Why?

Lesson 7

Variety

Paul Klee. *Fire at Evening,* 1929.
Oil on cardboard,
13 3/8 by 13 1/4 inches.
Museum of Modern Art, New York.

What provides variety in this composition? What provides unity?

An artwork with too many red lines and shapes can lack interest. To avoid this, artists think of ways to add variety to their compositions. **Variety** involves the use or combination of different elements to add interest to an artwork.

Techniques to Create Variety

Artists create variety in many ways. For example, they use objects that are similar, but have different details. Look at the similar shapes and colors Swiss painter Paul Klee (1879–1940) used to unify this painting. Then notice how he included the bright spot of orange among the cool and neutral hues to add variety.

Artists can add variety to their artworks in other ways. They might:

- Use a spot of color to contrast with the rest of the artwork
- Alter the size or shape of repeating elements
- Use a different line quality or texture on one element to contrast with the rest of the artwork
- Include a unique element, such as a shape or color, to draw the viewer's eye to a particular part of the artwork
- Use a different medium in a particular area of the artwork

Variety can be the ingredient you need to make your artwork pop!

Miriam Schapiro. *Wonderland,* 1983. Fabric and acrylic on canvas, 90 by 144 inches. National Museum of American Art, Washington, D.C. © Miriam Schapiro.

Unity from Variety

American artist Miriam Schapiro (1923–) made this collage with pieces of fabric art like lace. Look at the quilted pattern around the edge. How did the artist add variety to this repetitive pattern?

Wonderland is made up of objects of many shapes and colors. But these objects all have something in common. They used to be made almost entirely by hand, and usually by women. These common elements help provide unity. The artist added contrast with a plain rectangle in the center. How does the rectangle also provide variety?

Visual Culture

Study a quilt from your family's collection, a library book, or the Internet. Find the elements of art used to make the quilt. Describe how the artist used pattern and color in the design. If possible, ask the quilt's maker how he or she decided what colors and patterns to use.

Studio 7 Setup

Variety *Through Detail*

Ando Hiroshige. *Cats (Chats: extrait de l'album Schitsu gafu),* 1850. Pen and ink drawing. Bibliotheque nationale de France, Paris.

How do the details in this drawing add variety to the composition?

In this work of art, Japanese artist Ando Hiroshige (1797–1858) drew many cats in a variety of positions. Look for these details that show variety:

- Hiroshige changed the position and activity of each cat.
- The cats are all drawn in black ink. Some cats have patches, some have stripes, and some have neither.
- Some of the cats are drawn in funny positions. This humor provides interest that makes the viewer pause and look closer.

Value and Lines

At first glance, it might seem as though this artwork shows the same cat in many different positions. But, if you look closer, you can see that it shows many different cats. The repeated subject of cats drawn with the same medium provides unity. Some cats are drawn with bold lines to emphasize their position. Some are drawn with actual lines, while others include both actual and implied lines. In what other ways did Hiroshige add variety?

Technique Tip

Drawing Positions

To draw the position of an animal's body, study actual animals or pictures of animals. Look at the shapes that make up the body parts. This will help you position the head, torso, limbs, and tail. Draw lightly at first, then make the lines darker when you have a position you like.

Studio 7

Use Variety in a Drawing

Use what you have learned about variety to draw an animal in a number of different positions.

Materials

- ✓ pencil
- ✓ 12" × 18" white drawing paper
- ✓ black felt-tip markers

1 **Pick an animal to draw. Imagine how this animal looks, moves, and behaves.**

2 **Draw the animal many times on your paper. Each time, change the animal's position, activity, or appearance.**

3 **Use black felt-tip pens to add thick and thin lines and emphasize the shapes of each animal to add variety.**

Review and Reflect

- Describe how you showed variety in your composition.
- How did your placement of the animals show variety?
- Which of your animal poses do you find most humorous? Why?
- Which of the animal poses do you like best? Why?

Artist *at Work*

Careers in Graphic Design

Graphic design is the art of arranging words and pictures to state a message. Often, graphic design is an advertisement used to sell products, services, or messages. Good graphic design balances the art and text with the space on a page. It keeps in mind the viewer who will see the final design. Logos, brochures, newsletters, posters, signs, magazine and book pages are all types of graphic design.

Isaiah Sheppard is a senior designer at a publishing company. He leads a team of graphic designers. They all work together to brainstorm, design, and produce the pages of a book or magazine. To begin, Sheppard thinks about what the goal of the final design will be. Then he considers what principles of design are needed to meet that goal. For example, a page for a children's book will have a different look and message than a page for a magazine. Each publication has a different group of readers. Therefore, each one needs different principles of design, print styles, and images.

Isaiah Sheppard designs books and magazines to convey a message or information.

"To the Moon and Beyond," Designer Isaiah Sheppard. World Book illustration by Steven Seymour, Bernard Thornton, artists. From THE WORLD BOOK ENCYCLOPEDIA. © 1989 World Book, Inc. By permission of the publisher.

Where do you notice the artist's use of the principles of design?

A World Book special feature

To the moon...

and beyond

On July 20, 1969, two American astronauts from the *Apollo 11* mission became the first human beings to set foot on the moon. Millions of people back on earth sat spellbound as television pictures showed the astronauts exploring the lunar landscape. Four days later, *Apollo 11's* three-man crew splashed down safely in the Pacific Ocean. Yet as spectacular as the lunar landing was, it was only one of many space-age accomplishments. This special *World Book* feature commemorates the 20th anniversary of the first moon landing and traces the history of manned space travel from the Soviet Union's first earth orbit on April 12, 1961, to today's American space shuttles and Soviet space stations.

Keeping Up to Date

As a part of his job, Sheppard reads many different magazines and newspapers. This helps him stay up to date on current events. He also reads about new trends in design. It is important for Sheppard to know about new software and tools that can help him with his designs. Computers are an important graphic design tool. They are used to design a layout, produce text and artwork, and even create presentations.

The part of Sheppard's career that he likes best is helping children to learn. He thinks of himself as a visual communicator. He is able to share ideas with children and educators through his page designs.

Portfolio *Project*

Paint a Still Life

Paul Cézanne. *Ginger Jar and Fruit,* ca. 1895. Oil on canvas, 28 3/4 by 23 5/8 inches. Barnes Foundation, Merion, PA.

Plan

French artist Paul Cézanne (1839–1906) painted more than two hundred still lifes in his lifetime. In *Ginger Jar and Fruit,* he chose a simple arrangement of common objects. The rich colors and expressive brushstrokes are typical of Cézanne's style. Notice these details that show his use of the principles of design:

- The artist placed the jar and most of the towel on the left side of the table. The tinted stripe and the folds of the towel create a rhythm that draws your eye to the other objects on the table.
- Cézanne balanced the composition by placing most of the fruit on the right side of the table and the jar on the left. What type of balance does this composition show?
- The artist made the fruit the focal point by placing it in the center of the composition. How did Cézanne add emphasis to the fruit?
- Cézanne painted the background different shades of the same hue. He repeated the reds, greens, and yellows of the fruit as colors in the towels. This use of color helps unify the artwork.

Use your understanding of the principles of design to create a still-life painting. What theme will you show?

Sketchbook Journal

Set up some favorite objects from indoors or outdoors such as dishes or bicycles. Arrange them in a pleasing design. Make thumbnail sketches of the arrangement from different angles. Note which angle you prefer and why.

Materials

- ✓ various objects to arrange in a still life
- ✓ 12" × 18" white drawing paper
- ✓ markers
- ✓ acrylic or tempera paints
- ✓ brush
- ✓ container of water

Create

1 **Arrange a still life with seven different objects. Draw the objects using contour lines, concentrating on outlines.**

2 **Draw patterns on each object in your still life. Include lines, colors, and shapes inside of them.**

3 **Paint each large shape with a thin wash of color so that the lines of each object show through the paint.**

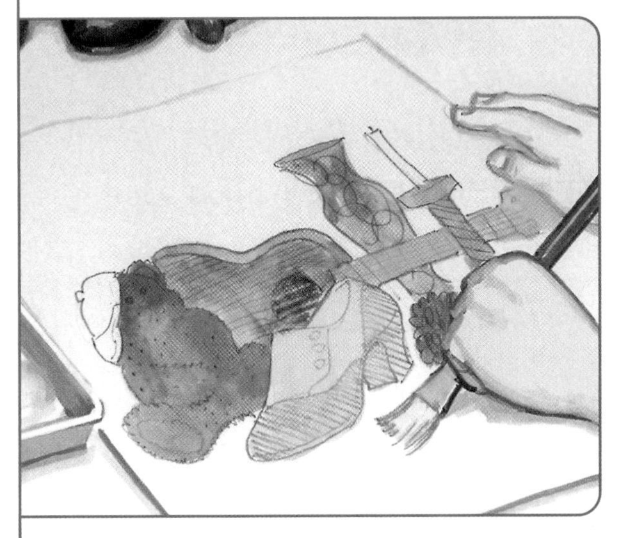

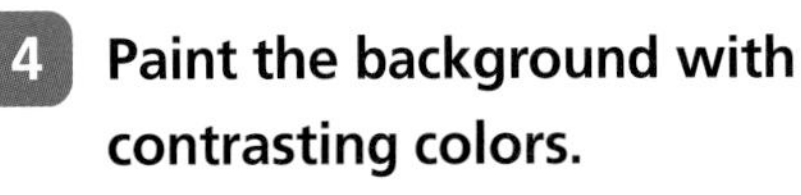

4 **Paint the background with contrasting colors.**

Reflect

- What mood did you choose to portray in your artwork? What elements of art did you use to support this mood?
- Did your use of the elements of art show movement in your artwork? Explain.
- How does the use of acrylic paints affect the mood of your painting?
- What problems did you encounter while completing your artwork? How did you solve them?

Unit 2 *Review*

Vocabulary Review

A **Match each art term below with its definition.**

rhythm	**variety**
balance	**proportion**
unity	**emphasis**
pattern	**monumental**
dominance	**style**

1. an artist's personal way of expressing ideas
2. when an artwork's elements of art and principles of design belong together
3. objects having larger-than-life proportions
4. repeated use of the same element in a regular way
5. how the parts of an artwork relate to each other and to the whole
6. using or combining one or more elements to add interest
7. a sense of real or visual motion in an artwork
8. a visual sense of importance given to a part of an artwork
9. when one element is the strongest or the most important in a composition
10. arranging elements of art according to their visual weight

Artists and Their Art

B **Each artwork listed in the box appears in this unit. Use the titles to finish the sentences.**

Breezing Up
Big Star
Red Cow
The Riches of California
Dancing in Colombia
Letter to the World—The Kick
System Drawing E66
Cataract III
Flood
Wonderland

1. Leonora Carrington demonstrates dominance in ___.
2. ___ by Melissa Miller shows how unity pulls elements together.
3. Winslow Homer used asymmetrical balance in ___.
4. Miriam Schapiro shows variety in ___.
5. M. C. Escher showed how pattern can be effective in ___.
6. Diego Rivera used exaggerated proportions in his mural ___.
7. ___ by Bridget Riley is an example of the rhythm of Op Art.
8. ___ by Andy Warhol is an example of progressive rhythm.
9. Altered proportions created emphasis in ___ by Fernando Botero.
10. ___ by Dawid Stanislawa is an example of radial balance.

Respond to Art

C **Look at the painting *Parade* by Jacob Lawrence. In a class discussion or on a sheet of paper, match each art term below with examples from the painting.**

Jacob Lawrence. *Parade*, 1960. Tempera with pencil underdrawing on fiberboard, 23 7/8 by 30 1/8 inches. Hirshhorn Museum and Sculpture Garden, Smithsonian Institution, Washington, D.C. Gift of Joseph H. Hirshhorn, 1966. Courtesy of the artist and Francine Seders Gallery, Seattle, WA. Photograph by Lee Stalsworth.

Art Terms

1. regular rhythm
2. standard proportion
3. pattern
4. asymmetrical balance
5. unity
6. emphasis
7. contrast
8. variety

Unit 2 *Review*

Write About Art

Descriptive Paragraph

D Copy the chart below and fill in the seven principles of design in the first column. Look back at the artworks in this unit. Select one artwork that shows your favorite principles of design. Circle those principles on the chart. In the second column, write descriptive details about those principles. Use the completed chart to help you organize a descriptive paragraph.

Your Studio Work

E Answer these questions in your Sketchbook Journal or on a separate sheet of paper.

1. What skill or principle of design did you find the most challenging? Which was the easiest? Explain.
2. Choose a studio artwork to put in your portfolio. What principles of design are reflected in this artwork? Why did you choose it?
3. What problems did you encounter with any of the studio techniques? What will you do differently next time?
4. Which artwork did you find the most inspiring? Why?

Name of Artwork

Principle of Design	Descriptive Details
	1.
2.	2.
3.	3.
4.	4.
5.	5.
6.	6.
7.	7.

Put It All Together

Claude Monet. *Rocks at Port-Goulphar,* 1886. Oil on canvas, 32 by 25 1/2 inches. Cincinnati Art Museum, Fanny Bryce Lehmer Endowment and The Edwin and Virginia Irwin Memorial 1985.282.

"These landscapes of water and reflection have become my obsession." —CLAUDE MONET

F **Discuss or write about Monet's *Rocks at Port-Goulphar,* using the four steps for critically viewing artwork.**

1. **Describe** What is the subject of this painting? Identify as many objects as you can.
2. **Analyze** How did the artist show the principles of design in this artwork? What elements of art provide unity? What type of balance does the painting show?
3. **Interpret** What time of day do you think it is? How do you think the artist felt about this place? What is the mood of this painting?
4. **Judge** Do you think Monet had a favorite principle of design? Explain.

Claude Monet found inspiration for his paintings in his gardens.

M. C. Escher. *Triangle System I A3 Type I,* 1938. Pencil, ink, and watercolor, 13 by 9 1/2 inches. Private collection.

Unit 3

Media and Methods

M. C. Escher used imagination, careful planning, and precise drawing to create this artwork. The path he took in imagining, developing, and creating this artwork is called the **creative art process.**

Many scholars agree that the creative process involves these general experiences:

- Getting an idea. Find inspiration as you review your Sketchbook Journal. Use your imagination, or notice things around you.
- Developing an idea. Make sketches of your idea. Then rethink it before beginning your artwork.
- Trying out ideas. Select materials for making artworks. Then express your ideas in a meaningful way.

Artists apply the creative process using a variety of **art media,** such as charcoal, paint, and clay. They use a variety of **methods,** or techniques, for using each medium.

M. C. Escher. *Self-Portrait,* 1943.

About *the Artist*

Dutch printmaker **M. C. Escher** planned to become an architect. Instead, he became a well-known graphic artist. Read more about Escher's life and his use of art media and methods on page 128.

Lesson 1

Drawing

Drawing is a visual record of how an artist's mind, feelings, and senses work together. A drawing can be a work of art itself. It can also be a plan for an artwork. Drawing helps artists improve their **perception,** or their ability to use their senses to observe the things around them.

Techniques for Shading

Artists draw with art media such as pencils, pen and ink, crayons, charcoal, chalk, and oil pastels. With these media, artists apply **shading techniques.** These techniques help show light and shadow. They give a feeling of depth and texture to a drawing. Artists choose from four main types of shading techniques.

Blending is a gradual change in value. **Stippling** shows a dot pattern to create dark values. **Hatching** involves creating thin parallel lines. **Cross-hatching** shows lines that cross each other.

blending

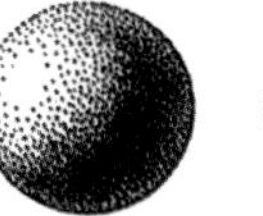
stippling

hatching

cross-hatching

Attributed to Rogier van der Weyden. *Men Shoveling Chairs,* date unknown. Pen and ink on paper, 11 3/4 by 16 3/4 inches. The Metropolitan Museum of Art, New York.

Notice how the artist used shading techniques to show light and shadow.

Eugène Delacroix. (Detail) *Une Femme d'Alger,* 19th century. Pen lithograph. The Metropolitan Museum of Art, New York.

Drawing and Details

French artist Eugène Delacroix (1798–1863) filled his notebooks with sketches of people and places to use later in his paintings. He made this drawing of an Algerian woman while traveling in Morocco. What shading technique did he use to give roundness and form to the woman's face and arms?

Notice how shading techniques show value and depth in the drawing. Compare the values in the woman's headdress with those in her arms. Delacroix placed the shading lines closer together to make the headdress look darker than the arms. Why do you think he chose the art medium he used?

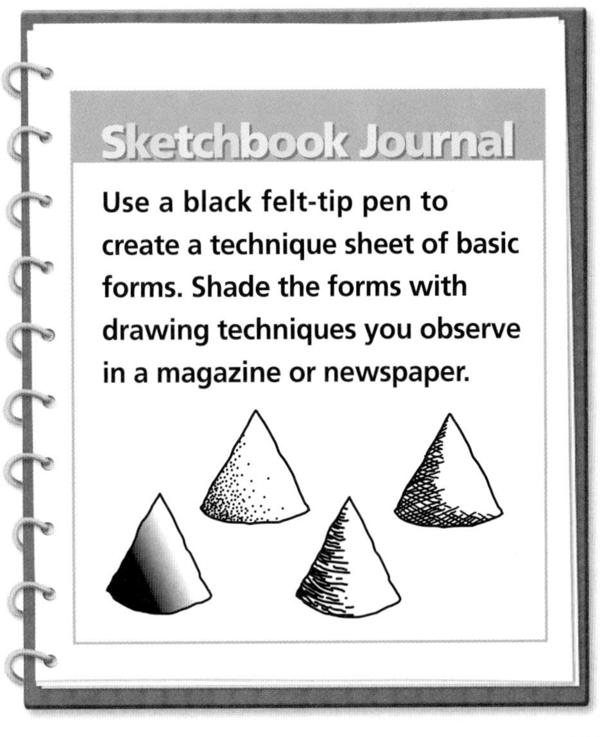

Studio 1 Setup
Gesture *Drawings*

Artist unknown, Italian. *Dancing Figure,* 16th century. Red chalk, 6 1/4 by 5 1/4 inches. The Metropolitan Museum of Art, New York.

How did the artists of these drawings show movement?

Honoré Daumier. *Street Show,* ca. 1868. Black chalk and watercolor on laid paper, 14 3/8 by 10 1/16 inches. The Metropolitan Museum of Art, New York.

Artists can use **gesture drawing** to loosen the mind and fire the imagination. In a gesture drawing, the artist captures a subject's actions by moving a pencil or other medium quickly and freely over a surface. Some gesture drawings are hardly more than scribbles. Others are more fully drawn. Look for these details:

- Scribbles around the limbs of the people in both artworks suggest movement.
- Curved lines around their bodies show how clothing moves during the gestures.
- Facial features and other details are barely sketched in.

Experiment with Position

Sometimes artists use gesture drawings to observe different positions of hands, feet, or heads. Look at the feet of the man on the chair. Notice how the scribbled lines suggest different placements for his left foot. What else do the scribble lines represent?

Technique Tip

Body of Circles

You can use circles and ovals to help you draw the human body. Larger circles can show the position of the torso. Smaller circles can be used for shoulders and knees. Smaller ovals can indicate the position of the head and hips. Limbs can be positioned by using long, thin ovals.

Studio 1

Create a Gesture Drawing

Use what you have learned to draw a sketch of a classmate in several poses through gesture drawing.

Materials

- ✓ 12" × 18" white drawing paper
- ✓ #2 pencil
- ✓ black felt-tip pen
- ✓ colored pencils, crayons, colored markers, pastels, or oil pastels

1 **Make a gesture drawing of a classmate in a stop-action pose. Use a pencil or felt-tip pen. Move the tool quickly and freely.**

2 **Make three more gesture drawings of different poses. Actions may include running, dancing, throwing, or walking.**

3 **Add contour lines around each gesture drawing to create a background. Use different colors.**

Review and Reflect

- Describe the lines you used to show the action of each pose.
- How do the lines in your gesture drawings work together to show movement?
- What do your gesture drawings say about each of the poses you drew?
- Which of your gesture drawings best shows movement? Explain.

Lesson 2

Painting

The art of painting dates back to the first recorded history of humankind. Cave dwellers used this artform as a means of expression thousands of years ago. Some of these paintings are preserved on cave walls in countries such as France, South Africa, and the United States.

Art Media for Painting

The artist of *The Great Hall of Bulls* made paint by grinding colored rocks into powder and mixing it with animal fat. The paint was then rubbed or brushed onto cave walls. Today, artists choose from a much larger selection of paints.

Paints are made by mixing a pigment and a binder. The **pigment** is the colored material, much like the cave dweller's rock powder. Pigments can also be made of chemicals, crushed minerals, and plants.

A **binder** holds the pigments together in the form of a paste. The cave dweller used animal fat. Other good binders include wax, egg, glue, resin, or oil. Paint can be thinned by adding a **solvent,** a liquid such as turpentine or water.

Artists use brushes, sticks, sponges, rollers, and other tools to apply paint. They may even use their fingers!

Artist unknown. *The Great Hall of the Bulls,* date unknown. Montignac-Lascaux, France.

Cave art may have been a record of a successful hunt or an artist's personal expression.

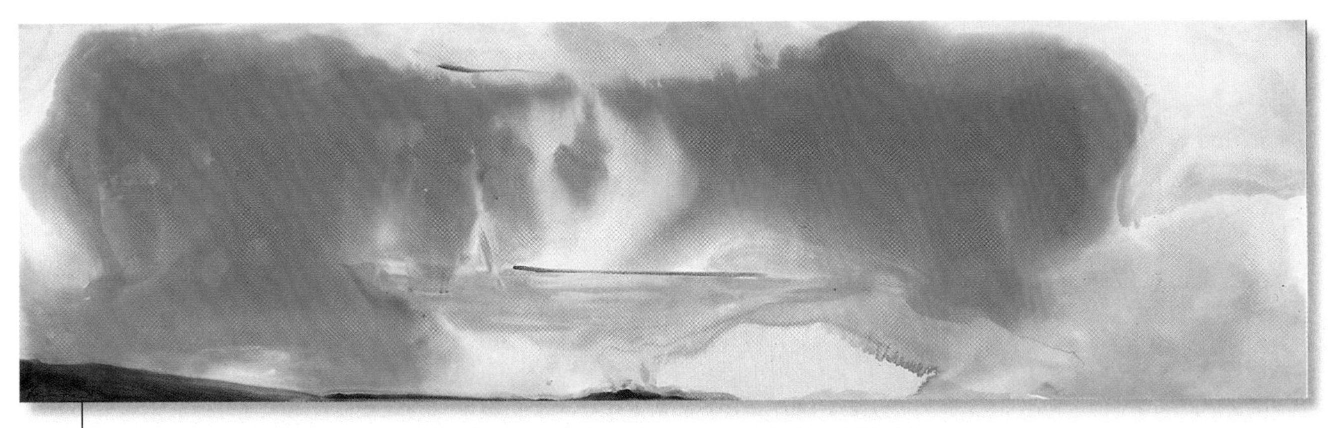

Helen Frankenthaler. *Moveable Blue,* 1973. Acrylic on canvas, 70 by 243 1/4 inches.
Courtesy of SBC Communications, Inc.

Painting and Expression

During the 1960s, a group of painters developed a style known as Color Field. To achieve this style, the artist brushes or pours thin paints onto large canvases. The wet blending of colors creates soft edges. American artist Helen Frankenthaler (1928–) demonstrated this style in *Moveable Blue.* Why do you think she chose this title?

Color-field paintings often show no subject. A **subject** shows what the artwork is about, such as a person or an animal. Color-field paintings are examples of Nonobjective Art. Nonobjective painters express their feelings through colors and shapes that look unfamiliar. What do you feel when you look at *Moveable Blue?*

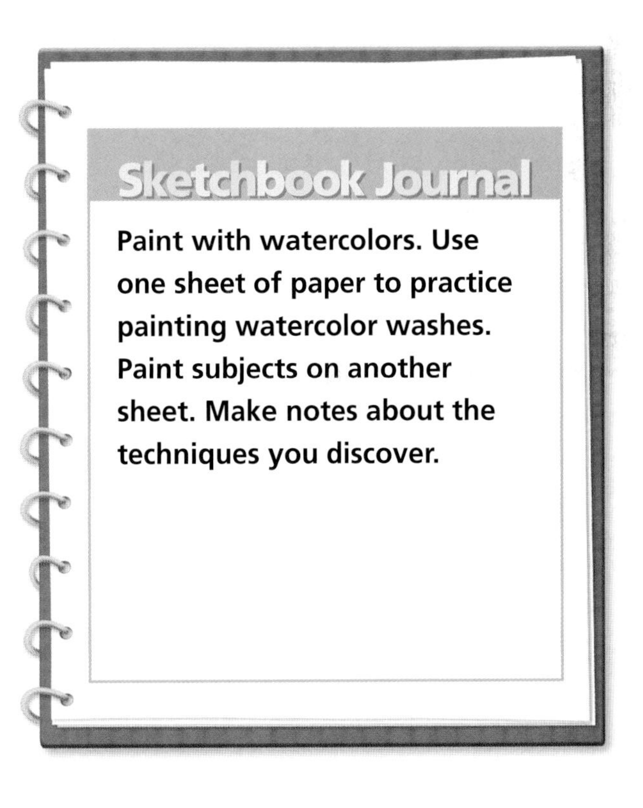

Studio 2 Setup

Art Media *for Painting*

Paul Cézanne. *Mont Sainte-Victoire Seen from the Bibemus Quarry,* ca. 1897. Oil on canvas, 25 1/3 by 31 1/4 inches. The Baltimore Museum of Art, Baltimore, MD.

How does the use of oil paints create texture and detail in this painting?

French artist Paul Cézanne (1839–1906) created this landscape with **oil-based paints.** The binder in oil-based paints is linseed oil. The solvent is often turpentine. Oil-based paints dry slowly. Artists have time to experiment with the paint as they work. Look for these details:

- Cézanne layered values of blue over white on the snow-covered mountain.
- Rough brushstrokes create texture in the paint on the shrubs and trees.
- Sharp lines of dark paint give details to tree limbs and rocks.

Water-Based Paints

Tempera, watercolor, and acrylic are all **water-based paints.** Their solvent is water, and they dry quickly. Water-based paints have different qualities. Tempera and acrylic paints are usually thick and **opaque.** You cannot see through them to the paper. Watercolor paints can be **transparent.** Light passes through them to reveal the paper. You can make tempera and acrylic paints transparent by mixing them with water.

Technique Tip

Watercolor Techniques

Experiment with watercolor on wet paper and on dry paper. Try sprinkling wet areas with salt. Blot an area of wet paint with a sponge. Scratch lines into wet or dry areas with a toothpick or pencil. As you try a technique, think about how it can be used for certain effects in your paintings.

Studio 2

Paint a Landmark

Use what you have learned about painting to create a watercolor painting of a landmark.

Materials

- ✓ 12" × 18" white drawing paper
- ✓ #2 pencil
- ✓ white crayon and/or white pastel
- ✓ watercolors, watercolor pencils, brushes, water container
- ✓ paper towels
- ✓ palette
- ✓ oil pastels, crayons, chalk pastels

1 **Lightly sketch a landmark from memory. Cover areas to remain white with white crayon or oil pastel.**

2 **Paint large areas with light tints. Let the paint dry. Add medium and dark shades by painting over some of the tinted areas.**

3 **Add more contrast with watercolor pencils, oil pastels, crayons, and chalk pastels.**

Review and Reflect

- Name the art media you used to paint your landmark.
- How do tints and shades create contrast and dominance in your painting?
- How would you describe the mood of your painting? What, if any, effect does the medium have on the mood?
- What areas of your painting please you most? Would you do anything differently next time? Explain.

Lesson 3

Printmaking

Printmaking is the process of transferring an image from an inked surface to another surface. Artists who make prints are called **printmakers.** They usually create many prints of the same image. One of these "multiple originals" that is signed, dated, and numbered by the printmaker is called an **impression.** The total number of prints made from one plate is called an **edition.**

Art Media for Printmaking

You can make a print with just your thumb and an inkpad. Most printmakers use a wider variety of tools.

The **plate,** or **block,** is the surface on which the artist creates the design to be printed. The design on the plate is a mirror image of what will appear on the print.

The printmaker often makes a test print, called a **proof,** and then carves more lines and shapes into the plate for the next print. The cycle is repeated until the artist is satisfied.

When the design is ready, the artist spreads ink across the plate with a **brayer,** a cylinder with a handle. Printmakers often have a brayer for each color of ink.

The artist covers the plate with thick, sticky ink called **printing ink.** The plate is then pressed to another surface, usually paper. Finally, the artist pulls the print, peeling it away from the plate to see how it looks.

M. C. Escher. *Rind,* 1955. Wood engraving in four colors, 13 1/2 by 9 1/8 inches. Private collection.

In this relief print, a spiral of a ribbon shape forms the features of a woman.

Karin Broker. *Boys 'n cat (notes of a mad girl),* 1996. Photo etching, 11 3/4 by 14 1/2 inches.

Intaglio Prints and Details

Houston artist Karin Broker used the **intaglio** technique to create *Boys 'n cat....* Artists make intaglio prints by cutting or scratching lines and details into a surface. These grooves in the intaglio print plate are then filled with ink and transferred to paper.

Intaglio printing is ideal for creating details. Artists can use a fine-tipped scratching tool to cut thin lines and precise detail into the plate. Look carefully at this print. How did Broker include fine details? What shape dominates the print?

Visual Culture

Study examples of printing on T-shirts, posters, newspapers, or other items. Find a newspaper's color comics page. When the page was printed, each color was applied with a separate plate. Describe what is printed with each plate.

Studio 3 Setup
Relief *Printing*

Describe the positive and negative space in this relief print.

Antonio Frasconi. *Weighing Fish,* 1919. Colored woodblock print, 10 1/2 by 7 3/4 inches. Norton Simon Museum, Pasadena, CA.

Weighing Fish is a **relief** print. In this printing technique, the plate is carved to leave a raised image. This raised image is then inked and transferred to paper or another surface. Look for these details:

- The paper is half yellow and half white. Notice how the paper shows through where no ink was applied.
- The positive space of the weighing scales, workers, and fish was carved out of the block. The carved-out areas did not receive ink.
- In the background, the yellow color of the paper and the heavy black ink create a sense of depth.

Relief Print in Reverse

The position of the fishermen creates an implied diagonal line that curves to the right. On the printing block, the artist carved the fishermen curving in the opposite direction. Why would he do this? Now look at the man holding the fish in the top right corner. On which side did the artist carve the fish on the original plate?

Technique Tip

Prints of Many Colors

There are many techniques to help you make multicolored prints. You can make a separate plate for each color. You can roll different colors onto different parts of the plate. Or you can print light colors first, and then add gradually darker colors with the same plate. Be careful to place the plate in the same position for each inking.

Studio 3

Create a Relief Print

Use what you have learned about printmaking to make a relief print showing an activity you enjoy.

Materials

- ✓ cardboard
- ✓ string
- ✓ scissors
- ✓ glue
- ✓ water-soluble printing ink
- ✓ brayer and inking surface
- ✓ 9" × 12" white drawing paper

1 **Create a contour drawing of yourself doing your favorite activity. On cardboard, arrange and glue strands of string over the lines of your drawing.**

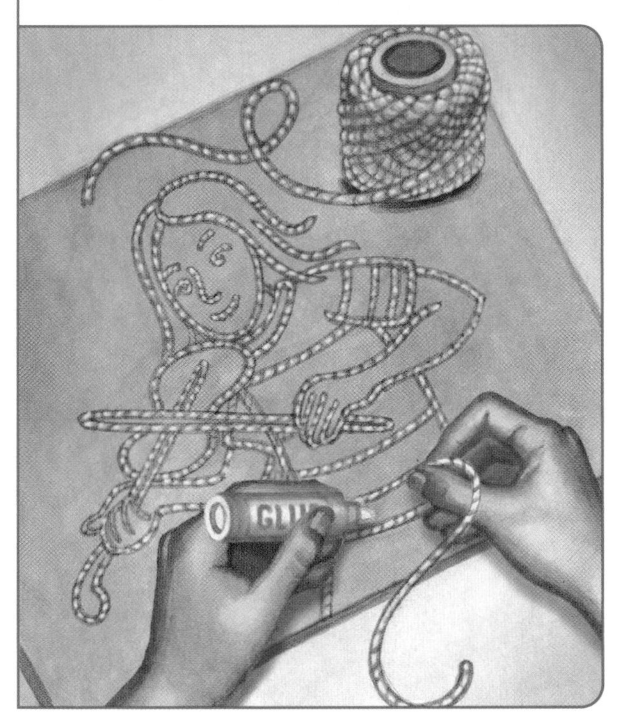

2 **Let the plate dry. Roll on a light color of printing ink with a brayer. Press paper on the inked plate. Pull the print.**

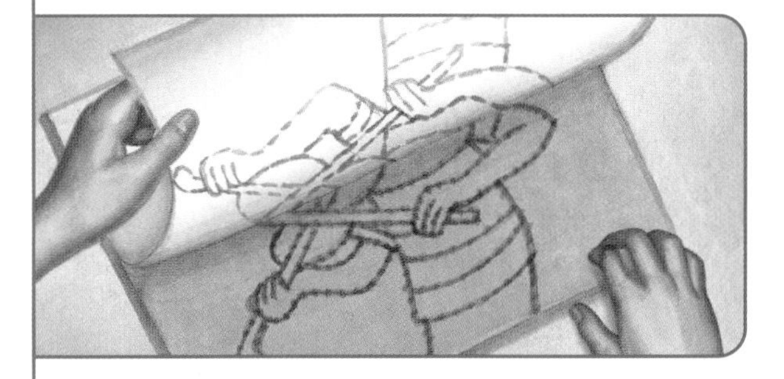

3 **Add details to the plate with string. Roll on a slightly darker ink and press again. Add details and print until you are satisfied.**

Review and Reflect

- Name the types of lines and shapes you used in your composition.
- How did the addition of colors change your print? Describe the changes you made to your plate. Explain why you made the changes.
- How would you describe the meaning of your print?
- Which part of printmaking did you enjoy most? Which was most difficult? Why?

Lesson 4

Collage

Artists sometimes express their ideas by arranging and gluing materials to a flat surface. This type of artwork is called a **collage.** An artist who makes it is called a **collagist.** Artists choose this artform for many reasons. Some like the way colors and shapes complement each other. Others find that collage is the best way to express certain personal or political messages.

Collagists include a variety of materials in their artworks.

Collage Media and Techniques

Some common materials for collage are magazine and newspaper pictures and brightly colored papers. Many artists also include pieces of fabric and hand-drawn images. Almost anything you can glue to cardboard could be material for collage.

Collagists glue the materials to a sheet of stiff paper or cardboard. Colored markers, pencils, or pastels can be used to add interest or emphasis. Paints can be applied. Objects can be drawn. With collage, the only rule is that there are hardly any rules!

Romare Bearden. *Sunset and Moonrise with Maudell Sleet,* 1978. Collage on board, 41 by 29 inches. Estate of Romare Bearden. © Romare Bearden Foundation/Licensed by VAGA, New York, NY.

How do exaggerated proportions create emphasis in this collage?

Collage and Cultural Themes

Collagist Romare Bearden (1912–1988) created this artwork of a woman he recalled from his childhood. Read the title and look at the details in the collage. Notice the time of day the artist chose to show.

Look for the painted paper and photographs Bearden used. Think about why he chose these materials. Notice the figures and objects that are in the foreground, middle ground, and background. How does this arrangement help you understand Bearden's meaning?

Bearden's collages often include cultural figures and symbols. This composition shows the subject working in her garden as the moon is rising. In what ways does she appear as a figure of strength?

Sketchbook Journal

Draw three sketches of yourself taking part in a favorite activity or hobby. Next to each sketch, make a list of materials you can use for a collage about the activity. Make notes about how the materials fit the theme of the collage.

Studio 4 Setup
Emphasis *in Collage*

Georges Braque. *Still Life with Tenora (formerly called "Clarinet"),* 1913. Pasted paper, oil, charcoal, chalk, and pencil on canvas, 37 1/2 by 47 3/8 inches. The Museum of Modern Art, New York.

How did the artist use colored paper to create emphasis in this collage?

French artist Georges Braque (1882–1963) used lines, shading, and pasted papers to draw your eye to the center of this collage. Look for these details:

- Braque used values of brown for his color scheme.
- The letters and the orange color draw your attention to the paper rectangle near the center.
- Curved shapes provide contrast to geometric ones.

The Simplicity of Shapes

Some of the first collages included only shapes cut from paper. In about 1913, Braque began adding wood, paint, and other materials to his collages. Notice the materials he used in this collage. He cut the materials into shapes that repeat the drawn shapes in the background. What effect do the vertical lines and shapes have? How do they contrast with other elements in the composition?

Technique Tip

Found Objects

As you look for collage materials, keep your mind and your eyes open. Often they are in your house or school. You might even find collage materials outdoors on the ground. You can cut or tear these materials into shapes and glue them to your collage.

Studio 4

Make a Hobby Collage

Use what you have learned to make a collage about yourself or someone you know who has an interesting hobby.

Materials

- ✓ collage materials
- ✓ scissors ⚠
- ✓ glue
- ✓ chipboard or posterboard
- ✓ felt-tip markers, pastels, or paint

1 **Collect a variety of collage materials. Focus on items that are related to your subject's hobby.**

2 **Arrange the items to create emphasis and interest. Cut them to size if necessary. Glue the items in place.**

3 **Use other art media to add details to help show your subject's hobby.**

Review and Reflect

- Which materials and objects did you use in your collage?
- What is the emphasis of your collage? Describe how the parts of your collage support the main part.
- How do you think other people will interpret your collage?
- Which part of your collage do you like best? Why?

Lesson 5

Fiber Artworks

Handmade quilts and knitted sweaters are examples of **textiles,** artworks made from fibers. **Fibers** are threadlike materials. They come from animals (wool), plants (cotton), or chemicals (nylon).

Textiles and other **fiber artworks,** such as embroidery and crochet, are a type of art called **crafts.** Fiber artists are craftspeople, highly skilled at making useful or decorative artworks by hand.

Types of Textile Arts

Textile and other types of fiber arts often involve weaving or stitchery. These are ancient techniques, but they remain popular with many craftspeople.

Artists **weave** by overlapping threads or fibers to create a fabric. Often the artist uses a **loom,** a frame that holds the fibers. All textile weavings have a **warp,** or lengthwise threads, and a **weft,** fibers that cross over and under the warp.

Other fiber arts use stitchery. It is made using a needle, thread or yarn, and cloth. One form of stitchery is appliqué, in which fabrics are stitched to a background. Quilting is another type of stitchery, in which the artist stitches together two layers of cloth with padding between them.

A design plan helps textile artists anticipate when thread colors need to be changed. Plans can be imagined, drawn on paper, or designed on a computer.

Quilt makers often combine shapes from different fabrics in their designs.

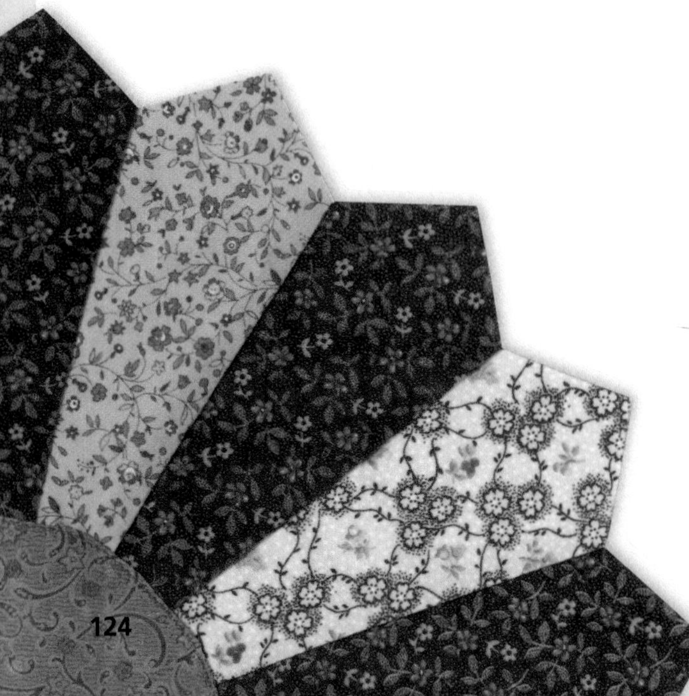

Notice how different fabric shapes can be applied using appliqué.

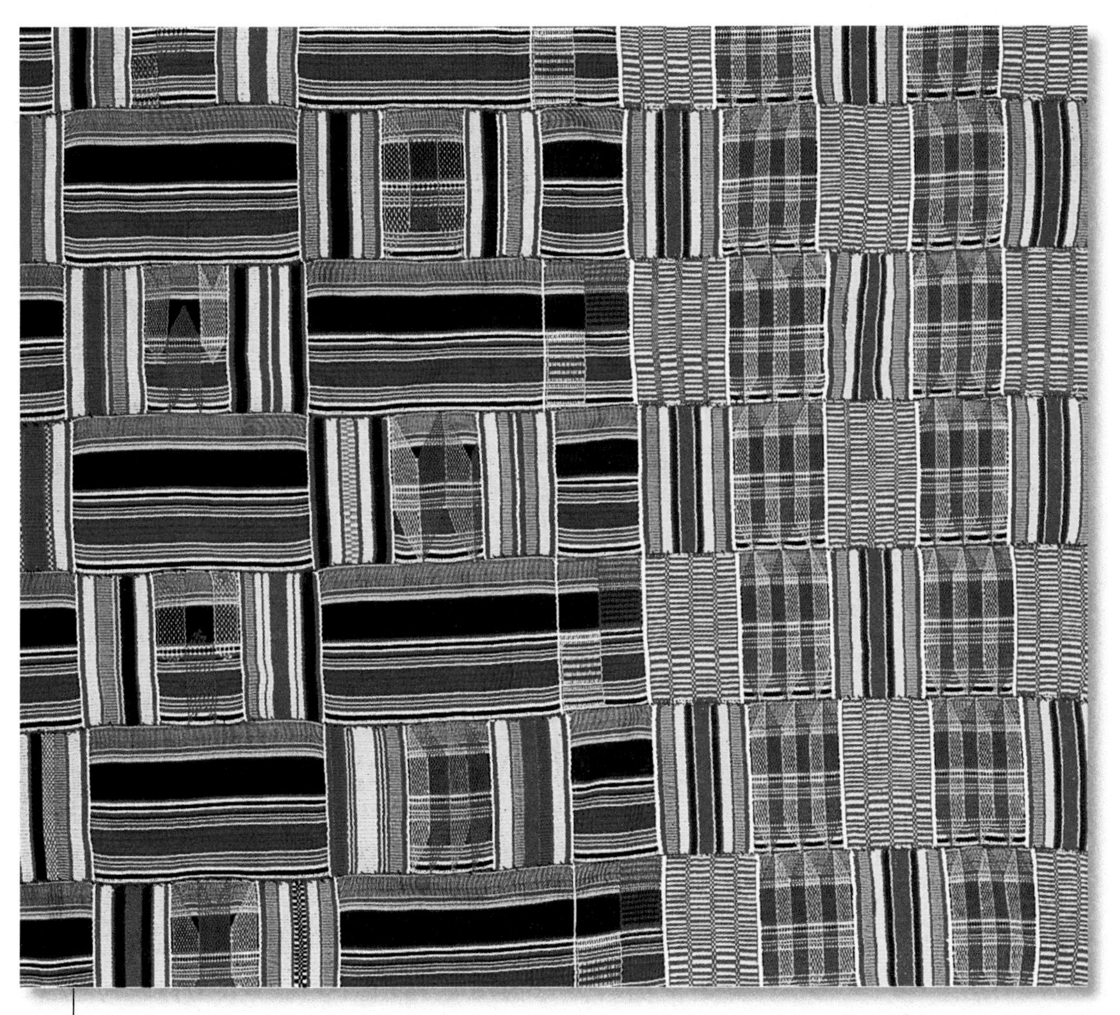

Artist unknown, Asante people, Ghana. *Kente Cloth,* 20th century. Silk, 120 by 71 1/3 inches. The British Museum, London, England.

Fiber Art and Culture

Kente cloth is woven by hand in Africa. The weaver creates the pattern by using different colors of fiber for the warp and weft. Read the credit line to discover the medium the artist used to make this kente cloth.

Notice how the vertical and horizontal lines are repeated to create a pattern. This repetition unifies the two color schemes of the design. Notice also how the same colors appear throughout the cloth. Blue, green, and black stand out on the left. On the right, yellow and orange are dominant. Why do you think the artist chose to do this?

Kente comes from the word *kenten*, which means "basket." Think of how the cloth and a basket are similar. Today, kente is a popular textile and is used by many cultures and appreciated for its artistry.

Research

Baskets are another type of textile art. Discover a variety of basket designs by searching for *basketry* on the Internet. Explore the materials basket weavers use. Make notes about the fibers used in each artwork.

Studio 5 Setup
Basket *Weaving*

Artist unknown, Aleut culture. *Twined Basket with Lid,* ca. 1900. Bowers Museum of Cultural Art, Santa Ana, CA.

How did the artist include pattern in this basket?

One of the first art skills early humans mastered was weaving lengths of reed into baskets. Artists of ancient cultures then used this same technique to create textiles.

The lidded basket above shows a basket weaving of the Aleut culture of Attu Island, Alaska. Look at these details:

- Unlike textiles, which are woven on a flat surface, reed baskets are woven in the round.
- Baskets, like textiles, can be made with warp and weft. A coarse fiber frame is the warp. Fine fibers, such as grasses or reeds, are the weft.
- Some fibers are dyed with colors made from plants. The violet and red fibers above form the design on the basket and lid.

Fiber Art and Function

Baskets can be functional items. The design of an artwork is often planned around its function. A quilt, for example, is designed for warmth. How might this basket be used?

Weavers experiment with decorations to distinguish their artwork from others or to please themselves. Some designs show symbols of the culture in which they were made.

Technique Tip

Watch That Weft!

Remember to alternate each weft fiber that you weave through the warp. If the previous weft goes over a warp, the next weft should go under. After each weft, push the fiber tight against the other wefts. A ruler or thin piece of wood can help you tighten the weft fibers. This will help you take your weaving off the loom when it is completed.

Studio 5

Make a Fiber Weaving

Use what you have learned about textile arts to make your own fiber weaving.

Materials

- ✓ cardboard
- ✓ yarn
- ✓ fibers, cloth strips, or other materials for the weft
- ✓ ruler
- ✓ clear tape

1 **Cut a small zigzag 1/4-inch deep across the top and bottom of the cardboard. Wind yarn around each "tooth" of the zigzag.**

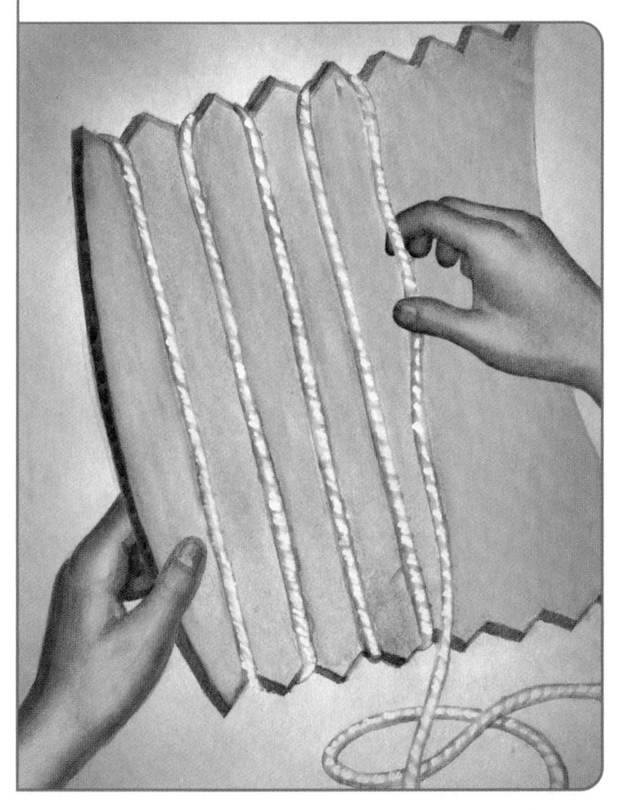

2 **Use different materials as wefts to weave over and under the yarn. Alternate warps with each weft. Push the wefts together.**

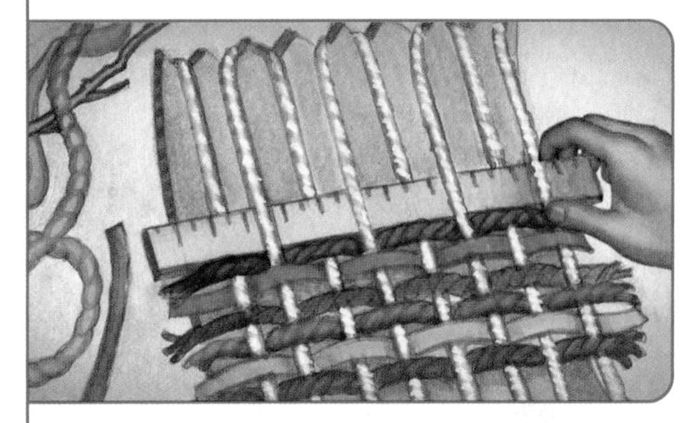

3 **When the weft is full, bend the cardboard and slide off your weaving.**

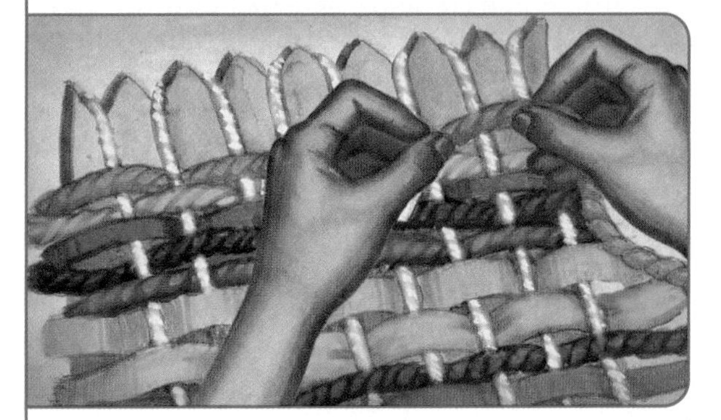

Review and Reflect

- Describe the colors, textures, and materials in your weaving.
- How do the textures and types of fibers add to the design of your weaving?
- What cultural symbol might you add to the design? Explain its meaning.
- What was most difficult about weaving? Would you do anything differently next time? Explain.

Meet *the Artist*

M. C. Escher

M. C. Escher is known for his carefully planned prints and paintings. He measured each shape in a design to fit with the other shapes like a jigsaw puzzle. But the artist longed for more.

The method that he used to present his images became less important. The message his artworks conveyed became Escher's focus. "Ideas came into my mind quite unrelated to graphic art," he said, "notions which so fascinated me that I longed to communicate them to other people."

He began to experiment with a wide range of subjects for his prints. Many of his subjects were inspired by his observations of people, places, and objects. Today, Escher's prints fascinate viewers around the world.

M. C. Escher. *Self-Portrait,* 1943. Lithographic ink, 9 3/4 by 10 inches. Private collection.

Escher manipulates perspective to intrigue the viewer.

"Only those that attempt the absurd will achieve the impossible."
—M. C. ESCHER

A Promising Youth

Escher was born in the Netherlands in 1898. Although he struggled in school, he showed a great talent for art. Escher decided to put to use his artistic skills and talent.

From 1919 to 1922, Escher attended a school for architecture and decorative arts. During this time, he studied graphic arts. He worked mainly in woodcuts, making prints with plates carved from blocks of wood.

A Leading Artist

Escher left school in 1922 and spent several years touring Europe. Every place he stopped, the artist drew landscapes and buildings. He also began to use dense patterns.

During his travels, Escher saw some beautiful mosaics in a palace in Granada. Mosaics include patterns that are made by attaching small pieces of glass or tile to a surface. These mosaics inspired Escher to create tessellations, or patterns of shapes that fit together, leaving no space in between.

Escher made some two thousand drawings and more than four hundred prints. *The World of M. C. Escher*, a major book about his art, was published shortly before he died in 1972.

Talk About It

Look back at *Triangle System I A3 Type I* on page 106. What effect does the system of triangles have on the artwork? Why do you think the artist chose this title?

The Life of M. C. Escher

1895

1898 Escher born on June 17

1915

Begins studying architecture **1919**

the Colosseum, Rome, Italy

Begins touring Europe **1922**

1924 Marries Jetta Umiker and moves to Rome

1935

Begins making tessellations **1936**

(detail) *Triangle System 1 A3 Type 1*

1938 Produces *Triangle System I A3 Type I*

1954 Artwork shown at math conference

1955

The Graphic Work of M. C. Escher published **1960**

Produces last graphic artwork, *Snakes* **1969**

1972 Dies in the Netherlands on March 27

1975

Look *and Compare*

Arts and Crafts

Can a craft be a work of art? Can a work of art be a craft? Consider M. C. Escher's artworks. His prints are as carefully crafted as are quilts. In fact, many of Escher's designs could be used as patterns for quilts. Likewise, it is not difficult to imagine the Mennonite quilt that could have inspired an Escher design.

What shape does this flock of geese form?

Repeating Patterns

Look at the blue birds in Escher's print at the top of the next page. Escher drew the birds nose to nose in groups of three. Notice how an implied line running along the birds' wings forms a circle. Look for other shapes that you recognize. Now look at the entire composition. Notice how Escher gave each part of the pattern its own color. The color scheme helps create the pattern.

Practical Patterns

Now look at the Mennonite quilt beneath Escher's artwork. Quilts serve a practical purpose. They help keep us warm. But they are also decorative items. Quilts are stitched from fabric pieces. Skilled craftspeople cut and arrange the fabric pieces into colorful shapes and patterns.

Look closely at the orange flower design in the Mennonite quilt. The red space inside each petal resembles a leaf. The shapes that at first appear to be background are actually other images you can probably recognize. Each of these designs uses three dominant colors and repeated shapes.

Color is an important element in creating patterns in these two artworks. Although the shapes each artist used differ, the patterns they create are similar. Notice how the larger shapes appear to be connected by smaller shapes. What other elements of art could be used to create patterns?

M. C. Escher. *Symmetry Drawing E69,* 1948. Ink and watercolor, 11 7/8 by 12 2/3 inches.

Artist unknown, American. *Mennonite Coverlet,* ca. 1880. Quilted, pieced, and appliquéd cotton.

Compare & Contrast

- **How do the different media in these artworks set the mood of each one?**
- **Where would you display each artwork? Tell why.**

Lesson 6

Sculpture

You have read that shapes are two-dimensional and forms have three dimensions. One way artists work with forms is by **sculpting,** taking material away from or adding it to the form. These artists are called **sculptors,** and their artworks are **sculptures.** Sculptors use media that range from hard marble to soft cloth. They may use stiff wood or pliable modeling clay. They might even use rusted old iron or shiny new copper.

Francisco Matto. (Detail) *Red Relief with Masks and Animals,* 1960. Carved and assembled wood, painted with oil, 77 2/3 by 29 1/2 by 2 inches. Museo de Arte Americano de Maldonado, Uruguay.

This South American artwork is an example of a wooden relief sculpture.

Sculpting Techniques

Sculptors create artworks by using one or more of four basic processes.

In **modeling,** the sculptor builds up and shapes a pliable medium. Clay, which is taken from the earth, is ideal for modeling.

Assembling is the technique of building a sculpture by attaching old or new objects together. Sculptures created through this process are called **assemblages.**

Casting is another way to build a sculpture. Sculptors often begin casting by making a wax model of the sculpture. The wax is then covered with a heat-resistant mold, then melted away. The sculptor pours molten metal into the hollow space. When the metal cools, the mold is removed to reveal a cast metal sculpture.

In the sculpting technique of **carving,** the sculptor cuts or chips pieces from a block of material such as stone or wood.

This detailed sculpture of a horse was made by casting.

Artist unknown, Chinese. *Lokapala, the Guardian King*, ca. A.D. 700–755. Earthenware with three-color lead glaze, 32 1/2 inches. The Nelson-Atkins Museum of Art, Kansas City, MO.

Sculpture and Expression

This Chinese artwork is an example of sculpture in the round, or freestanding sculpture. It is surrounded by space. What might you see from the back?

The artist modeled this sculpture in clay. Since clay is pliable, it is easier to capture facial expressions and fine details. Look closely at the king and the figure on which he stands. Notice how their expressions and postures differ.

The king is prepared for battle in his warrior uniform. What message do you think the artist was trying to convey?

Sketchbook Journal

Use construction paper to work out different ways to sculpt paper. You might try cutting and tearing or scoring and shaping. You can also try curling, folding, or pleating the paper. In your Sketchbook Journal, make sketches of each technique and take notes about how you achieved different results.

Studio 6 Setup
Sculpture *in Relief*

Francisco Matto. *Red Relief with Masks and Animals,* 1960. Carved and assembled wood, painted with oil, 77 2/3 by 29 1/2 by 2 inches. Museo de Arte Americano de Maldonado, Uruguay.

How is this carved wood sculpture different from a sculpture in the round?

Francisco Matto (1911–1995), a sculptor from Uruguay, created this artwork by carving and assembling wood. Matto's work is an example of relief sculpture, in which forms project from a background. Look for these details:

- A variety of geometric and organic shapes project outward from a wooden background.
- Matto used shapes that suggest certain animals or objects.
- The sculpture is painted with one color of oil paint. The shapes are defined by the shadows they cast.

Sculpture and Symbolism

In this sculpture, Matto used a number of **symbols** —letters, figures, or signs that stand for real objects or ideas. Symbols often have fewer details and simpler shapes or forms than the objects they represent. What animals do you recognize in this sculpture?

Technique Tip

Create in Layers

One way to create a relief sculpture is by gluing objects to a background. When you use this technique, make sure you plan ahead. Sometimes you will need to glue more than one layer of objects to the background. Glue the larger objects to the background first, then add the smaller pieces. Remember that each layer will cover the previous layer.

Studio 6

Create a Relief Sculpture

Use what you have learned about sculpting to create a relief sculpture of a house you would like to live in.

Materials

- ✓ drawing paper
- ✓ pencil
- ✓ large piece of cardboard
- ✓ cardboard, matte board, or foam core scraps
- ✓ glue and scissors
- ✓ white latex paint
- ✓ paintbrush and water container
- ✓ tempera paint

1 **Draw the front of a house on paper. Include symbols and details you want to show in relief. This is your building plan.**

2 **Cut the scraps in shapes that match your drawing. Arrange the scraps on a large piece of cardboard and glue them in place.**

3 **Let the glue dry. Paint the sculpture a single color. When the paint is dry, add color to only the top layer.**

Review and Reflect

- Describe the shapes and forms you used in your relief sculpture.
- Which principle of design stands out most clearly in your relief sculpture? Explain.
- Tell about the meanings the symbols hold for you.
- If you could use this design as the front of a real house, would you make any changes? Why or why not?

Lesson 7

Architecture

Architecture is the art and science of planning buildings and other structures. **Architects** are artists who plan and design sturdy, functional structures with balance and style. They mix and match traditional geometric and organic forms to create attractive and functional designs. An example of a traditional form is a **dome,** such as the one below.

Planning Designs for Structures

An architect begins planning by asking questions such as: Who will use the building? Where will it be? What is its purpose? How much space is needed?

Next, the architect makes sketches showing the arrangement of rooms inside the building, called a **floor plan.** Talking with the client helps the architect make adjustments before preparing the **blueprint,** a photographic print used to show the final drawing.

The architect also makes an **elevation,** a drawing that shows one side of the structure.

Architects often ask a **landscape architect** to design the grounds around a building. The landscape architect creates a pleasing outdoor design using plants, rocks, trees, water features, and other materials.

Architect Filippo Brunelleschi (1377–1446) faced a great challenge during the building of *Dome of the Florence Cathedral.* Imagine trying to build the enormous dome atop the cathedral without modern machinery. Today, the dome stands as a reminder of the architect's design skills.

Filippo Brunelleschi, architect. *Dome of the Florence Cathedral,* 1420–1436. Florence, Italy.

It is estimated that the Florence Cathedral dome weighs more than 35,000 tons!

I. M. Pei, architect. *West Facade of The Morton H. Meyerson Symphony Center,* 1989. Dallas, TX.

I. M. Pei, architect, and Russell Johnson, acoustician. *Eugene McDermott Concert Hall,* of *The Morton H. Meyerson Symphony Center.* Dallas, TX.

Architecture and Proportion

Architect I. M. Pei (1917–) was born in China and moved to the United States to study architecture. He is known throughout the world for his public building and urban center designs.

Pei often designs buildings for the arts, such as the Meyerson Symphony Center. Notice the sweeping curves of the center's **exterior,** or outside, in the top photograph. What other shapes do you see?

Now look at the **interior,** or inside, in the bottom photograph. How do the exterior curves affect the design of the center's interior?

A building's setting is an important part of an architect's design. Both Brunelleschi and Pei created public spaces that embrace their surroundings. Each building takes advantage of the views offered by its respective city. What type of structure might you design for your community?

Sketchbook Journal

Draw a floor plan for an art, science, or other museum. Include areas for galleries, meeting rooms, restrooms, offices, a restaurant, and a gift shop. Then draw a landscape plan for the building. Include trees, benches, sidewalks, and so forth. Finally, draw the front elevation of the museum.

Studio 7 Setup

Classic *Architecture*

Callicrates, architect. *Temple of Athena Nike,* 427–424 B.C. Acropolis, Athens, Greece.

Architects often are inspired by designs of ancient buildings. *Temple of Athena Nike* was planned and built around twenty-five hundred years ago in Athens, Greece. Look for these details:

- Greek architects often used **columns,** vertical posts that carry weight. Columns, like those holding up the temple's roof, have three parts. At the top is a **capital,** at the bottom is a **base,** and in between is a **shaft.**
- The temple is made of stone blocks. Stone was a favorite building material of the ancient Greeks because it was abundant and durable.

A Model of Design

The model below shows the Acropolis, a group of buildings that includes the temple. A **model** is a small version of a larger object. Architects use models to show how a completed building will look. Where is the temple in this model? How does the temple compare to the other structures?

Artist unknown. *Restoration Model of the Acropolis,* 5th Century B.C. The Royal Ontario Museum, Toronto.

What details of this structure are characteristic of Greek architecture?

Technique Tip

Build a Basic Structure

Building a model will be easier if you remember this before you cut: measure twice, cut once. This will help save time in having to cut some parts over again. Also, use small pieces of masking tape to hold your walls together while the glue dries.

Studio 7

Create an Architectural Model

Use what you have learned about architecture to build a model of a museum.

Materials

- ✓ museum plan from Sketchbook Journal (optional)
- ✓ cardboard or foam core
- ✓ glue
- ✓ masking tape
- ✓ found objects, such as toothpicks, wood blocks, buttons
- ✓ tempera paint

1 **Cut and arrange the cardboard or foam core to resemble the museum plan from your Sketchbook Journal, or other design.**

2 **Glue the forms together. Add details to your model by gluing on found objects.**

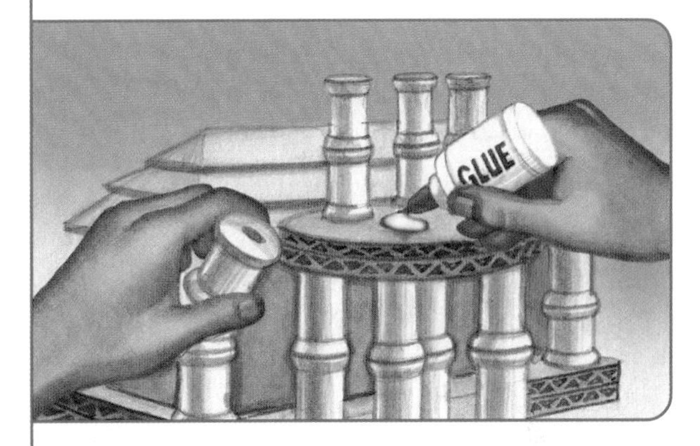

3 **When the glue has dried, paint your model in an appealing color scheme.**

Review and Reflect

- What organic and geometric shapes and forms did you use in your model?
- How closely does the model resemble your plan? How and why is it different?
- What is the purpose of your museum? How might your community use such a building?
- What is the best feature of your design? Explain.

Lesson 8

Pottery and Ceramics

In most parts of the world, you can find **ceramics,** or **pottery,** made of clay that has been hardened by intense heat. Some clay artworks are made to hold liquids or store food. Others are made for decoration. Clay is made of fine particles of minerals that are found in the earth. Most clay particles are made when rocks break down over time. Others are formed by the grinding action of glaciers.

Stages in Creating Pottery

Potters, artists who make pottery, begin by wedging the clay to remove air bubbles. Then the clay is modeled by hand or thrown on a wheel to create a desired form.

As clay dries, it becomes delicate. This occurs in the **greenware** stage. The greenware is then **fired,** or baked, to make it hard. Historically, people have fired pottery over hot coals. Today most potters use an electric or gas kiln.

When the pots cool, potters apply decorative designs. Some potters use thin layers of transparent paint made of minerals, called **glazes.** Making glazes with different minerals produces a wide range of colors. When the glazed pots are refired, the minerals in the glaze fuse to the clay.

Notice the designs the artist created on *Stirrup Jar with Octopus.* The swirling tentacles of the octopus create symmetrical balance. The curved lines on either side of the octopus's body are repeated in the fish.

Artist unknown, Mycenaean culture. *Stirrup Jar with Octopus,* ca. 1200–1100 B.C. Terra-cotta, 10 1/4 by 3 5/16 inches. The Metropolitan Museum of Art, New York.

This jar, used by seafaring Greeks to hold liquid, is both decorative and functional.

Fannie Nampeyo carried on her mother's tradition of creating hand-built Hopi pottery.

Pottery and Culture

Fannie Nampeyo's mother began making pottery as a young girl. She taught the craft to her three daughters, including Fannie (ca. 1900–1987). They became well known for their artistic designs. Some of the Nampeyos continue making pottery in the Hopi tradition.

Fannie Nampeyo and her great-niece, Dextra Quotskuyva, used designs and forms from ancient Hopi pottery. Notice the symmetrical shape of the pots shown below. Look closely at the designs glazed on the surfaces. How do these decorative designs compare with those on the Greek stirrup jar?

Native American potters often draw inspiration from ancient cultural designs. Notice how the artists painted the glazes. Many of the designs are stylized reptiles, birds, or feathers. What other stylized designs do you see on these ceramic pots?

Fannie Nampeyo and Dextra Quotskuyva. *Polychrome Ceramic Pottery,* ca. 1900–1980. Private collection.

Sketchbook Journal

In your Sketchbook Journal, draw designs for several different pieces of functional pottery. Make notes about the purpose each pottery vessel could serve. Choose one design that you would like to build. Make notes about how you would build, fire, and glaze your clay vessel.

Studio 8 Setup

Pottery *and Symbols*

Artist unknown, Greek. *Sphinxes, Dance Scene and Procession of Chariots,* ca. 700–680 B.C. Height 31 3/5 inches. Musée du Louvre, Paris.

Why do you think the artist chose these symbols to decorate this pottery?

Potters usually add decorative touches to functional pots. A Greek *loutrophoros* is a tall, long-necked pot used in rituals such as weddings and funerals. It has a functional purpose, but it is also highly decorated. Look for these details:

- Two long handles with finger holes make the pot easy to carry or pour from.
- The surface of the pot is covered with symbols, pictures, and designs. Some are decorative. Others seem to tell a story.
- The artist decorated the vessel with several different bands of repeated objects and lines. How did the artist use lines and shapes to create patterns?

A Story in Clay

The surfaces of many Greek pots tell stories. Potters often painted mythological creatures, heroic deeds, or historical events. The symbols on a *loutrophoros* would sometimes tell about the life of the person being buried or the bride being married. Look closely at the images on this vessel. What story might the symbols used by the artist tell?

Technique Tip

Wedging Clay

Wedging clay removes air bubbles that can expand during firing and explode your greenware. Take a large lump of clay and thump it down on a hard, flat work surface. Push your palms into the clay to form a wedge shape. Pull the back of the clay toward you and wedge it again. Keep wedging the clay for about five minutes to make sure all the air bubbles are removed.

Studio 8

Make a Hand-Built Pottery Vessel

Use what you have learned about ceramics to build your own pottery vessel.

Materials

- ✓ clay
- ✓ rolling pin
- ✓ plastic knife
- ✓ found objects
- ✓ toothpicks or toothbrushes
- ✓ kiln ⚠S
- ✓ clay glazes
- ✓ paintbrush

1 **Roll a ball of clay and hold it in one hand. Push the thumb of your other hand into the ball's center. Score the top edge and add slip.**

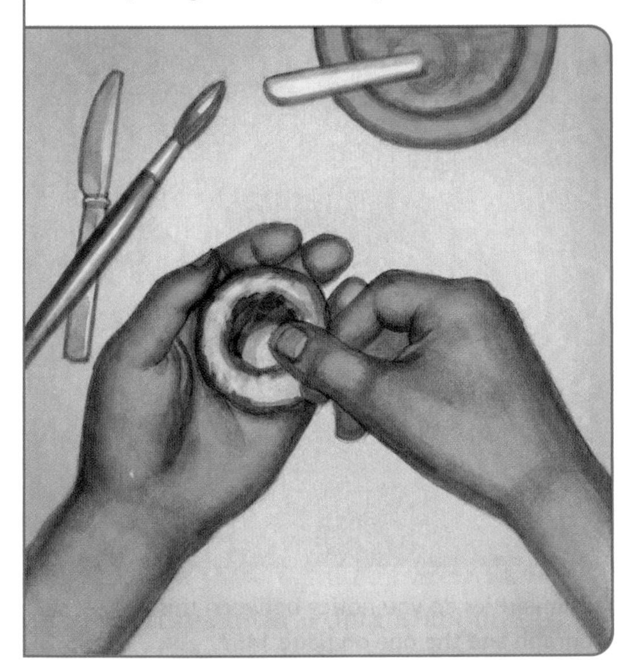

2 **Roll clay coils and wrap them around the top. Continue adding slip and coils to create your design. Cut a clay slab for the lid.**

3 **Use a toothpick or toothbrush to scratch designs or symbols. Add marks by pressing with found objects. Dry, fire, glaze, and fire again.**

Review and Reflect

- What types of marks or impressions did you use to decorate your pot?
- How do the lines, shapes, and textures you created show symbols and patterns?
- How might your pottery vessel be used? Who might use it?
- Which tool was best for making designs on your pot? What other tools might you use on a future pot?

Portfolio *Project*

Tessellation Design

M. C. Escher. *Symmetry Drawing E58*, 1942. Watercolor and ink, 11 7/8 by 9 inches.

Plan

M. C. Escher created this tessellation by repeating fish shapes. Notice that there is no space between the shapes. Making a tessellation requires careful planning. The artist must design interesting shapes that fit together with no space in between. Once that is achieved, the artist creates variety with no more than a few simple shapes. Escher does this by making the fish different colors, facing left or right, and positioning their bodies up or down.

- Look for the variety of fish shapes Escher used. Notice the similarities and differences between the shapes.
- The colors help show pattern and provide unity. There is no space between the many shapes.
- How does the artist's use of colors and shapes create rhythm?

Now use your understanding of the creative process, principles of design, and elements of art to make a tessellation.

Sketchbook Journal

Plan a tessellation by drawing geometric shapes that fit together. Begin with one shape, such as a circle. Draw several reproductions of the shape on construction paper. Cut the shapes out and arrange them in different patterns, two on top and two on bottom. Make sure all the shapes are touching.

Materials

- ✓ 3" × 5" index cards
- ✓ scissors
- ✓ tape
- ✓ #2 pencil
- ✓ 12" × 18" drawing paper
- ✓ colored pencils, markers, or watercolors
- ✓ black felt-tip marker

Create

1 **Begin a tessellation shape by cutting a shape from the left side of an index card and taping it to the right side.**

2 **Cut another shape from the top of the index card. Tape it to the bottom of the card.**

3 **Put the shape on the paper and draw around the shape's edges with a pencil. Repeat, fitting the shapes as in a puzzle.**

4 **When the paper is filled, outline each shape with a marker. Choose an art medium and add color to create rhythm and unity.**

Reflect

- What principles of design and elements of art did you use in your tessellation?
- How did the art medium you chose contribute to the composition?
- What meaning do the shapes hold for you?
- What problems did you have creating your shape? How did you solve them?

Unit 3 *Review*

Vocabulary Review

D **Match each art term below with its definition.**

cross-hatching	intaglio
perception	relief
opaque	collage
transparent	fibers
pigment	assemblage
blending	floor plan
glaze	greenware

1. not allowing light through
2. natural or synthetic threads
3. a shading technique using lines that cross each other
4. colored powder used to make paint
5. a mixture applied to clay before firing to create a thin, glassy coating
6. unfired pottery
7. clear enough to see through
8. a sculpture made by combining and connecting objects
9. the arrangement of rooms inside a building
10. a type of sculpture in which forms project from a background
11. using one's senses to be aware of the elements in one's surroundings
12. a technique that gradually changes the value of a color
13. artwork made by gluing different materials to a flat surface
14. a printing technique in which an image is cut or scratched into a surface

Artists and Their Art

E **Each artwork listed in the box appears in this unit. Use the titles to finish the sentences below.**

Une Femme d'Alger
Moveable Blue
Street Show
Sunset and Moonrise with Maudell Sleet
Kente Cloth
Red Relief with Masks and Animals
Portrait of a Kenyan Elder
Triangle System I A3 Type I

1. ___ is an example of fiber art.
2. ___ by Helen Frankenthaler shows a blending of liquid colors.
3. Honoré Daumier used gesture drawing to show movement in ___.
4. ___ is a collage by Romare Bearden that shows emphasis.
5. ___ is a still photograph by Judy Walgren.
6. Eugène Delacroix demonstrated shading techniques in ___.
7. M. C. Escher used precisely arranged shapes in ___.
8. Francisco Matto created the monochrome relief sculpture ___.

Respond to Art

C **Look at the fabric and paint collage *Master of Ceremonies* by Miriam Schapiro. In a class discussion or on a sheet of paper, match each art term below with examples from the collage.**

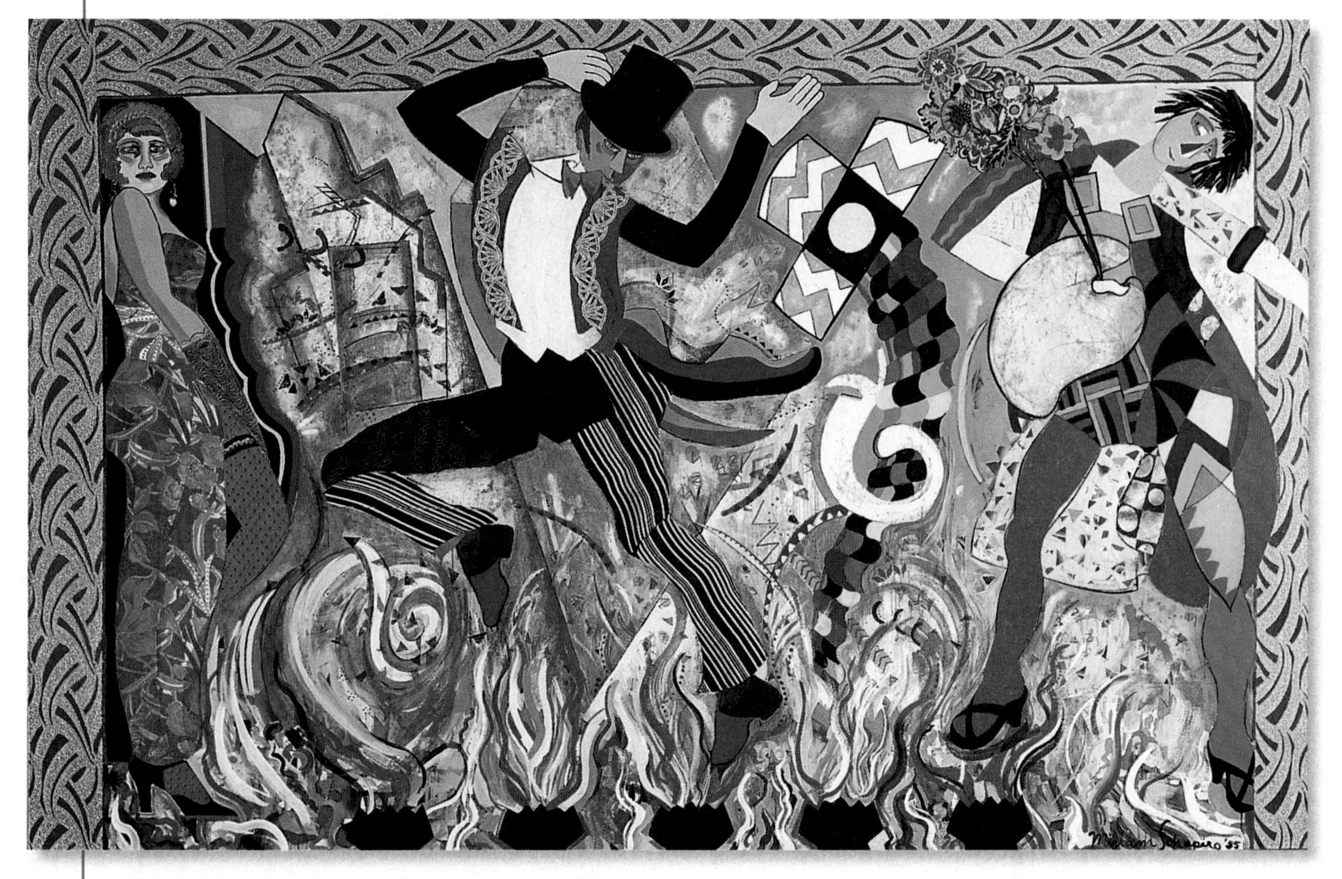

Miriam Schapiro. *Master of Ceremonies,* 1985. Acrylic and fabric on canvas, 90 by 144 inches. Collection of Elaine and Stephen Wynn. © Miriam Schapiro.

Art Terms

1. negative space
2. repetition
3. palette
4. pattern
5. intensity
6. overlapping

Unit 3 *Review*

Write About Art

Explanatory Writing

D **Look back at the artworks you created in this unit. Choose one to analyze in a paragraph. Copy the chart below and add details about the media and methods you applied. Use the filled-in chart to organize your writing.**

Title:	
Media and Size:	
Original idea:	
Problems or changes during development:	
Problems or changes during creation:	

Your Studio Work

E **Answer these questions in your Sketchbook Journal or on a separate sheet of paper.**

1. Which art medium did you most enjoy using? Why? Which art medium was most difficult? Why?
2. How did you come up with ideas for your compositions? In what other ways could you develop ideas?
3. Choose your most successful artwork. Why is this artwork successful?
4. How did experimenting with different media affect your creative process? How did you refine your ideas along the way?

Put It All Together

Janet Fish. *Kara*, 1983. Oil on canvas, 70 1/4 by 60 1/2 inches. The Museum of Fine Arts, Houston, TX.

F Discuss or write about Janet Fish's painting *Kara*, using the four steps for critically viewing artwork.

1. **Describe** What is the subject of *Kara?* What objects did the artist show in the painting? What is happening in the artwork?

2. **Analyze** Why do you think the artist chose to use oil paints for this painting? How would the artwork be different if she had used a different medium? Write several words about each medium listed below.

watercolor	**photography**
collage	**pastel drawing**

3. **Interpret** What mood did Fish establish in this artwork? What might Kara be thinking about? How would the mood change if Kara were smiling?

4. **Judge** American artist Janet Fish (1938–) paints images of realistic reflective surfaces, such as glass, mirrors, or shiny plastic. Was she successful in showing how light plays off surfaces in this painting? Why or why not?

"I feel as though I haven't seen an object until I actually start painting it."

—JANET FISH

Janet Fish's paintings show her interest in the reflective quality of shiny surfaces.

Diego Rivera. *The Making of a Fresco Showing the Building of a City,* 1931. Fresco, 271 by 357 inches. San Francisco Art Institute. Photograph by David Wakely.

Unit 4

A World of Art and Artists

At first glance, this Diego Rivera mural might look like a work in progress. But look closer. The artists, sitting on scaffolding, are actually part of this artwork. Rivera painted a mural of people painting a mural.

Rivera believed that art could change society by showing social and political themes. Art can also define society by making a visual record of different ages and cultures. **Art history** is the study of this record. **Art historians,** the people who study art, look at artworks as closely as art critics. But they go much further. They also record turning points and changes in the art world. They learn about artists and the context, or setting, in which they lived and worked. This gives them a deeper understanding of each artwork.

In this unit, you will find out what art historians have learned about the cultural and artistic traditions of societies throughout history. You will also have opportunities to use what you have learned to create original artworks that reflect art history.

About *the Artist*

Diego Rivera was as interested in politics as he was in painting. His bold works of art often reflect social and political issues. Read more about Rivera's life and work on page 182.

Diego Rivera. *Self-Portrait,* 1930.

Lesson 1

Mysteries of Long Ago

Art and people go together. Whether painting on cave walls or designing on computers, people have always found ways to create. In some of its earliest forms art was functional, or used for a purpose. Artists made masks and costumes for ceremonies and tools for hunting or cooking. But from the beginning, art has also been a way to communicate.

The history of art is divided into ages. The earliest works of art are called **Prehistoric Art** and were made before written records appeared. Tests on rock carvings found in the Blombos Cave in South Africa show that people have been making art for more than seventy thousand years!

Some of Europe's oldest works of art that still exist were painted on cave walls in France and Spain. The pigments used to create the paintings show some to be more than thirty thousand years old. When these cave paintings were made, people moved from place to place and lived by hunting and gathering food.

Works of art created around 3500 B.C. to A.D. 400 are called **Ancient Art.** During this period, some people began to settle into villages and grow their food.

Artist unknown. *Pictograph,* ca. 30,000 B.C. Chauvet Grotto, France.

Notice the dates of these two cave paintings. What similarities and differences can you identify?

Artist unknown. *Hall of the Bisons,* Paleolithic cave painting, ca. 15,000–8000 B.C. Altamira Caves, Spain.

Artist unknown. *Stonehenge,* ca. 1800–1700 B.C. Stone, height approximately 13 feet. Salisbury Plain, Wiltshire, England.

Stonehenge is sometimes referred to as "the riddle of Salisbury Plain."

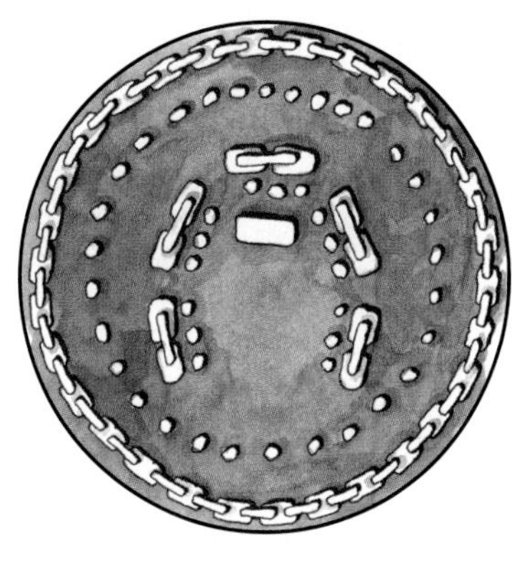

This diagram shows what the original structure may have looked like from above.

Ancient Architectural Forms

Stonehenge is an example of Ancient Art. It was built sometime between 1800–1700 B.C. on Salisbury Plain in England. Some of the stones fell over or were carried away to build other structures. From the remaining stones, scholars guessed what the original structure looked like. The huge stones form a circle 105 feet around. Near the center curve of the inner horseshoe shape was a marble slab that may have been an altar. This stone lines up with other stones to point toward the rising sun on the longest day of the year.

Sketchbook Journal

Look at cave paintings in this book, in the library, or on the Internet. In your Sketchbook Journal, take notes about the types of animals you see in the paintings. Make several gesture drawings of the animals. Describe the different positions of the animals you find.

Studio 1 Setup
Cultural *Cave Paintings*

Artist unknown. *Shepherds and Cattle,* 1300–1 B.C. Djado Massif, Niger, Africa.

How does this rock painting differ from those on page 162?

Artworks of Prehistoric and Ancient artists that remain today reflect life in their cultures. The cave paintings on page 162 and the one above show the importance of animals to hunting cultures. The cave painting above about shepherds and cattle shows symbols that communicate ways of life. By looking closely, you can discover some things about life three thousand years ago! Look for these details:

- A human figure seems to be herding or directing the cattle.
- The animals appear as simple shapes in a single color and show little detail.
- The size proportions of the animal figures are mostly the same.
- One animal near a human figure looks different from the cattle. What do you think its purpose was?

Movement

The human figure in this cave painting might be the artist. Perhaps the person painted this image to record the day's activities. Notice how some animals appear to be moving. They are all positioned in the same direction. What tells you that the person is moving too? What other information can you gather from this painting about the artist's culture?

Technique Tip

Artists of Prehistoric Times

Of course, Prehistoric artists did not have as many tools and materials as today's artists. Their color choices also were limited. As you study Prehistoric Art, think about what media you can use to create a similar look. Make notes about the colors you see to help you pick your color scheme.

Studio 1

Create a Cave Painting

Use what you have learned about Prehistoric Art to create a painting like those on cave walls.

Materials

- ✓ brown paper bag or craft paper
- ✓ charcoal
- ✓ natural dyes, such as berry juice, crushed leaves, or crushed rock, mixed with water
- ✓ brushes made from frayed sticks or bundles of grass

1 Crumple the paper into a ball. Flatten it again to create a texture similar to a cave wall.

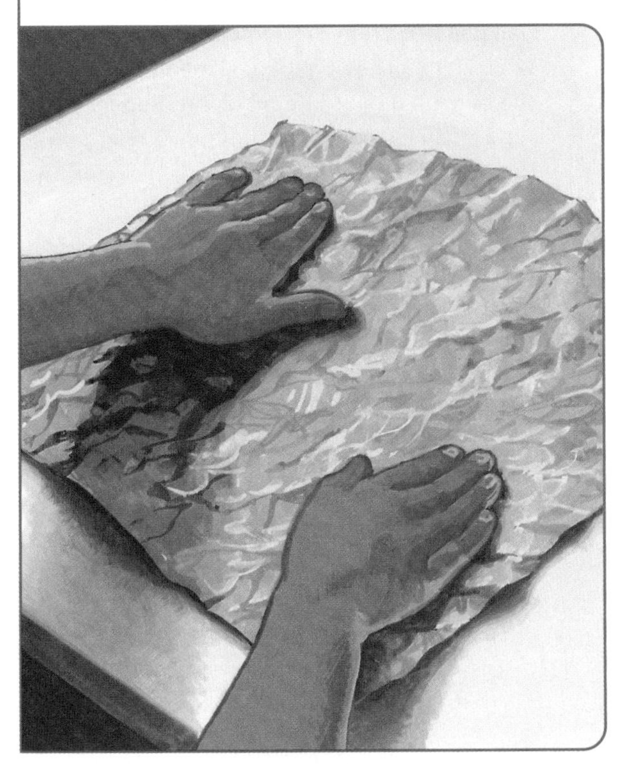

2 Draw some charcoal sketches of prehistoric animals in different positions. Add human figures if you wish.

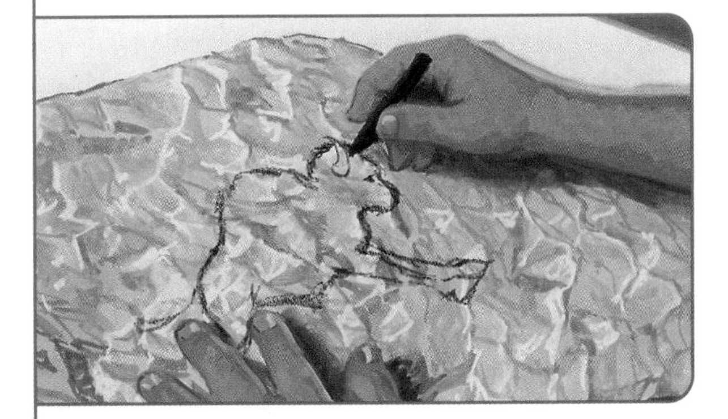

3 Use your homemade tools and paints to add color and shading to your "cave painting."

Review and Reflect

- Describe the positions of the animals in your painting.
- How do the tools and materials you used affect your painting?
- What actions or events do your drawings suggest? How did you show movement?
- What changes would make the animals you painted more realistic? Explain.

Lesson 2

Art of Ancient Egypt

Ancient Egyptian civilization began developing along the Nile River in Africa in about 5000 B.C. Farmers grew crops and craftspeople made pottery and jewelry. Boats carried goods from village to village along the Nile. Paintings of bloody battles during this time suggest the villages were at war. Towns in Upper Egypt banded together to support a king who wore a white crown. A king with a red crown controlled towns in Lower Egypt.

About 3100 B.C. the army of Upper Egypt defeated Lower Egypt. All of Egypt was now united under one king. The middle crown in the stone relief carving above symbolizes, or stands for, this victory. Notice how the middle crown is made up of parts of the crowns on either side.

This king became Egypt's first pharaoh, or ruler. The pharaohs hired artists and craftspeople to make beautiful objects such as pottery, jewelry, sculpture, and furniture. They also decorated the tombs and coffins of wealthy people. These tomb paintings often show scenes from daily life, like *Fishing Scene.*

These two artworks show the typical Egyptian artistic style. The head and lower body are shown in profile, or from the side. The eye and upper torso are shown in frontal view.

Artist unknown, Egyptian. (Detail) *Egyptian Rulers and Their Crowns,* date unknown.

Why do you think the center crown contains elements of the crowns on each side?

Artist unknown, Egyptian. *Fishing Scene: Attendants with harpoons and string of fish,* 1436–1411 B.C. Copy of the original wall painting from the Tomb of Kenamun, 17 by 20 2/3 inches. Egyptian Expedition of The Metropolitan Museum of Art. Rogers Fund, 1930 (30.4.67). Photograph © 1984 The Metropolitan Museum of Art, New York.

What does this painting tell you about life in ancient Egypt?

Artist unknown, Egyptian. *Tutankhamen, mask from mummy case,* ca. 1340 B.C. Gold, lapis lazuli, and cornelian, height 21 1/4 inches. Egyptian Museum, Cairo.

The Riches of Ancient Egypt

The pharaohs believed they could take their riches into an afterlife. They filled their tombs with dazzling works of art. This golden mask was found in the tomb of the pharaoh Tutankhamen. King Tut, as he is sometimes called, became pharaoh when he was about nine years old. He ruled until his death at age eighteen.

Read the information next to the artwork to learn the materials the artist used. What do these materials say about King Tut?

Research

Read about other famous treasures from King Tut's tomb by visiting http://touregypt.net/museum/tut.htm. The Cairo Museum site is filled with facts about King Tut and the riches in his tomb. It also has details about other Egyptian pharaohs. Note the similarities and differences of the pharaohs you find.

Studio 2 Setup
Royal *Symbols*

Artist unknown, Egyptian. *Throne of Tutankhamen,* ca. 1340 B.C. Gold-sheathed wood, carved and inlaid with precious stones. Egyptian Museum, Cairo.

What do these decorative images tell you about the owner of this throne?

This royal throne is one of almost five thousand treasures found in King Tut's tomb. It was meant to be used by the boy king in an afterlife. Although it is a royal throne, it is only slightly larger than a chair at your dinner table. Look for these details:

- The detailed carving is covered in gold and gems.
- A pair of lions protect the throne. Their faces appear at the front corners of the seat. The chair's legs end in carvings the shape of a lion's paw.
- The darker skin tones add interest by contrasting with the gold that covers much of the throne.

Symbolic Images

Many of the images on this throne have special meaning. The king sits upon a throne that symbolizes his power. Next to him stands a woman wearing a tall crown. She is touching the king's arm. What does the woman's attire and posture hint about her position in Egypt? At the top of the throne, the sun god beams down on the two people. What might this symbolize?

Technique Tip

The Power of Symbols

One way to come up with a symbol for a human trait is to think about animals that have that trait. For example, lions are powerful animals. They can be used to symbolize power. Cheetahs run fast and can be used to symbolize speed. Dogs are considered trusty and devoted. They can symbolize loyalty.

Studio 2

Design a Symbolic Throne

Use what you have learned about ancient Egyptian art to design and build a throne.

Materials

- ✓ cardboard boxes or an old chair
- ✓ tape, glue, or glue gun ⚠
- ✓ 9" × 12" white drawing paper
- ✓ pencil
- ✓ colored pencils or markers
- ✓ water-soluble paint
- ✓ brushes
- ✓ scissors ⚠
- ✓ plastic jewelry, gold or silver foil, or found objects

1 **With several classmates, plan a design for a throne. Use cardboard boxes or an old chair as your base.**

2 **Individually, make several design sketches for decorating your throne with symbols and color.**

3 **Work with your group to pick the best parts of each person's design. Then decorate your base with craft materials.**

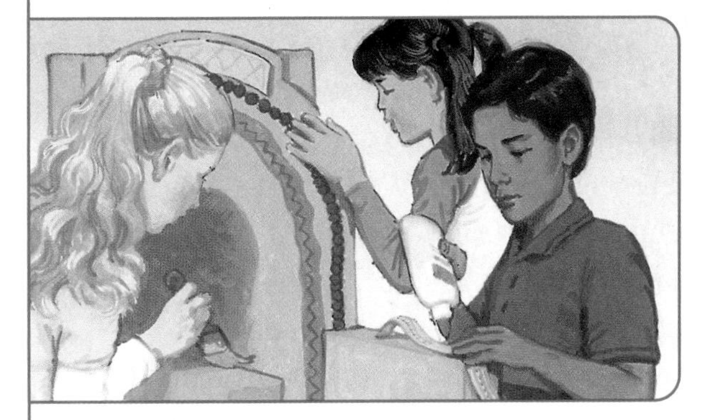

Review and Reflect

- What symbols did you use on your group's throne?
- How is your throne similar to those of other groups? How is it different?
- Describe the Egyptian king or queen who might sit on your throne.
- In what setting should your throne be placed? Explain.

Lesson 3

Art of Ancient Greece

Egyptians focused on life after death. But ancient Greeks (650–150 B.C.) turned their attention to their time on Earth. They valued the human ability to think and reason. Above all, though, they prized the human form and praised physical fitness. Works of art from ancient Greece often showed images of what the artists felt was the perfect human form.

Artist unknown, Greek. *Women Gathering Fruit,* ca. 5th century B.C. Red-figured cup. Musée Vivenel, Compiègne, France.

What does this painting indicate about the lifestyle of women in Athens?

The Art of Sparta and Athens

Many artifacts have been preserved from Sparta and Athens, two ancient Greek city-states. The tools and objects made by Greek artists offer clues about the differences between the two city-states.

Bronze figure of a running girl shows an athletic woman running. The men and women of Sparta were expected to be strong. Spartan children began athletic training at age seven. Boys learned to read and write and trained to be soldiers. Girls trained to become strong mothers of strong children.

Growing up in Athens was different. Boys worked with their fathers as farmers, stonemasons, or potters. Some wrestled or boxed after work. Athenian girls did not practice sports. They were not encouraged to ask questions or enter into discussions. *Women Gathering Fruit* shows activities that were thought proper for Athenian women.

Artist unknown, Greek. *Bronze figure of a running girl,* 6th century B.C. Bronze, height 4 1/2 inches. The British Museum, London. Courtesy of the Trustees of the British Museum. © The British Museum.

What does this sculpture say about life in the Spartan culture?

Painter of Micali. *Hydria with Running Figures,* date unknown. Museo Gregoriano Etrusco, Rome.

Greek Painting

Ancient Greek writings tell us that some of their best artists were painters. Sadly, no wall- or panel-paintings have been found. We can only get a glimpse of Greek painting by studying Etruscan pottery.

Etruscans, who lived in Italy, often imitated works of art from Greece. This Etruscan vase uses the Greek "black-figured" style. The figures were painted in black glaze on clay. How did the artist create a sense of movement?

This decorative vase also served the practical purpose of holding olive oil. Do these figures have more in common with Spartan or Athenian culture? Why?

Visual Culture

Look through magazines and newspapers to find pictures of modern athletes in action. Compare these pictures with the athletes on Greek vases and sculptures. How do the positions of their bodies and limbs create a sense of movement? What types of equipment do they use? How does their clothing differ?

Lesson 4

Art of Ancient Rome

Not far from Greece, the ancient Romans (753 B.C.–A.D. 476) built a republic in what is now Italy. The Romans eventually conquered Greece. By 100 B.C. Rome had built an empire that circled the Mediterranean Sea. Millions of people were subjects of the Roman Empire. The Romans admired Greece and they collected and copied many Greek works of art. The art of both Greece and Rome spread through the empire.

The Romans did not just copy the Greeks. Greek art emphasized ideal beauty. Romans were more concerned with art that was realistic and functional.

Roman artists often painted or sculpted **portraits,** artworks showing one or more people. These portraits focused on how people really looked. Roman artists showed their subjects' flaws and personal traits, which bring character to a person's face. This style may have started with the custom of making wax death masks of ancestors for family shrines. These death masks were sometimes made into marble portraits.

The Roman *Portrait Bust* shown here may have been created from such a death mask. Notice the realism the artist used to show the areas around the eyes and mouth. The features are of standard proportion, which adds to the portrait's realistic quality.

Artist unknown, Roman. *Portrait Bust,* ca. A.D. 54–117. Marble, life-size. Museo Lateranense, Vatican Museums.

What features do you see in this sculpture that would not be present in a Greek sculpture?

Artist unknown, Roman. *Ducks and Ducklings,* 1st century B.C.–A.D. 1st century. Marble mosaic, 28 by 28 inches. The Metropolitan Museum of Art, gift of Mrs. W. Bayard Cutting, 1932 (32.141). Photograph © 1980 The Metropolitan Museum of Art, New York.

Roman Mosaics

Romans also expressed ideas and feelings in **mosaics.** These works of art are made by attaching small bits of glass, stone, tile, or similar material to decorate a surface. These bits of material are called **tesserae.**

Romans made mosaics on walls, furniture, and other surfaces. This mosaic is made with small bits of marble. The tesserae are arranged to show a family of ducks at the edge of a body of water.

Many Roman mosaics were so carefully crafted that the tesserae show shadows. How did the artist make shadows on the head of the male duck in the foreground?

Sketchbook Journal

Cut and tear different colors of construction paper into small bits. Using white chalk on black paper, create a sketch for a design. Arrange and glue the bits of paper onto the black paper. Glue the design in your Sketchbook Journal. Make notes about the process you used.

Studio 4 Setup

Roman *Architecture*

Architect unknown, Roman. *Colosseum,* ca. A.D. 72–80. Rome, Italy.

What repeating element do you see in this ruin of the Roman Colosseum?

Roman buildings showed the empire's power and wealth. One of the most famous of the Roman buildings is the Colosseum in Rome. Gladiators fought for their lives in this huge stadium. Look for these details:

- The tiny people outside show the stadium's vast proportions. It seated fifty thousand people.
- The outer wall is made of a series of arches, openings with round tops.
- The repeated arches and columns create a pattern as well as serve a function.
- Most earlier stadiums were dug into hillsides for support. The strong arches provide the support for the freestanding *Colosseum*. Roman arches were so strong that this building has stood for almost two thousand years!

The Classic Arch

The arch may be the most outstanding feature of Roman architecture. The diagram above shows a variety of Roman arches. Arches allowed architects to leave openings in walls without weakening the wall. How might these openings have been used?

A strong type of cement is another Roman gift to architecture. Romans made this cement by mixing sand and lime with bits of bricks or stone. It took two thousand years for people to invent a stronger form of cement.

Technique Tip

Tools of the Trade

Architects use tools to help them draw building designs. They make straight lines with a straightedge or ruler. A compass is a tool for drawing circles or measuring distances. A French curve is a thin sheet of plastic with different curved shapes. Whatever tool you use, a sharp pencil will make things easier.

Studio 4

Design a Model with Arches

Use what you have learned about Roman art and architecture to design a model of a space station with arches.

Materials

- ✓ 9" × 12" white drawing paper
- ✓ pencil
- ✓ 12" × 18" white drawing paper
- ✓ colored pencils

1 **Research examples of arches that you see in books, on the Internet, or in your community. Make practice sketches.**

2 **Design an arch of your own. You might combine details from the arches you have studied.**

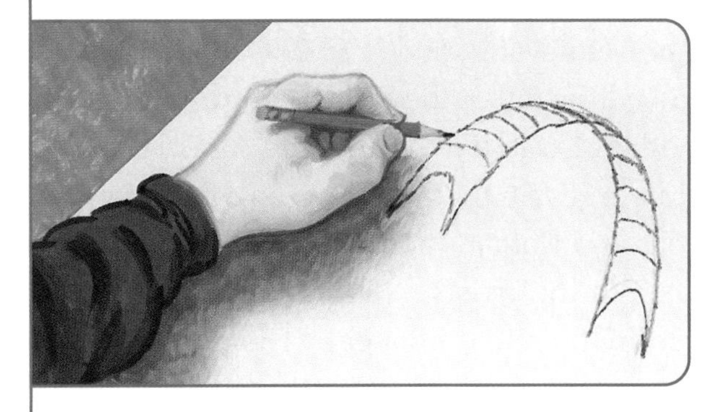

3 **Use colored pencils on clean paper to draw an imaginary design of a space station that shows off your arch and others.**

Review and Reflect

- Describe the line, shape, color, and texture of your design.
- What type of balance does your design have? What role do the arches play in creating balance?
- What music would be appropriate to play in your space station? Explain.
- Would your space station be a comfortable place to live? Explain.

Lesson 5

Art in the Middle Ages

The Medieval period (A.D. 400–about 1400) followed the fall of the Roman Empire. This period is also called the **Middle Ages.** The Middle Ages fill the gap between the ancient Greeks and Romans and the rebirth of their ideas. But the artists of the Middle Ages did more than just fill a gap. The creative energy that flowed through these ten centuries resulted in some of the world's most remarkable works of art.

Animal Symbolism

Animals were a common subject for artists of the Middle Ages. They used animals on jewelry and as decoration. Art historians call these works of art **animal style,** which was most popular in Germany and Scandinavia.

Sculptors in Norway carved fine animal-style works of art for Viking ships. Vikings felt that these works of art were powerful spirits. By their own laws, they had to take these figures off of their ships before they landed in port. They were afraid these mighty spirits would frighten the land spirits.

This animal head was made by carving away wood. The artist carved complex patterns and textures in the wood. Notice the variations in textures and patterns. Where would you display such a sculpture today? Why?

Artist unknown, Scandinavian. *Carved Viking Ship Post,* A.D. 850. Carved wood. Viking Ship Museum, Bygdoy, Norway.

Which animals would you choose as symbols for ships today?

Architect unknown. *Caerlaverock Castle,* ca. A.D. 1270. Dumfries, Scotland.

What special design features helped to protect the inhabitants of this castle?

Medieval Castles

During the Middle Ages, wars broke out among kings and other wealthy landholders. As protection from invaders, these people had architects design castles. These dwellings had high stone walls and strong towers. Notice the **crenations,** or curved edges, around the top of each tower. Why do you think the windows are small and narrow?

This seven hundred-year-old Scottish castle was often attacked during wars with England. Like most castles, this one is surrounded by a moat to help keep invaders out.

Sketchbook Journal

A coat of arms is a design that stands for a family, school, or city. Look on the Internet or in your school library for ideas for a coat of arms. Draw several designs for a coat of arms that represents your family or school. Make notes that explain the meanings of the symbols you used.

Studio 5 Setup

Art *and Religion*

Artist unknown, French. *Wenceslaus Psalter,* ca. 1250–1260. Ink, tempera colors, and gold leaf on vellum, bound between pasteboard covered with deep violet morocco, 7 9/16 by 5 1/4 inches. The J. Paul Getty Museum, Los Angeles.

Artist unknown, French. *Rose de France,* ca. A.D. 1200. Stained-glass window. Chartres Cathedral, Chartres, France.

What stories are told by the details in these artworks?

In the Middle Ages, European art was usually made to adorn the church. **Illuminations,** pictures painted by hand in books, often showed scenes from Bible stories. Soaring cathedrals featured stained-glass windows that served a similar purpose. Look for these details:

- Each frame in the illumination on top tells part of a story, sort of like a comic book.
- The five vertical windows in the bottom image each has a portrait of a religious figure.
- Sunlight streams through the windows, making the colors bright and rich.

The Power of Pictures

Few people could read during the Middle Ages. Those who could not read learned church history through images and symbols. This illumination tells the stories of events and history of the church. What type of balance does each of these works of art have?

Technique Tip

Illuminated Style

In the Middle Ages, books were written by hand in fancy writing called calligraphy. You can imitate this type of writing with a pen that has a broad, flat tip. As you write, hold the pen so the tip stays at the same 45-degree angle at all times. Practice on a sheet of scrap paper before writing on your artwork.

Studio 5

Make an Illuminated Storybook

Use what you have learned about art in the Middle Ages to make your own illuminated manuscript.

Materials

- ✓ three sheets of 9" × 12" white drawing paper
- ✓ stapler
- ✓ pencil
- ✓ colored pencils, markers, and other media
- ✓ gold or silver nontoxic markers or paint and brush

1 **Place three sheets of paper together and fold them in half. Staple them together on the center fold.**

2 **Write one or two sentences of a story on each page. Use an interesting lettering style, and leave blank spaces for illustrations.**

3 **Illustrate each sentence with colored markers. Add gold or silver with markers or paint to each page.**

Review and Reflect

- What is happening in your illumination?
- Compare the illustrations from page to page. How are they similar? How are they different?
- How does the setting of your story affect the mood of the illustrations?
- Which page of your storybook would you select to include in an advertisement for your book? Explain.

Meet *the Artist*

Diego Rivera

Diego Rivera mastered the classic European style of painting as a youth. Then he went to Europe and studied under artists Pablo Picasso and Georges Braque. But in the end, Rivera turned his back on classic art. Political revolution was in the air. Rivera wanted to create a new art for a new age. He combined classic art with Mexican folk art. Then he painted his murals on the sides of buildings and other public spaces. Rivera realized his dream of bringing art to the masses.

Diego Rivera. *Self-Portrait,* 1930. Lithograph, 15 3/4 by 11 inches. Fine Arts Museums of San Francisco, San Francisco, CA.

"One of my earliest memories of my youth is that I was always drawing."

—DIEGO RIVERA

A Born Artist

Rivera began drawing at the age of three. He was a serious art student by the time he was ten. In 1907, the twenty-one-year-old Rivera moved to Europe to study art.

But change was in the air. In 1911, rebels drove Mexican dictator Porfirio Díaz from power. Six years later followers of Karl Marx seized power in Russia.

Rivera was influenced by the revolutions. He decided that art should empower working people and help them understand their own histories. He wanted art to be visible to everyone, not just those who visit museums and galleries.

A New National Art

Rivera went back to Mexico in 1921. He began developing his own style of public paintings that "spoke" to the working people. He painted huge murals in public spaces where they could be seen by the masses. These murals honored Mexican culture and history with simple forms and bright colors.

In 1930, Rivera was commissioned to paint his first mural in the United States. He later received five more commissions for murals in San Francisco, Detroit, and New York.

Rivera continued painting murals for the rest of his life. He died while working on an epic mural telling the history of Mexico.

Talk About It

Look back at the mural by Diego Rivera on page 160. How is this mural like a time line covering the life of a city?

The Life of Diego Rivera

1885

1886
Diego Rivera born December 13 in Guanajuato, Mexico

1905

1907
Travels to Spain and France to study art

Plaza de España, Seville, Spain

1910
Successful show of Rivera art opens in Mexico; Mexican Revolution begins

1921
Begins his first mural in Mexico City

1925

1929
Marries artist Frida Kahlo

Diego and Frida

1930
Begins his first U.S. mural

1932
Begins mural for Detroit Institute of Art

Mural from *Portrait of Detroit* series

1939
Divorces Kahlo

1940
Remarries Kahlo

1945

1957
Dies on November 24 in Mexico City

1965

Look *and Compare*

Faces of Motherhood

Portraits can show us what life was like in different cultures at different times. Rivera's works of art often show people from Mexico's native cultures. Mary Cassatt painted many pictures of mothers caring for small children. Her works of art offer a look at daily life in France.

Motherhood in Mexico

Look at *Mother and Child* by Diego Rivera at the top of page 185. Rivera showed an Indian mother and her child in shades of gray. The mother wears simple clothes with a wrapped load on her head and a basket at her side. She seems to be briefly resting from her labors. Rivera did not show the child. He used shading and the position of the woman's arm to suggest a child tucked into its mother's clothing. What does this artwork tell you about the mother?

Motherhood in France

Now look at *Mother and Child* by Mary Cassatt at the bottom of page 185. Cassatt (1845–1926) was born in Pennsylvania, but lived and worked most of her life in Paris. Her artworks show the dignity of women as caretakers of children. In this painting, Cassatt showed the mother wearing a dress with a colorful flower print. A child sits on the mother's lap. This child seems bigger and older than the one in Rivera's painting. What do you think each artist was saying about motherhood?

Diego Rivera. *Mother and Child,* 1927. Graphite drawing on cream laid paper, 24 1/2 by 18 1/2 inches. Worcester Art Museum, Worcester, MA.

Mary Cassatt. *Mother and Child,* ca. 1890. Oil on canvas, 35 1/2 by 25 3/8 inches. The Roland P. Murdock Collection, Wichita Art Museum, Wichita, KS.

Compare & Contrast

- **How does each artist's choice of medium help express their thoughts and feelings?**
- **What mood did each artist create? How does this mood and other details show how Rivera and Cassatt felt about their subjects?**

Lesson 6

Architecture in the Americas

In the 1400s and 1500s, Europeans explored the Americas. They found many ancient cultures. Each had its own language and art. Some of these cultures were among the world's oldest. They are said to be **pre-Columbian,** which means they were in the Americas before Columbus. The Maya and the Anasazi are two examples. Each culture created its own style of architecture.

The Mayan Culture

The Maya (ca. A.D. 300–900) built a mighty empire in what is now Mexico and Central America. The Maya developed a calendar and a written language. They studied astronomy and built huge stone temples.

At the top of the two hundred-foot pyramid below is a temple with three rooms. Farmers depended on their predictions about agricultural cycles based on the refined Mayan calendar.

Artists painted the walls and roofs of Mayan temples. What comparison might you draw between the Maya and the Ancient Egyptians?

Architect unknown, Mayan culture. *Temple I,* ca. A.D. 300–900. Tikal, Guatemala.

Scholars think the Mayan city of Tikal surrounded this temple.

Architect unknown, Anasazi culture. *Cliff Palace,* ca. A.D. 600. Mesa Verde National Park, Colorado.

Anasazi Architecture

The Anasazi get their name from the Navajo word for "ancient ones." They have lived in North America for more than seventy-five hundred years. Some fourteen hundred years ago, they built homes into cliffs in what is now Colorado. The village is called Mesa Verde. The Anasazi lived there from about A.D. 600 to 1300. The Cliff Palace, shown above, was the center of religion and trade. In many ways, the Cliff Palace is like a modern office building. The inside is divided into rooms. The outside is used as a common space. Where in your community do you notice the influence of Anasazi architecture?

Research

Use *Mesa Verde National Park* as your keywords for an Internet or library search. Find out what it was like to live on the side of a cliff. Take a closer look at the Cliff Palace, and then take a virtual tour of some of the other Mesa Verde cliff dwellings. Note any similarities and differences in these and other structures you have read about.

Studio 6 Setup

The Impact *of Proportion*

Artist unknown. *The so-called Castle, the pyramid of the Tulum ceremonial center, and the surrounding temples,* 12th–15th century. Tulum, Quintana Roo, Mexico.

How do you think it would feel to stand at the foot of this huge Mayan temple?

Architects often want their designs to have a certain effect on people. This Mayan temple, for example, may well create a sense of awe in the viewer. Look for these details:

- The main building towers high above the land. This gives the temple at the top an aerial view.
- A wide, steep staircase creates a pattern of geometric shapes.
- The massive building is wider at the bottom, which makes the building seem strong and solid.

Size and Power

The architects designed this building with monumental proportions. By making it so large, they gave the temple a sense of importance. This also added to the power of the temple's priests. Compare the size of the temple pyramid to the building in the foreground.

Technique Tip

Human Scale

To show the size of a building, architects sometimes include people in their drawings. People can be added to the foreground, the middle ground, and the background. This use of scale helps the viewer judge the size of different parts of the building in the architect's plan, and shows proportion.

Studio 6

Design a Mayan-Style Movie Theater

Use what you have learned about Mayan architecture to design a modern movie theater in the same style.

Materials

- ✓ 12" × 18" white drawing paper
- ✓ pencil
- ✓ colored pencils, markers, or watercolors and brush

1 **Draw a plan for a movie theater with a marquee, a ticket booth, and a concession stand. Add people to show the theater's size.**

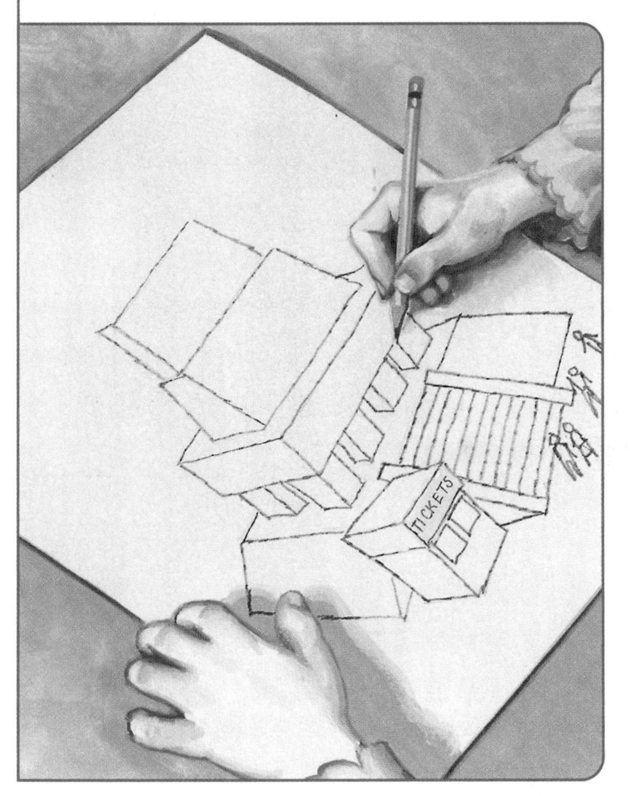

2 **Add elements from Mayan architecture, such as sides with steps, wide staircases, and horizontal bands of stone.**

3 **Choose an appropriate color scheme. Select a media and add color to your composition.**

Review and Reflect

- What elements of your design reflect Mayan architecture?
- Describe the proportion and design of your theater.
- What meaning do you think people will gain when they see your theater for the first time?
- What features of your theater do you like most? Explain.

Lesson 7

The Art of Renaissance Europe

In the 1400s, exciting changes were taking place in Italy, which soon spread across Europe. People became more interested in exploring their world. Art and science flourished. This period, lasting three hundred years, is called the **Renaissance,** or "rebirth." Reborn were the ideas and art of ancient Greece and Rome. This period laid the foundation for modern art and society in Europe and in the United States.

The Artist as Genius

After the Renaissance, people began to recognize artists as creative individuals. Some were hailed as geniuses.

Leonardo da Vinci was born in Italy in 1452. He began his long career as an apprentice when he was fifteen years old. When he died at sixty-seven, he had left his mark in art, science, math, and philosophy. This wide range of interests is the mark of what we now call a "Renaissance person."

Leonardo invented a painting technique called **sfumato,** in which the background shows blurry edges. His use of sfumato on the landscape adds to the mystery of the *Mona Lisa.*

The effects of the sfumato technique are similar to those of atmospheric perspective. Mona Lisa is shown in darker colors and greater detail. The background landscape appears distant and less detailed.

Leonardo da Vinci. *Mona Lisa*, 1503–1506. Oil on wood, 30 1/4 by 21 inches. Musée du Louvre, Paris.

The blurry background focuses attention on the subject, Mona Lisa.

Sofonisba Anguissola. *Portrait of Amilcare, Minerva, and Astrubale Anguissola*, ca. 1559. Oil on canvas, 61 13/16 by 48 1/32 inches. Nivaagards Malerisammling, Niva, Denmark.

Expressive Portraits

Sofonisba Anguissola was the first well-known woman artist of the Renaissance. She was born in Italy about 1532 and became skilled in portraiture. Her art won her international fame, as well as praise from Michelangelo, another well-known artist of the time.

This portrait shows Anguissola's father, brother, sister, and family dog. She created an implied line along the children's diagonal gaze. The background was painted in the sfumato style. Look closely and you will see what looks like Roman ruins. Why would a Renaissance artist include such a detail?

Sketchbook Journal

Make sketches of one or more family members in natural poses as they read or watch TV. Then choose two or three of your sketches to combine into a single sketch. Redraw the figures as they appeared in your original sketches. Make notes about how the figures you drew work together in the single drawing.

Studio 7 Setup

Emphasis *in the Renaissance*

Leonardo da Vinci. *The Virgin and Child with St. Anne,* ca. 1510. Oil on wood, 65 1/2 by 50 1/10 inches. INV 776. Musée du Louvre, Paris.

What elements of art create emphasis in this painting?

Leonardo's use of value, line, and overlapping in this painting lead your eye from one object to the next. Look for these details:

- The lighter values on the face and shoulders of the woman and the child in the middle draw attention to them.
- The implied line created between the eyes of these two figures strengthens their importance.
- The woman in the back is painted a slightly darker value, and the woman in the middle overlaps her.
- All four figures, including the lamb, stand out against the blurred background.

Light and Emphasis

Leonardo added emphasis to his subjects by creating the illusion of light shining on their faces. His use of value helped create this illusion of light. By carefully applying highlights, Leonardo made it seem as if his subjects were bathed in light from above. What might the directions of the light indicate?

Technique Tip

Sfumato Shortcuts

There are many ways to create a sfumato background. For example, you can draw the background with pastels or charcoal, and then smudge the medium to blur details. Or you can blend charcoal over the background to give it a smoky look. Either way, make objects blurrier as they get farther away.

Studio 7

Create a Renaissance-Style Portrait

Use what you have learned about Renaissance art to create a portrait with a sfumato background.

Materials

- ✓ 9" × 12" white drawing paper
- ✓ pencil, chalk pastels
- ✓ tempera or acrylic paints
- ✓ brushes and water container

1 **Use chalk pastels to create a sfumato background for a portrait.**

2 **Draw a realistic portrait of a friend in the foreground. Paint the portrait with tempera or acrylic.**

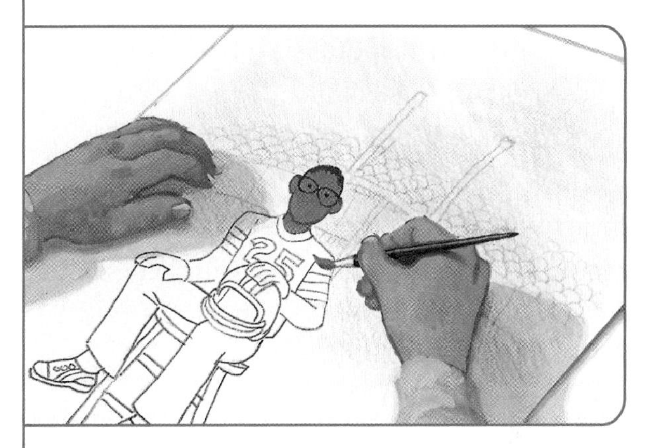

3 **Use a small brush to add detail to the foreground.**

Review and Reflect

- Describe the person you chose for your composition.
- How did you show contrast between the background and foreground?
- What mood does your sfumato background create with the portrait?
- What effects do you like best about your composition? Explain.

Lesson 8

Early Eastern Art

Eastern art—the art of Asia—has a long history. Artists from Asian countries such as China, Japan, and India have been creating dazzling works of art for thousands of years. Their artworks range from massive mosques and temples to delicate ceramics and silks. In this lesson you will explore the art of two Eastern cultures: India and China.

The Art of India

The earliest known Indian works of art were sculptures created by the Indus civilization (2500–1700 B.C.). The rise of Eastern religions from about 550 B.C. to A.D. 700 brought many new art forms. Indian artists designed temples and mosques. They sculpted mythological characters and animals. They painted religious murals. They covered walls with mosaics of tile and semiprecious stones.

Buffaloes in Combat was made in India at about the time the Renaissance was happening in Europe. It features bulls fighting and men dancing. This was a common subject in Indian art. How does this work of art compare to cave paintings in France and South Africa? What might you conclude about art around the world?

Attributed to Miskin. *Buffaloes in Combat,* late 16th century. Brush and ink with color on paper, 6 7/8 by 9 1/2 inches. The Metropolitan Museum of Art, Harris Brisbane Dick Fund, 1983 (1983.258). Photograph © 1984 The Metropolitan Museum of Art, New York.

How did the artist emphasize the bulls?

Artist unknown, Chinese. *Winged Tiger,* 19th century. One of a pair of banners, silk embroidery on silk, 46 1/2 by 46 inches. The Metropolitan Museum of Art, gift of Mrs. John H. Ballantine, 1947 (47.75.1). Photograph © 1990 The Metropolitan Museum of Art, New York.

The Art of China

While the Renaissance swept across Europe, art was also thriving in China. During the Ming Dynasty (A.D. 1368–1644) Chinese artists made fine porcelain. Dishes and vases of this delicate ceramic are among the most prized Chinese works of art.

Chinese artists also turned silk into excellent works of art. This lively silk banner was made in the nineteenth century. Notice the tiny stitches embroidered, or sewn, onto the silk. The diagonal lines in the border lead the viewer's eye to the tiger as the focal point. What element of art is the same in the border and the winged tiger?

Visual Culture

Research ancient Asian art in the library or on the Internet. Draw subjects and images that appear often. Include notes about what you think these might represent. Then, think about other symbols you have seen. Add these to your Sketchbook Journal along with notes about what you think the symbols represent.

Studio 8 Setup
Color *and Pattern*

Yang Fang Nhu. *Hmong Skirt,* ca. 1965. Batik, embroidery and appliqué on cotton, 25 by 43 inches. International Folk Art Foundation Collections at the Museum of International Folk Art, Santa Fe, NM. Photograph by Michel Monteaux.

How does this textile demonstrate pattern and repetition?

Eastern artists are well known for their textile artworks. They create patterns and designs by adding embroidery or dyes to the fabric. Look for these details:

- Tiny pleats, or folds, add texture and interest to the skirt.
- Repeated lines of color form horizontal bands around the skirt.
- The lightest color values are at the top of the skirt. In the middle the artist used darker colors. As the pattern moves to the skirt's hem, colors become brighter.

The Process of Batik

The artist created part of the pattern in this skirt by using a process called **batik.** To make batik, artists first create patterns on fabric with melted wax. The fabric is then dipped into a colored dye. The wax keeps the fabric from soaking up the dye. When the wax is removed, the dyed areas contrast with the areas that are not dyed. Where was the batik process most likely used on this skirt?

Technique Tip

Transfer By Proportions

A grid can help you turn a small image into a larger one. Draw a grid of one-inch squares over your own drawing. Then draw a grid of three-inch squares on a blank sheet of paper. Transfer what you see in each small grid to the larger grid in the same position. Your new drawing will be three times larger!

Studio 8

Make a Banner

Use what you have learned about Eastern art to make a banner.

Materials

- 9" × 12" drawing paper
- 36" × 54" sheet of white butcher or craft paper
- ruler
- pencil
- tempera paint or other art media

1 **On drawing paper, create a vertical design for a banner. Include personal symbols and images from the Eastern art style you have studied.**

2 **Use a ruler to draw a grid over the design. Draw a larger grid on the butcher or craft paper, and then transfer the drawing.**

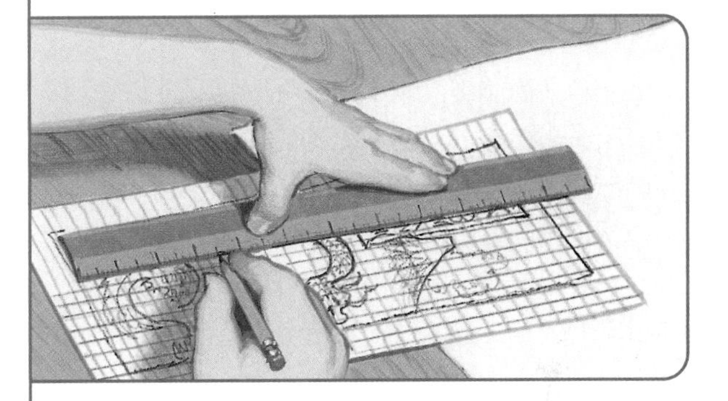

3 **Add color to the banner with your choice of art media. Use colors that attract attention or add to the message on your banner.**

Review and Reflect

- Describe the symbols and images you used in your design.
- How did you use pattern in your banner to convey your message?
- What feelings and emotions does your banner evoke? Explain.
- If you were to add a written message to your banner, what would it be? Why?

Lesson 9

Modern Western Art

The art of the past two hundred years is known for its many artistic styles and movements. For the first time, artists felt free to try different ways to express their ideas and emotions. No sooner had one art movement begun than it seemed to be replaced by another. In the past, art seemed to be filled with rules. For a modern artist, the only rule is that there are no rules.

Styles of Artistic Expression

For the most part, modern Western art falls into one of three main styles. In *Realism,* artists show objects much as they actually appear. This style, also called **Realistic art,** was the dominant art form of the second half of the nineteenth century. *The Horse Fair* is an example of realistic art.

Nonobjective art uses color, form, and texture, but does not have a recognizable subject. Different viewers see different things.

Abstract art focuses on mood and impressions. It may have an identifiable subject, but it usually has been simplified or changed in some way.

Rosa Bonheur. *The Horse Fair,* 1853. Oil on canvas, approximately 8 by 16 feet. The Metropolitan Museum of Art, gift of Cornelius Vanderbilt, 1887 (87.25). Photograph © 1997 The Metropolitan Museum of Art, New York.

Why is this a good example of Realistic art?

Wassily Kandinsky. *Improvisation 19a,* 1911. Oil on canvas, 38 1/4 by 41 3/4 inches. Städtische Galerie im Lenbachhaus, Munich. GMS 84.

German Expressionism

By the time the twentieth century arrived, artists had developed many styles of art. In Germany, a group of artists began painting simple designs with vivid color. This style was called **German Expressionism.**

Improvisation 19a by Russian artist Wassily Kandinsky (1866–1944) is an example of German Expressionism. Kandinsky used bold colors and organic shapes that overlap. His painting does not have a recognizable subject. What style of artistic expression does this painting represent? Notice how Kandinsky's placement of shapes and colors creates implied lines.

Sketchbook Journal

Choose a subject and make a realistic sketch of it in your Sketchbook Journal. Then draw the same subject as an abstract artwork. Change certain features of the object, but make sure you can recognize it. Finally, draw the object in a nonobjective style. Make notes about the effect of the different styles.

Studio 9 Setup
Abstract *Maquette*

Henri Matisse. *Ivy in Flower,* 1953. Colored paper and pencil, 112 by 112 inches. Dallas Museum of Art, Foundation for the Arts Collection, gift of the Albert and Mary Lasker Foundation. © 1999 Succession H. Matisse, Paris/Artists Rights Society (ARS), New York.

How would you describe the style of this artwork?

This collage by Henri Matisse is a **maquette,** or model for a larger work of art. Matisse created this abstract design when he was working on a stained-glass window. Look for these details:

- Matisse used only a few colors and no shading. The lack of shading gives a flat appearance to the shapes.
- A grid divides the artwork into windowpanes. This geometric element provides contrast to the organic shapes.
- The title of the artwork gives the viewer a better idea of what the shapes and colors represent.

Simplified Shapes

Matisse created this artwork late in his life. Though his eyesight was failing and he could no longer stand at his easel, he found a way to keep creating art. Matisse cut large, bold shapes with scissors. He then directed an assistant where to place the shapes on a wall across the room. How might this technique have contributed to the abstract appearance of the art?

Technique Tip

Focus with a Viewfinder

A viewfinder can help you find abstract compositions. Make a viewfinder by cutting a rectangle out of the center of a three-by-five-inch card. Hold the viewfinder at arm's length to frame details of objects around you. Or frame details of artworks in your portfolio. Make sketches of the abstract compositions you frame.

Studio 9

Create an Abstract Collage

Use what you have learned about modern Western art to create an abstract collage.

Materials

- ✓ viewfinder
- ✓ composition from your portfolio
- ✓ 12" × 18" drawing paper
- ✓ pencil
- ✓ colored tissue paper
- ✓ glue and water mixture
- ✓ paintbrush
- ✓ oil pastels
- ✓ black felt-tip pen

1 **Use a viewfinder to frame a nonobjective design in one of your own compositions. Draw the design on drawing paper.**

2 **Glue colored tissue paper to your design to show color and shape.**

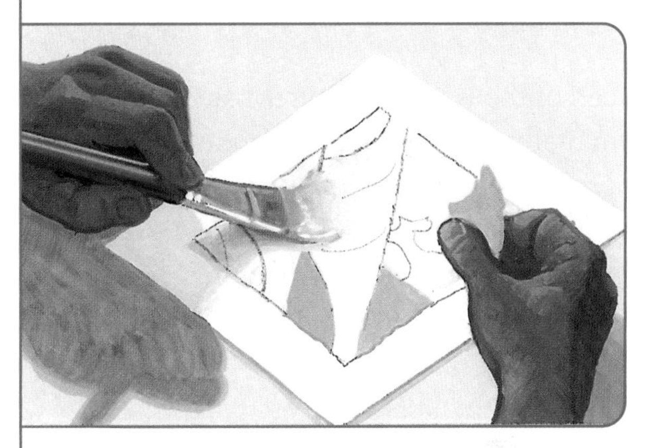

3 **When the tissue paper is dry, add more color using oil pastels. Outline some shapes with a felt-tip pen.**

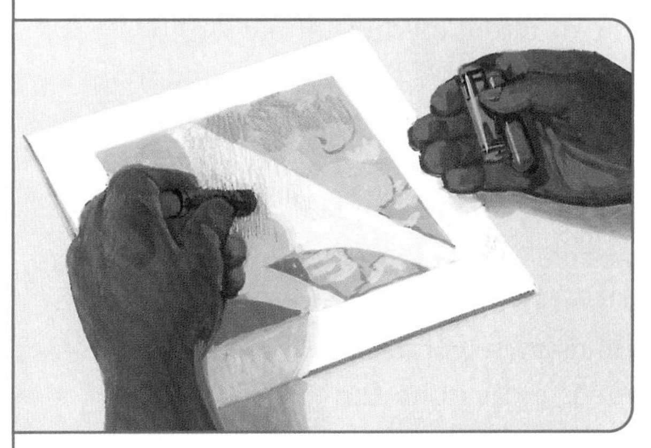

Review and Reflect

- Describe the use of texture and color in your collage.
- How does your abstract design differ from realistic designs you have created?
- How would you describe the mood of your collage?
- How would a color change make your design different?

Lesson 10

Modern Global Art

Each of the world's cultures has its own art. In many cultures, special ceremonies are important sources of group identity. Artists make **ceremonial artworks** for these events. These works of art show the group's values and beliefs. The cultures of the world also make an array of **crafts,** useful handmade items. Crafting skills often are passed down through generations. Over time, they become part of a culture's identity.

A Blending of Ideas

The different cultures of the world have traded goods such as food and tools for centuries. But this trade is not limited to goods. When cultures come into contact, artistic ideas flow freely back and forth. Artists blend new ideas from other cultures into their own works of art. As the world becomes more connected, this exchange happens more often.

This Beaded Zemi shows a likeness to artworks of Africa, Europe, and the Caribbean. Some art historians say this work of art is a spiritual figure from South America. Others say it is a portrait of a chief of the Taíno. This Caribbean culture was all but wiped out five hundred years ago. What materials can you identify in this sculpture?

Artist unknown. *Beaded Zemi,* ca. 1515. Wood, cotton, shell, and glass, height 12 1/2 inches. Collection of Museo Nazionale Preistorico ed Etnografico "Luigi Pigorini," Rome, Italy. Photo by Daniela Masci, courtesy El Museo del Barrio, NY.

Straight lines form geometric patterns on this artwork.

Artist unknown, Nkanu culture. *Figure (drummer),* date unknown. Carved wood with pigments, height 27 3/4 inches.
© The Tervuren Museum, Royal Museum for Central Africa, Belgium.

What might the artist have used to add color to this sculpture?

Ceremonial Art and Purpose

Drummer figures like this African sculpture are often used for rituals of initiation. These rituals mark the passing of young people into adulthood. Traditionally, sculptures such as this one are burned once the ceremony is completed.

In the past, African artists usually worked for kings or chiefs. They rarely signed their names to their works of art. Many of these artists are lost to history.

Many African artists, then and now, excel at carving wood sculptures. After carving, they smoke the sculpture and rub it with oil, clay, or other substances. This creates the desired finish, or **patina.** A patina can be created by natural aging or imitated with different techniques. Notice the artist's use of color on this figure. The neutral black and white on the figure's face contrast with the red-orange on the body.

Sketchbook Journal

Draw several objects that have special meaning to you. The objects may be an animal, a medal, or other meaningful symbol. Choose parts from each sketch. Then draw a design for a symbolic sculpture. Make notes about the personal meaning the sculpture holds for you.

Studio 10 Setup
The Message *of Global Art*

Artist unknown, Nagano, Japan. *Horse,* ca. 1960. Wrapped fiber, height 7 3/8 inches. From the Girard Foundation Collection in the Museum of International Folk Art, a unit of the Museum of New Mexico, Santa Fe, NM. Photograph by Michel Monteaux.

How did the artist create a sense of movement in this sculpture?

Artists create sculptures that have special meaning in their cultures. In Japan, this horse sculpture used to be a religious symbol. Today it is a good luck charm. Look for these details:

- Fibers are bundled together to form the head, neck, body, and legs. Fibers are wrapped around these bundles to hold everything in place.
- The artist used fibers to add the details of ears, mane, and tail. These loose fibers add contrast and interest to the bundled fibers.
- The loose and bundled fibers create textures that add interest to the artwork.

Sculpture and Motion

In *Horse,* the horizontal and vertical lines of the mane and tail create a sense of movement. The horse leans slightly forward, as if it is facing a strong wind. The mane and tail seem to be rippling in the wind. Is this work of art realistic or abstract? Explain.

Technique Tip

Make an Armature

An armature is a frame for a sculpture made of stiff material. Armatures add support to sculptures that might have trouble standing. To make an armature, bend the wire into a skeleton of the shape you want to sculpt. Then attach your sculpting medium to the wire.

Studio 10

Create a Ceremonial Sculpture

Use what you have learned about global art to create a ceremonial sculpture.

Materials

- ✓ wire
- ✓ raffia
- ✓ buttons, ribbons, pipe cleaners, or other found objects
- ✓ glue

1 **Make an armature for an animal sculpture. Bend, twist, and wrap wire to create the position you want.**

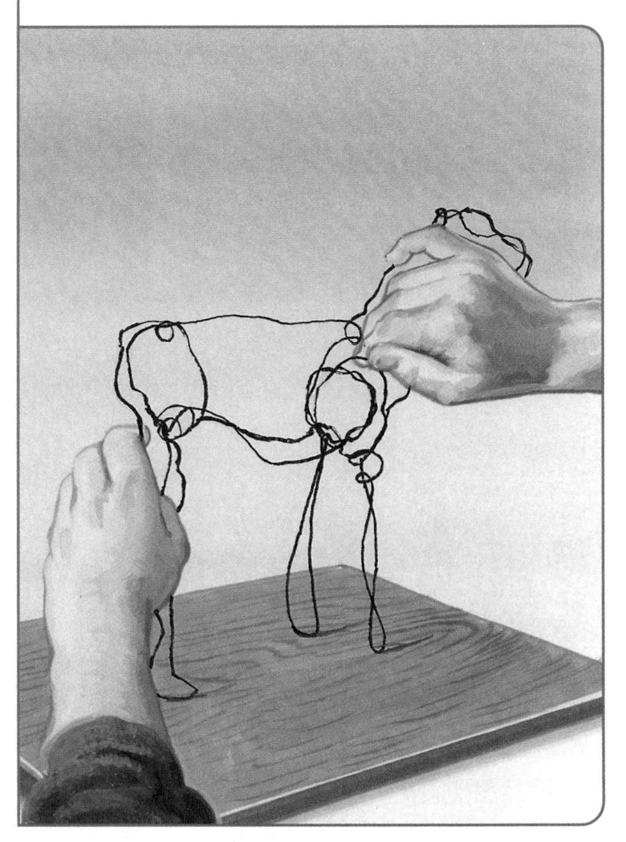

2 **Wrap the armature with dampened raffia. Twist the raffia in various directions or use it to tie other raffia in place.**

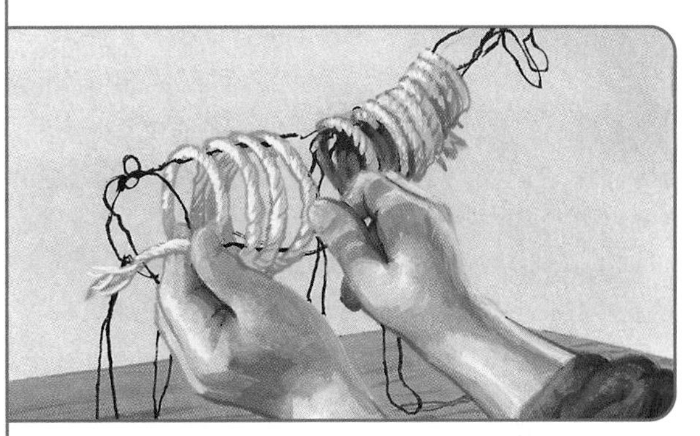

3 **Once the raffia has dried, add details with found objects. Attach them with glue or tie them to your sculpture.**

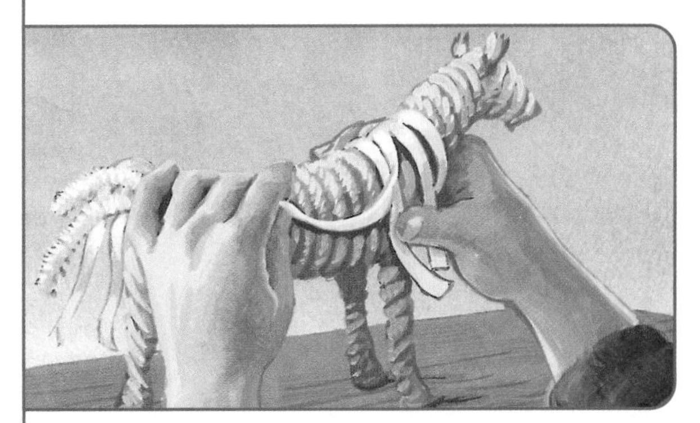

Review and Reflect

- Describe the animal you used for your sculpture.
- How did the form of your armature change when you added the raffia?
- What mood does your sculpture create? What symbol or message does it convey?
- How does your sculpture reflect the styles of global art? Explain.

Artist *at Work*

Sculptural Career

Sculptors can model, carve, cast, or join their materials into expressive three-dimensional forms. They work in wood, stone, clay, metal, and a variety of other materials. Some are hired to design and create a sculpture to add meaning, function, or beauty to a building or an outdoor space. Others choose to use their art form simply as a means of expression. Still others combine this expression in their sculptural careers. Sculptors like Francisco Matto sometimes create sculptures in relief. Matto also creates three-dimensional sculptures. Monumental concrete sculptures by the artist are landmarks in South America.

Sculpture and Symbolism

Francisco Matto (1911–1995) was a painter and sculptor from Uruguay. He started his art career by teaching himself how to paint when he was fifteen years old.

In 1939, Matto met Joaquín Torres-García, a famous teacher and artist in Uruguay. Matto showed him some of his paintings on wood. Torres-García encouraged Matto to continue working in the same style.

The two friends started a school for artists like Matto who made abstract artworks. The school, *El Taller Torres-García,* was a respected art center from 1944 to 1962.

Members of the *taller,* Spanish for "workshop," expressed their ideas in many ways. They made paintings and sculptures, and crafted ceramics. They carved reliefs, painted murals, and designed furniture and buildings.

Francisco Matto. *Removedor,* 1959. Oil on wood relief, 15 by 20 7/8 inches. Cecilia de Torres Gallery, New York.

Cultural Symbols

Matto's favorite art medium was wood. He used the material to create relief carvings and sculptures. Matto became interested in pre-Columbian art during a trip to Argentina. These works of art and other cultural art from around the world inspired him. He started adding signs and symbols from these works to his own art.

Matto studied cultural totems, or symbols that represent certain groups. A totem might represent a family, a culture, or a religious figure. Matto included these totems in his sculptures, often in abstract form.

Francisco Matto combined symbolic images from various cultures in his sculptures.

Portfolio *Project*

Create a Clay Vehicle

Artist unknown, Greek. *Two Warriors with Helmet and Shields in a Horse-Drawn Chariot,* 6th century B.C. Clay. Musée du Louvre, Paris.

Plan

The ancient Greeks created thousands of sculptures from limestone, marble, bronze, gold and ivory, terra cotta, and wood. Of these materials, terra cotta was the most common. Today, only a few dozen of the original sculptures remain.

The artist who created this sculpture is not known, but the artwork gives us a sense of what life was like in ancient Greece. The artist shaped the figures of the chariot, warriors, and horses from terra-cotta clay. Their features are not clearly shown. However, the position of the horses creates a sense of movement.

- What items had been invented by the time this artwork was made?
- What does this sculpture tell us about how ancient Greeks traveled?
- Look at the position of the horses. What mood is created by these details?
- What do you notice about the proportion of the figures in relation to the horses?

Use your own understanding of the world of art and artists to create a clay vehicle of the future.

Sketchbook Journal

Use the library or the Internet to research a time in history that interests you. Make notes and sketches in your Sketchbook Journal about how people dressed. Include information about their cities and the customs they practiced. How did their society differ from society today?

Materials

✓ sketch paper
✓ pencil
✓ clay, clay tools, and slip
✓ tempera or glazes
✓ brush

Create

1 **Draw a design of a futuristic vehicle with wheels.**

2 **Use ceramic clay to re-create your design in three dimensions.**

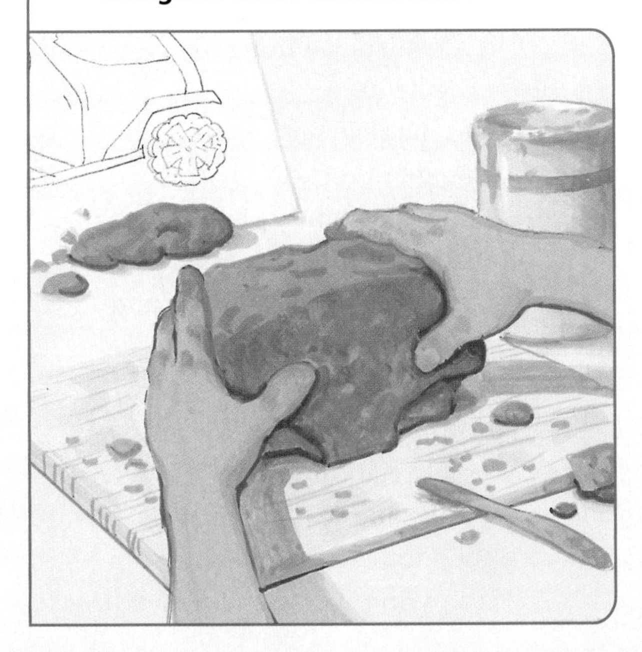

3 **Remember to score any parts that fit together and attach them with slip. Use clay tools to add details.**

4 **After your clay vehicle has been dried and fired once, paint it with tempera or glazes.**

Reflect

- Describe your vehicle of the future.
- What types of patterns, color, and line did you use?
- Compare your vehicle with a classmate's artwork. How do the details in each one show meaning?
- What problems did you face building your vehicle? How did you solve them?

Unit 4 *Review*

Vocabulary Review

A **Match each art term below with its definition.**

Prehistoric Art	**illumination**
tesserae	**abstract**
animal style	**mosaic**
sfumato	**nonobjective art**
maquette	**Realistic art**
Renaissance	**portrait**

1. a style of art that represents objects or scenes as they actually appear
2. a hand-painted illustration for a book
3. a small model of a larger artwork
4. artworks created before 3500 B.C.
5. a technique used to paint blurry backgrounds
6. small pieces of material used to make a mosaic
7. a simplified style of art that is not realistic
8. work of art that shows a person, group, or animal, usually focusing on the face
9. artwork from the Middle Ages that used animals as the subject
10. a type of art that has no recognizable subject
11. artwork made by fitting together small pieces of material to form a picture
12. a period marked by the rebirth of ideas from ancient Rome and Greece

Artists and Their Art

B **Each artwork listed in the box appears in this unit. Use the titles to finish the sentences.**

Ivy in Flower
Temple I
Improvisation 19a
Rose de France
The Horse Fair
Portrait of Amilcare, Minerva, and Astrubale Anguissola
Ducks and Ducklings
Tutankhamen, mask from mummy case
Stonehenge
The Virgin and Child with St. Anne

1. ___ shows how ancient Egyptian artisans prepared royalty for the afterworld.
2. Henri Matisse used abstract shapes and bold colors to create ___.
3. ___ is a realistic painting by Rosa Bonheur.
4. ___ was made in ancient times by stacking giant rocks.
5. ___ shows the family of painter Sofonisba Anguissola.
6. Leonardo da Vinci used a sfumato background in ___.
7. ___ is a Roman mosaic.
8. An example of nonobjective art is ___ by Wassily Kandinsky.
9. ___ is an example of medieval art designed for a cathedral.
10. ___ is a pyramid created by the Maya.

Respond to Art

C **Look at these two versions of the mosaic *The Court of Empress Theodora.* Match each art term below with the letter in the illustration of the mosaic.**

Artist unknown. *The Court of Empress Theodora,* A.D. 547. Early Christian mosaic. S. Vitale, Ravenna, Italy.

Art Terms

1. tesserae
2. arch with vaulted dome
3. symbol designating royalty
4. portrait

Unit 4 *Review*

Write About Art

Comparative Writing

D **Look back at the artworks you studied in this unit. Choose two from different historical periods to compare in a paragraph. Copy the Venn diagram below. Compare elements of art, principles of design, subjects, and historical context for the two artworks, placing the information in the correct area of the diagram. Use the completed chart to organize your writing.**

(Title of Artwork)

Both

(Title of Artwork)

Your Studio Work

E **Answer these questions in your Sketchbook Journal or on a separate sheet of paper.**

1. How does art provide clues about what life was like in ancient cultures?
2. How did the Renaissance change people's opinions of artists?
3. Which studio artwork did you most enjoy creating? Why?
4. Which artworks and historical periods are your favorites? Why?

Put It All Together

Pablo Picasso. *Baboon and Young,* Vallauris, 1951. Bronze (cast 1955), after found objects, 21 by 13 1/4 by 20 3/4 inches. The Museum of Modern Art. Mrs. Simon Guggenheim Fund. Photograph © 1996 The Museum of Modern Art, New York.

F **Discuss or write about Picasso's sculpture *Baboon and Young,* using the four steps for critically viewing artwork.**

1. **Describe** What has the artist shown? Describe the subject or theme. Describe the visual qualities of the artwork using the elements of art and principles of design listed below.

texture	**contrast**	**emphasis**
shapes	**proportion**	**art medium**

2. **Analyze** What do you think the artist was trying to say about animals in this artwork?
3. **Interpret** Look at the details of this sculpture. What does it tell you about the historical period in which it was created?
4. **Judge** Pablo Picasso (1881–1973) used his art to challenge people to look at the world in a different way. Why do you think Picasso chose to show animals in this manner?

"Everyone wants to understand painting. Why is there no attempt to understand the song of the birds?" —PABLO PICASSO

Picasso defied artistic conventions to find the unusual in ordinary subjects.

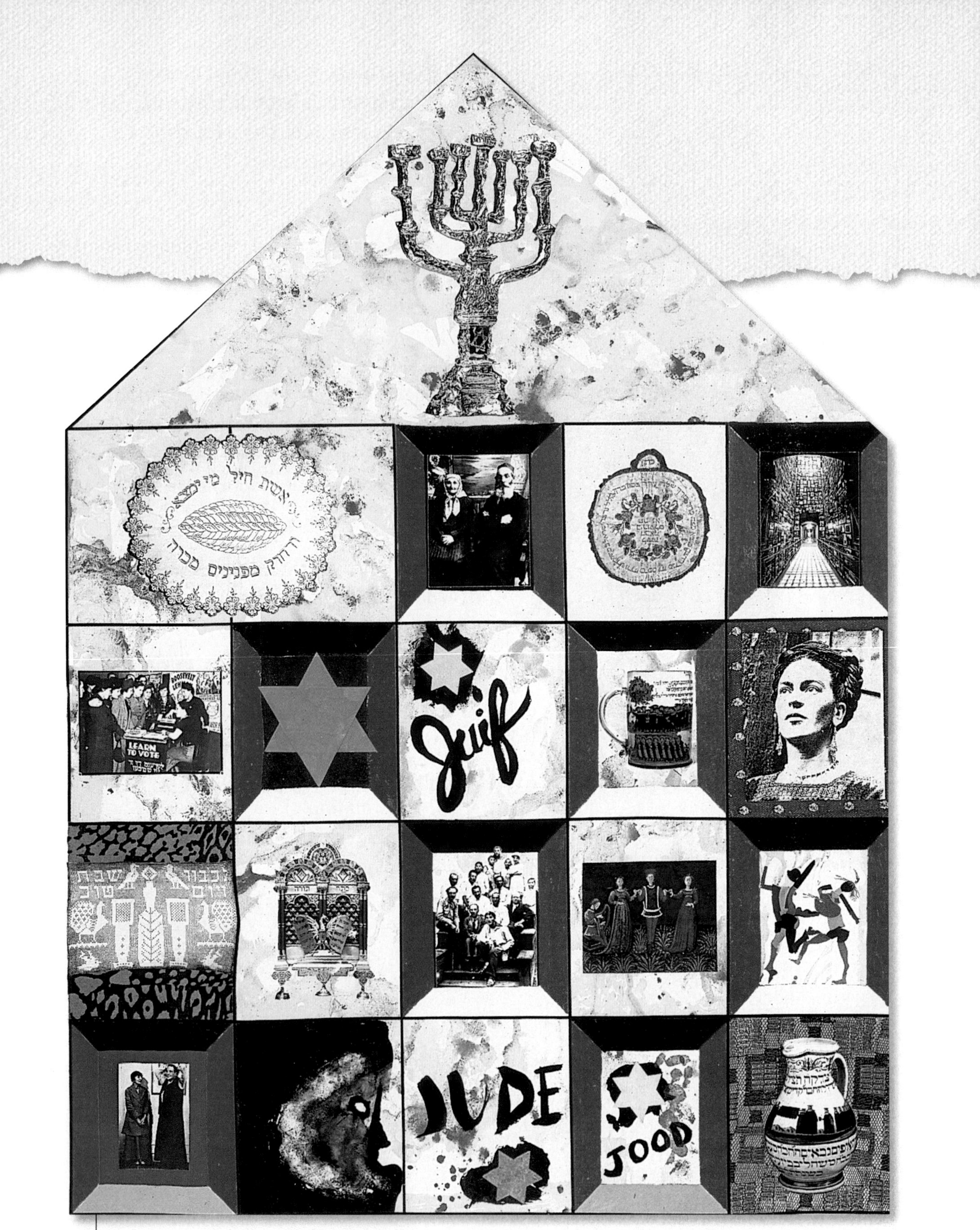

Miriam Schapiro. *My History,* 1997. Paper, acrylic, and fabric on paper, 33 3/4 by 25 1/4 inches. Collection of Eleanor and Len Flomenhaft. © Miriam Schapiro.

Unit 5

Subjects and Styles

Have you ever heard someone say "I like her style" or "He has a style of his own"? **Style** is an artist's personal way of combining media, techniques, and subjects to create a work of art. An artist can develop her or his own style by studying the works of other artists. They can also explore their own ideas and try new ways of expression.

Style can refer to qualities shared by works of art from the same geographic region or historical era. Today many art styles focus on the same types of **subjects,** such as people, animals, objects, or scenes. For example, paintings from one region may show tigers or birds. Paintings from another region might show dogs or horses. Animals are the common subject in the paintings from each region.

As you read this unit, take notes and make sketches of the ways artists express themselves. Try imitating their styles and subjects as you work in your Sketchbook Journal. As you practice, develop your own personal style to give your compositions a special quality.

About *the Artist*

Miriam Schapiro brought her own style to the collages she made. In the process, she created a whole new kind of collage. Read more about Schapiro's style and her contribution to art on page 236.

Lesson 1

People as Subjects

Have you ever spent time observing people in their daily routines? If so, you probably saw a variety of faces, sizes, ages, and types of people. Perhaps you asked yourself questions about their character, beliefs, or lifestyles. Maybe you even created stories about some of them in your imagination. As a general rule, people fascinate other people. People have been a favorite subject of artists throughout the history of art.

Drawings of People

John Biggers (1924–2001) chose African Americans as subjects for his drawings for more than fifty years. As an art student in college, Biggers began exploring the meaning of family and community. He learned about the roles of elders and young people, of men and women.

Three women are the subjects of *Three Quilters (Quilting Party)*. Their bodies are turned slightly toward each other. The expressions on their faces show they are good friends. How would the drawing be different if the women were looking toward the viewer or to one side?

Biggers drew the women's hands larger than the standard size. This emphasis shows the important role of hands in quilting.

John Biggers. *Three Quilters (Quilting Party),* 1952. Conté crayon, 30 by 40 inches. Dallas Museum of Art. © John Biggers. Photograph by Earlie Hudnall.

Why do you think the artist exaggerated the size of the women's hands?

Honoré Daumier. *The Third-Class Carriage,* ca. 1863. Oil on canvas, 25 3/4 by 35 1/2 inches. The Metropolitan Museum of Art, H. O. Havemeyer Collection, bequest of Mrs. H. O. Havemeyer, 1929 (29.100.129). Photograph by Schecter Lee. © 1986 The Metropolitan Museum of Art.

Paintings of People

The subject of this painting by French artist Honoré Daumier (1808–1879) is a group of people riding in a train. Daumier added drama to the scene with a carefully selected light source. A **light source** is a point from which light seems to shine in a work of art. Artists use light sources to emphasize or contrast objects. A light source also can provide unity or drama to a work of art.

Light sources often seem to come from outside artworks. In Biggers' drawing, light appears to be coming from above. In Daumier's painting, light seems to shine from a third window that is not visible in the painting. How can you tell?

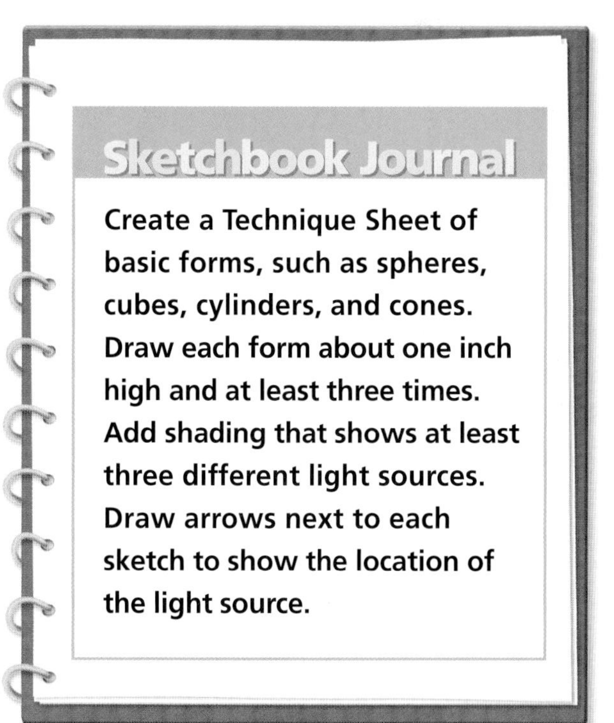

Sketchbook Journal

Create a Technique Sheet of basic forms, such as spheres, cubes, cylinders, and cones. Draw each form about one inch high and at least three times. Add shading that shows at least three different light sources. Draw arrows next to each sketch to show the location of the light source.

Studio 1 Setup

The *Human Form*

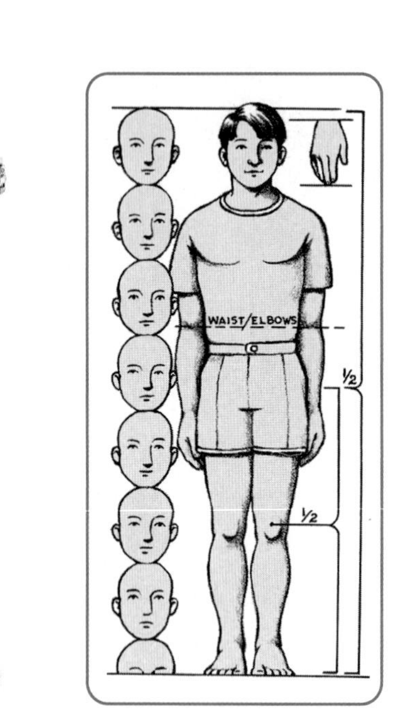

Viola Frey. *Grandmother Series: July Cone Hat,* 1982. Glazed earthenware, four parts, overall 86 ½ by 21 by 18 inches. The Nelson-Atkins Museum of Art, Kansas City, MO. Gift of Byron and Eileen Cohen.

How do the proportions in this sculpture relate to the standard human form shown in the illustration?

Artists portray the human form in many ways. California artist Viola Frey (1933–) created the sculpture from her *Grandmother Series* by molding four separate parts of clay. She joined the parts together to make a **figure,** or human form. Look for these details:

- If you were looking at the sculpture in person, you could move around it and study it from different angles. This type of artwork is called **in the round.**
- The artist showed the subject from head to toe as a **full figure.**

Guidelines

Proportion is an important principle of design to portrait artists. Artists use these guidelines to create full figures with typical proportions.

1. The height of most adults is about seven or eight times the length of the head.
2. The hands are about as large as the face.
3. The knees are about halfway between the hips and the bottom of the feet.
4. The hips are about halfway between the top of the head and the bottom of the feet.
5. The elbows are about parallel to, or even with, the waist.

Technique Tip

Wire Options

Use pliable or flexible wire to make sculptures. Insulated phone wire and soft copper wire are good options. Sharp scissors will often cut thin wire. Wire cutters may be necessary for heavier wire, but use caution with wire cutters. If you cut the wire too short, simply twist another length of wire onto the end.

Studio 1

Create a Wire Sculpture

Use what you have learned about human proportion to make a wire sculpture.

Materials

- ✓ 12" × 18" paper
- ✓ drawing media, such as pencil or charcoal
- ✓ pliable wire
- ✓ sharp scissors or wire cutters
- ✓ self-hardening clay
- ✓ acrylic paints
- ✓ paintbrushes

1 **On a 12" × 18" sheet of paper, create several full-figure contour drawings of a human in an action pose.**

2 **Make a sculpture of your favorite drawing. Bend the wire to show the same proportions you used in your drawings.**

3 **Cover your wire sculpture with self-hardening clay. Let your sculpture dry. Add color with acrylic paints.**

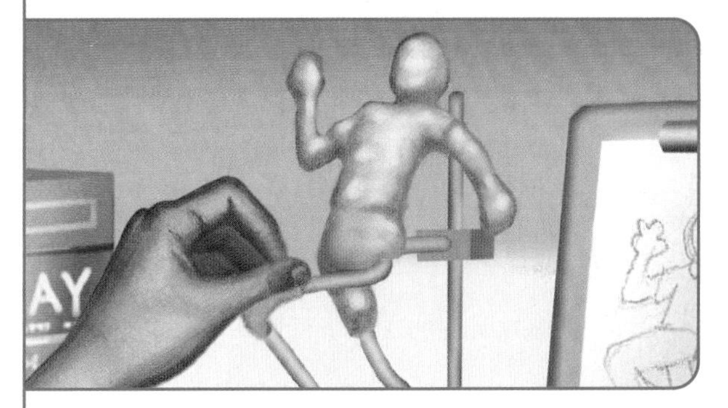

Review and Reflect

- What action is indicated by the position of your sculpture?
- How did the guidelines for human proportion help you position your sculpture?
- How does standard human proportion affect the meaning of your artwork?
- How does your sculpture reflect your own art style?

Lesson 2

Proportion and Faces

Look at the facial features, such as the eyes, nose, mouth, and ears, in the portraits on these two pages. Artists call the size relation between these features facial proportions.

A good way to learn about facial proportions is to ask a friend to be your **model.** A model **poses** as you sketch. Artists often draw their models in one of three views: frontal, profile, or three-quarter.

A **frontal view,** as in *Head of Queen Tiy,* shows the front side of a person or an animal. Artists often begin such a portrait by drawing the basic lines and shapes of the facial proportions. Next, the lines are changed to reflect the qualities of the actual person or model. Finally, special qualities are added. These might be laugh wrinkles around the eyes to show a sense of humor or a distinguishing birthmark on the cheek.

A **profile view,** such as *Roy II* by Chuck Close, shows the subject from one side. You can see only one of the subject's eyes. Notice how Close defined the jaw with a shadow.

A **three-quarter view,** as in *Lady Wearing a Gauze Headdress,* is positioned in between a frontal view and a profile. You can usually see both eyes, the nose, and the mouth.

Artist unknown, Egyptian. *Head of Queen Tiy,* ca. 1391–1353 B.C. Yew wood with silver and glass, height 3 1/2 inches. Ägyptisches Museum und Papyrussammlung. © BPK, Berlin, 1998. Photo by M. Büsing.

From what view is this sculpture shown?

Chuck Close. *Roy II,* 1994. Oil on canvas, 102 by 84 inches. Collection of Hirshhorn Museum and Sculpture Garden, Smithsonian Institution, Washington, D.C.

Miriam Schapiro. *Anna and David,* 1987. Painted steel and aluminum, 35 by 31 by 9 feet. Commissioned for J. W. Kaempfer Building, Rosslyn, VA. © Miriam Schapiro.

Niki de Saint-Phalle. *Oiseau sur l'arche (Bird on the Arch),* 1993. Mosaic of mirrors, approximately 18 by 12 1/3 by 5 1/2 feet. Paris, France. Photo by Laurent Condominas, courtesy of Archives Niki de Saint-Phalle, Paris.

Compare & Contrast

- **How are the sculptures the same? How are they different?**
- **Where might you place each of these sculptures in your community? Why? How would each sculpture alter the mood of the location you chose?**

Lesson 6

Impressionism

Claude Monet. *Arrival of the Normandy Train, Gare Saint-Lazare,* 1877. Oil on canvas, 23 1/4 by 31 1/4 inches. The Art Institute of Chicago, Mr. and Mrs. Martin A. Ryerson Collection, 1933.1158. Photograph © 1998 The Art Institute of Chicago. All rights reserved.

In 1874 a critic made fun of a Claude Monet painting called *Impression—Sunrise.* Monet was among a group of Paris artists who wanted to paint in a new way. They were tired of the strict rules of art contests and the dark colors of the Realistic paintings. They called themselves *Independents.*

What Is Impressionism?

As the movement grew, it became known as **Impressionism.** These artists, known as **Impressionists,** painted or drew impressions—moments in everyday life—as they saw and felt them.

Impressionists were excited about the play of light and color. They painted or drew outdoor scenes to show the effect of light on their subjects. Notice how the large patch of light in the left center helps draw your eye into Monet's painting.

This new style featured a fresh way of filling spaces. Impressionists began using hundreds of energetic strokes and dabs—straight, curved, thick, thin, broken, smooth, dotted, blurry, and sharp. This technique stressed each stroke rather than broad areas of color. Look for dabs of color on the floor of Monet's train station and in the steam rising from the train.

Camille Pissarro. *Place du Havre, Paris,* 1893. Oil on canvas, 23 1/2 by 28 2/3 inches. The Art Institute of Chicago, Mr. and Mrs. Potter Palmer Collection. Photograph © 1998 The Art Institute of Chicago. All rights reserved.

Subjects and Techniques

French artist Camille Pissarro (1830–1903) used the effects of light to show this busy Paris street scene. He and other Impressionists saw that objects in the distance seemed lighter and blurrier. They showed this using the technique of atmospheric perspective, painting light tints on faraway objects. Notice how each artist used this technique to show distance, air, and light. These and other Impressionist painters felt their artworks were realistic. But they did not follow the traditional Realistic style. How did Monet and Pissarro show a realistic scene with atmospheric perspective?

Research

You can form your own impression of the Impressionists by visiting your local library or the Internet. Use key words such as *Impressionism* in your Internet search. Or visit the Art Institute of Chicago's Impressionist collection at www.artic.edu. Make notes about similarities and differences between each artwork.

Studio 6 Setup

Impressionist *Drawings*

Edgar Degas. *The Large Green Dancers,* 1898–1900. Pastel on paper, 29 1/4 by 27 1/4 inches. Ny Carlsberg Glyptotek, Copenhagen, Denmark.

How does the artist's use of color and movement affect the mood of this drawing?

French Impressionist artist Edgar Degas (1834–1917) often showed the human figure in motion. He created this drawing with his favorite art medium, pastels. Look for these details:

- Degas used a cool color scheme featuring shades and tints of green and blue. Light tints provide highlights, while darker shades show shadows and form.
- The ballerinas' positions show Degas's interest in depicting movement.
- The scene is indoors. Unlike other Impressionists, Degas rarely painted outdoors.

Everyday Ballet

Degas spent a lot of time at the Paris Opera Ballet, where the everyday scenes usually included ballet dancers. Degas drew the dancers with pastels. He painted them with oil on canvas and board. He made sculptures in wax that were later cast in bronze. In all, Degas produced more than fifteen hundred works of art set at the opera house.

Technique Tip

Paint Like an Impressionist

Impressionists often use different brushstrokes to paint objects in the foreground, middle ground, and background. Use large brushstrokes on foreground objects. Make your strokes smaller on middle ground objects. Save your smallest strokes for background objects.

Studio 6

Draw Like an Impressionist

Use what you have learned about Impressionism to create an Impressionist drawing.

Materials

- ✓ 12" × 18" white drawing paper
- ✓ pencil
- ✓ colored pencils
- ✓ oil pastels
- ✓ chalk pastels

1 **Select a landscape, seascape, cityscape, portrait, or still life from your Sketchbook Journal or create a new sketch.**

2 **Draw the design lightly on 12" × 18" drawing paper. Make a mental note of the direction of your light source.**

3 **Use colored pencils, chalk pastels, oil pastels, or all three to add color to your design in an Impressionist style.**

Review and Reflect

- How did you use color and line?
- What makes your drawing appear Impressionistic rather than Realistic?
- If you could visit the place as it is shown in your drawing, how would it make you feel?
- How does the style of your drawing compare with other styles you have explored? Which do you prefer?

Lesson 7

Expressionism

All styles of art are expressive. Realistic artists express their ideas of how subjects actually look. Cubists express their perception of subjects from many angles. Impressionists express their impressions of subjects and light. Indeed, all artists express themselves. So why are some works of art called **Expressionism** with a capital *E?*

Early in the twentieth century, a group of German artists formed a group called *The Blue Rider.* This group created the style called German Expressionism, which you read about in Unit 4. Their artworks expressed thoughts, moods, and feelings with simple designs and vivid colors. Their main goal was to express a strong mood or feeling.

German artist Gabriele Münter was a founder of *The Blue Rider.* The subject of *Portrait of Marianne von Werefkin* is another group member. Münter painted her subject using abstract techniques, such as omitting or changing details. Notice the bold color scheme and the unusual hues on the subject's face.

This radical use of color stemmed from Münter's interest in **Fauvism.** The Fauve group of artists lived and worked in France from 1905–1907. Their bold use of color was so shocking that people called them **Fauves,** or "wild beasts."

Gabriele Münter. *Portrait of Marianne von Werefkin,* 1909. Oil on cardboard, 31 7/8 by 21 5/8 inches. Städtische Galerie im Lenbachhaus, Munich. GMS 656. © 1999 Artists Rights Society (ARS), New York/VG Bild-Kunst, Bonn.

Joan Mitchell. *George Went Swimming at Barnes Hole, But It Got Too Cold,* 1957. Oil on canvas, 85 1/4 by 78 1/4 inches. Albright-Knox Art Gallery, Buffalo, New York. Gift of Seymour H. Knox, 1958. © Estate of Joan Mitchell.

Abstract Expressionism

Abstract Expressionism started in the United States during the middle of the twentieth century. These artists also focused on expressing a strong mood or feeling. American artist Joan Mitchell (1926–1992) used bold movements as she painted this energetic artwork. Why do you think this style is also called *action painting?*

Mitchell's painting shows the effects of the techniques of the Abstract Expressionists. Notice the slashing, swooping, active brushstrokes. They also splattered, dripped, and poured paint on canvas.

"The lake is with me today," Mitchell once said. "The memory of a feeling. And when I feel that thing, I want to paint it." How might this statement apply to this painting?

Sketchbook Journal

Create several thumbnail sketches of people and places that arouse an emotion within you. Make notes about the emotions you feel. What colors could you use to match these feelings? What abstract techniques could you use to communicate your feelings?

Studio 7 Setup

Expressive *Fauve Colors*

André Derain. *Mountains at Collioure,* 1905. Oil on canvas, 32 by 39 1/2 inches. National Gallery of Art, Washington, D.C.

How does this painting reflect the style of the Fauves?

French painter André Derain (1880–1954) did not feel bound to use the colors nature chose for objects. Look for these details:

- Cool shades and tints of blue and green provide unity. These colors are in the foreground trees, the middle ground mountains, and the background sky.
- Shades and tints of orange and red draw your eye to the mountains and provide contrast. Placing orange next to its complement, blue, makes both colors seem more intense.
- Derain painted the grass and the leaves on the trees with short brushstrokes. This technique adds texture and variety to the painting.

Unnatural Color

Realists used color to show how things really looked. The Fauves chose colors for compositional reasons, however, or to convey an emotion or feeling. In this painting, Derain painted the grass and some of the trees with realistic colors. But some leaves are blue. The mountains are orange and the sky is green. Why did he choose to use these colors?

Technique Tip

Finding Complementary Colors

A complementary color scheme can lend a Fauvist touch to a work of art. You may recall that putting complementary colors next to each other makes them seem more vibrant. This can have a jarring effect on a work of art.

Studio 7

Paint in Fauve Colors

Use what you have learned about Expressionism to create a painting using Fauve colors.

Materials

- ✓ watercolor paper
- ✓ chalk
- ✓ tempera paint
- ✓ brushes and water container
- ✓ tissue
- ✓ India ink

1 **Use chalk to draw an Expressionist scene on paper. With tempera paint, add bright Fauve colors inside the chalk lines.**

2 **When it is dry, wipe away the chalk lines with tissue. Gently brush India ink over the entire painting.**

3 **Place the painting on a board. Rinse under running water. The ink will wash off the painted areas and stay on unpainted areas.**

Review and Reflect

- What objects did you paint using Fauve colors?
- How would you describe the rhythm you created with pattern and color?
- Tell how the Fauve colors affect the meaning of your artwork.
- What do you like best about your composition? What do you like least? Explain.

Lesson 8

Surrealism

René Magritte. *The Mysteries of the Horizon,* 1955. Oil on canvas, 19 1/2 by 25 1/3 inches. Private collection. © 1999 Charly Herscovici. Brussels/Artists Rights Society (ARS), New York.

Magritte once said, "The mind . . . loves images whose meaning is unknown since the meaning of the mind itself is unknown."

Have you ever woken from an amazing dream and written down what you remembered about it? The events may have seemed real, but perhaps the dream seemed a bit odd. Some artists produce realistic works of art that have a dreamlike quality. They create a feeling or mood that comes from their memory or imagination. This style of art is called **Surrealism.**

In a Strange Land

Have you ever arrived at a strange place in the middle of the night and been surprised by how it looks the next morning? Places and objects often look different at night. Shapes and forms are twisted. Objects cast distorted shadows in the moonlight and streetlights. Is it any wonder that many Surrealist painters have chosen to show night scenes?

Strange dream-world scenes characterize Belgian artist Réne Magritte's (1898–1967) paintings. In *The Mysteries of the Horizon,* Magritte created a strange mood by painting three crescent moons in the night sky.

Look at the three men painted under the moons. They all have the same stiff posture, but face different directions. Lighter values on their faces and necks indicate a light source not from the three moons, but from someplace to the right of the painting. This makes a strange scene even stranger.

Lee N. Smith III. *Intruder in the Port,* 1993. Oil and 3D construction on panel, 78 by 96 by 7 inches. Private collection. Courtesy of Lyons Matrix Gallery, Austin, TX.

The Colors of Surrealism

American painter Lee N. Smith III contrasted bright colors against a dark sky in his artwork *Intruder in the Port.* Like Magritte, Smith used paint to show color, space, and texture. Implied lines made by flashlight beams lead your eye around the canvas.

Smith attached three-dimensional airplanes at the bottom of his composition. Are the planes flying near the ground, or are they actually on the ground? Why are those people moving around in space? Or is that the ground they are on?

As you can see, Surrealist art can leave a viewer with more questions than answers.

Research

Salvador Dalí is known for his Surrealist artworks. Three museums are dedicated to his work in Spain alone. Use resources such as your media center or Internet to find artworks by Dalí and other Surrealists. Make notes about what makes each artwork surreal.

Studio 8 Setup

Meanings *in Surrealism*

Salvador Dali. *The Elephants,* 1961. Pencil, watercolor and gouache, 27 1/2 by 27 1/2 inches. Indianapolis Museum of Art, gift of Mr. and Mrs. Lorenzo Alvary. Photograph © 1975, Indianapolis Museum of Art. © 1999 Artists Rights Society (ARS), New York.

What parts of this Surrealist painting appear to be realistic?

Spanish Surrealist Salvador Dalí (1904–1989) turned visions from his dreams and subconscious into works of art. *The Elephants* was a study for a backdrop for a 1960s opera, *The Spanish Lady and the Roman Cavalier.* Look for these details in the artwork:

- The elephants appear realistic, except for their long, thin legs and bird feet. They tower over a giraffe that also appears realistic except for the flames on its back.
- Dalí used a cool color scheme. A bright red curtain draped on the top right corner of the artwork provides contrast. How might the curtain be used in an opera?

Symbols

Dalí was fascinated by the workings of the human mind that occur without our awareness. Like other Surrealists, he used symbols to represent words, messages, or ideas. Since these symbols are often drawn from the subconscious mind, their meanings are not always clear even to the artists. What might some of Dalí's symbols mean?

Technique Tip

Colors and Highlights

You can add realistic touches with chalk pastels. Mix colors by putting one color on top of another. Blend the colors with your fingertip, a tissue, or shading stump. Add highlights to certain objects by using a kneaded eraser. Gently erase parts of the pastel to show the reflection of light or to create lighter areas.

Studio 8

Create a Surrealist Painting

Use what you have learned about Surrealism to create a Surrealist painting.

Materials

- ✓ 9" × 12" drawing paper
- ✓ pencil
- ✓ 12" × 18" white drawing paper or illustration board
- ✓ tempera or acrylic paints, paintbrushes, water container
- ✓ chalk pastels

1 **Make practice drawings of Surrealist elements on 9" × 12" drawing paper. Include symbols, fantasy scenes, or unusual objects.**

2 **Pick one or more sketches. Enlarge the sketches and redraw them into a single composition on 12" × 18" drawing paper.**

3 **Select a cool, bold, or neutral color scheme. Add color with tempera or acrylic paints and chalk pastels.**

Review and Reflect

- Describe what is happening in your composition.
- What techniques did you use to show Surrealistic objects?
- What meaning might you give this dreamlike composition?
- What person do you know who might especially like your Surrealist painting? Explain why.

Lesson 9

Pop Art

Roy Lichtenstein. *Nurse,* 1964. Oil and magna on canvas, 48 by 48 inches. Private collection. © Estate of Roy Lichtenstein. Photograph by Robert McKeever.

How does this artwork resemble a comic strip?

People have always had ideas and opinions about subjects for art. Subjects were usually religious during the Middle Ages. Later artists felt that daily life was the best subject. A new idea developed in England during the 1950s. It spread to the United States in the 1960s. Artists of this new art style felt that the products and images of popular culture were good subjects for art. The works they created were called **Pop Art,** short for *popular art.*

Pop Art on the Comics Page

American artist Roy Lichtenstein (1923–1997) was a founder of Pop Art. In about 1957, he shocked critics by making art that looked like a newspaper comic strip. Look closely at *Nurse.* This work of art is made up of thousands of tiny dots. The artist used oil and a special type of acrylic paints to give the painting a comic strip appearance. Notice how each dot is evenly spaced, making it look as though it had been printed by a machine.

Lichtenstein turned to Pop Art because he was tired of Modern Art. "... Everybody was hanging everything. It was almost acceptable to hang a dripping paint rag; everyone was accustomed to this," he said. "The one thing everyone hated was commercial art." Then, referring to the success of Pop Art, he added, "Apparently they didn't hate that enough either."

James Rosenquist. *Telephone Explosion,* 1983. Oil on canvas, 78 by 66 inches. Courtesy of SBC Communications, Inc. © James Rosenquist/Licensed by VAGA, New York.

Pop Art Subjects

Pop Artists found their subjects in almost every aspect of modern life. Their subjects included product ads and consumer goods. Some showed food packaging and movie stars. Others included billboard posters.

American artist James Rosenquist (1933–) used a common object as a subject in *Telephone Explosion.* The artist used diagonal lines to lead your eye to the telephone as the focal point. Smiling faces also help emphasize the subject.

Was Rosenquist saying that talking on the telephone is fun? Or was he saying that advertisers want you to *think* that it is fun?

Visual Culture

Newspapers and magazines strive to stay on top of the latest trends in popular culture. Study the photographs and drawings in ads for a variety of consumer products. What techniques do the designers use to lead your eye to the product? How do they emphasize the message of the ad?

Unit 5 *Review*

Vocabulary Review

A **Match each art term below with its definition.**

utilitarian art	pointillism
subject	Impressionism
light source	Expressionism
still life	Surrealism
Pop Art	Fauvism

1. a style of art that shows the effect of light on moments in everyday life
2. a person, animal, object, or scene represented in an artwork
3. a style of art that concentrated on popular culture
4. a style of art that used bold colors in unusual combinations
5. art that serves a useful purpose
6. a style of art in which the main idea is to portray a strong mood or feeling
7. a technique in which tiny dots of color are blended by the viewer's eye
8. a point from which light seems to shine in an artwork
9. a style of art that makes realistic objects seem strange and dreamlike
10. an artwork that shows an arrangement of objects that cannot move on their own

Artists and Their Art

B **Each work of art listed in the box appears in this unit. Match each artwork with its description below.**

The White Soup Bowl
Stirrup Spout Vessel in the Form of a Seated Deer
The Mysteries of the Horizon
Roy II
My History
Nurse
Grandmother Series: July Cone Hat
Arrival of the Normandy Train

1. Miriam Schapiro included objects made by anonymous craftswomen in ___.
2. ___ is an example of utilitarian art.
3. Claude Monet used atmospheric perspective in ___.
4. Anne Vallayer-Coster used Realism to show a still life in ___.
5. René Magritte created a mysterious landscape with three moons in ___.
6. Roy Lichtenstein adapted a newspaper printing technique to make ___.
7. Chuck Close painted ___ by dividing his canvas into grids.
8. Viola Frey created the full-figure sculpture, ___, using clay.

Niki de Saint-Phalle

Joan Mitchell

Respond to Art

C **Look at the painting *Autumn,* by Giuseppe Arcimboldo. In a class discussion or on a sheet of paper, match each art term below with examples from the painting.**

Giuseppe Arcimboldo. *Autumn,* 1573. Oil on canvas, 29 2/3 by 24 3/4 inches. Musée du Louvre, Paris.

Art Terms

1. light values
2. texture
3. secondary color
4. organic shape
5. geometric shape
6. neutral color
7. profile view
8. negative space

Unit 5 *Review*

Write About Art

Explanatory Paragraphs

D **Look back at the works of art you saw in this unit. Choose one that inspires you to create an artwork with a similar style or subject. Write three paragraphs about the artwork you would make. First explain your idea, and then list the steps you would take to complete your work of art. Use the chart below to organize your thoughts before you start writing.**

Name of Artwork

A. Idea

1. Subject: ____________
2. Style: ____________
3. Media: ____________
4. Other: ____________

B. Steps to complete

1. ____________
2. ____________
3. ____________
4. ____________

Your Studio Work

E **Answer these questions in your Sketchbook Journal or on a separate sheet of paper.**

1. How did you generate ideas for subjects of your artworks?
2. How did you develop and refine your ideas in your artworks?
3. What style and medium did you most enjoy? Why?
4. How did you reflect your own style in your artworks?
5. Choose one of your artworks from this unit that best expresses your personal style. Explain why you think this artwork is successful.

Put It All Together

Marisol Escobar. *The Family,* 1962. Painted wood and other materials in three sections, overall 82 5/8 by 65 1/2 by 15 1/2 inches. The Museum of Modern Art, New York, Advisory Committee Fund. Photograph © 1996 The Museum of Modern Art, New York.

F Discuss or write about Marisol Escobar's *The Family* using the four steps below for viewing artwork critically.

1. **Describe** What is the subject of *The Family?* Look carefully. How would you describe the expressions of the figures? What is the setting? Describe the objects and symbols you see.
2. **Analyze** How did the artist use the elements of art and principles of design to represent the subject? Analyze the visual qualities of the artwork by writing three or more words that describe each example of the elements and principles listed below:

pattern	**rhythm**	**space**
color	**texture**	**emphasis**
shape	**value**	

3. **Interpret** What is the meaning of this artwork? What might each figure be thinking about? What does this assemblage remind you of? How does the artwork make you feel?
4. **Judge** How do the subject and the style work together to make this assemblage special? Explain. How might you represent your family?

"Whatever the artist makes is always some kind of self-portrait."

—MARISOL ESCOBAR

Marisol's artworks sometimes show portraits in a humorous, Pop Art style.

Georgia O'Keeffe. *From the Lake No. I,* 1924. Oil on canvas, 37 1/8 by 31 inches.
Des Moines Art Center, Des Moines, IA.

Unit 6

Expression and Meaning

A common challenge facing artists is finding personal ways to express ideas and feelings. **Expression** is an artist's way of using symbols with personal meaning. Artists strive to express themselves in a style of their own. This special way of showing ideas and feelings results in an artist's **originality.**

Georgia O'Keeffe developed her own way of expression. *From the Lake No. I* is an example of her personal style. Her originality made it possible for people to identify her paintings without looking at the signature. She used her paintings to convey ideas and feelings that she sometimes could not express in words.

This unit will help you discover how artworks showing the same subject can be quite different. You may also discover how thoughts and ideas can express meaning in art. The studio activities invite you to express your own thoughts and ideas. How will symbols help you show your intended meaning?

About *the Artist*

Georgia O'Keeffe painted in a realistic style during her younger years. Soon she rejected realism to develop a style of her own. How might you describe O'Keeffe's style in *From the Lake No. I?* Read how she developed the style that made her a well-known artist on page 282.

Lesson 1

Murals Tell Stories

The first known artists painted large visual stories, or **murals,** on the walls and ceilings of caves. These murals offer clues about ideas, beliefs, and values of long ago. Modern artists can choose from a wide variety of media, but many still paint murals. You may have seen some in your community. They may be painted on billboards or buildings, walls or ceilings. They often tell historical, cultural, or political stories.

Murals and Messages

Political messages are common in murals. For example, Mexican murals painted in the early twentieth century often show the struggle of the people of Mexico against their government.

Murals tell other stories as well. They might tell about a religious event. They might show how people celebrate a special day. Some murals entertain viewers with humor or call attention to something unusual.

American artist Kent Twitchell (1942–) drastically changed an urban environment with this huge mural. The title offers a clue to its meaning. California Pop Artist Edward Ruscha, the subject, often poked fun at billboards that focused on products instead of people. What makes this mural funny?

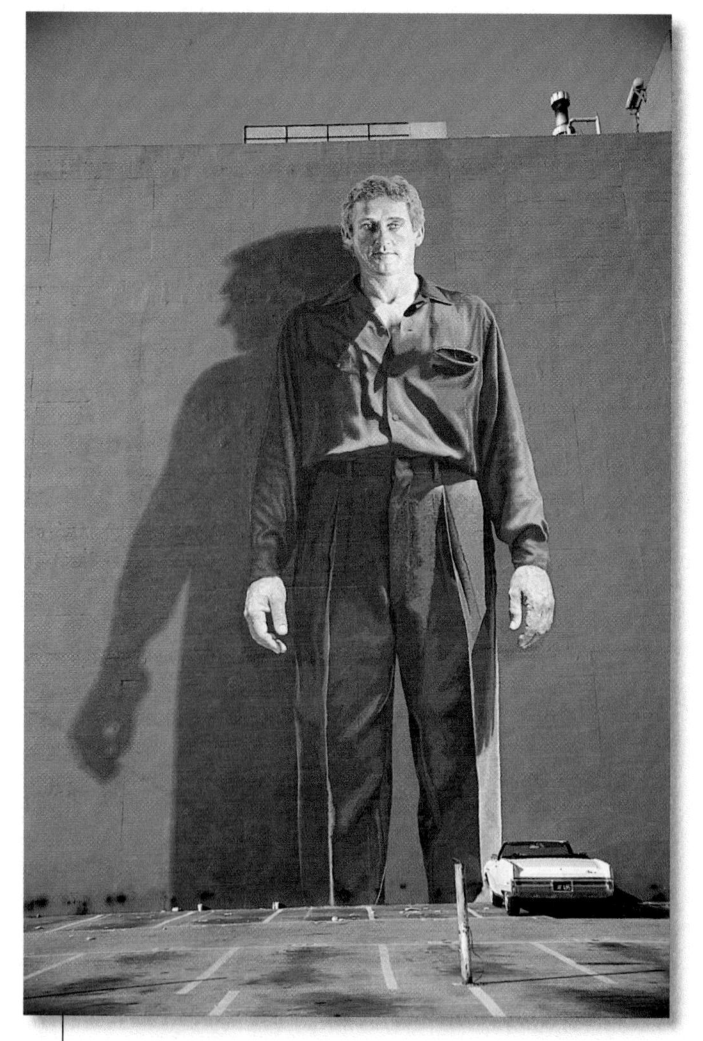

Kent Twitchell. *Edward Ruscha Monument,* 1978–1987. Mural, height 70 feet. Los Angeles, CA. © Kent Twitchell.

The car parked in front of this mural gives you an idea of the artwork's size or scale.

Judith F. Baca. *The Farmworkers of Guadalupe,* 1990. Acrylic mural on wood, 9 by 9 feet. Los Angeles, CA. © Judith F. Baca. Photo courtesy of SPARC (www.sparcmurals.org).

How did the artist show depth in this mural?

Murals and Messages

A **muralist** is an artist who designs a mural and manages the team of artists that helps paint it. Muralists work with a theme, or ideas about broad topics such as nature, love, beauty, or humor.

Mexican American muralist Judith Baca (1946–) chose the difficult labor of farm workers as the theme of this mural. On an arch over the workers are several crates like those used to harvest fruits or vegetables. Each crate has a different scene painted on it. How do these scenes differ from the actual work in the field? Notice how Baca used the techniques of linear perspective to show space and depth.

Sketchbook Journal

Think of some ideas for a school mural. You can show a sports, social, or classroom event. In your Sketchbook Journal, make notes about the theme you want to address and the colors that will support your theme. Draw pictures of details that support your theme.

Studio 1 Setup
Murals *of Daily Life*

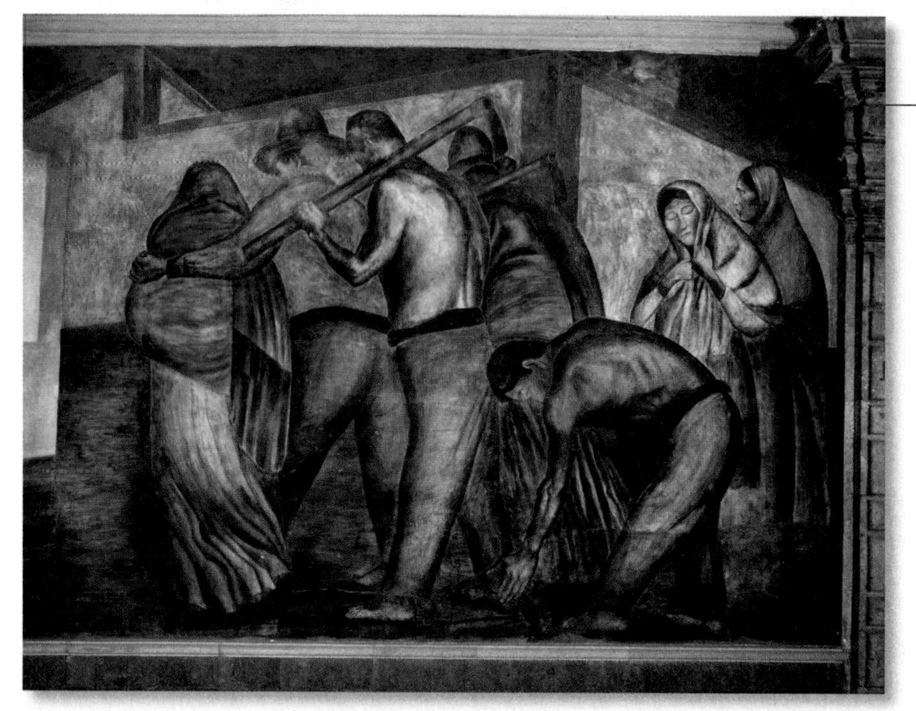

José Clemente Orozco. (Detail) *The Working Class.* Fresco. Escuela Nacional Preparatoria San Ildefonso, Mexico City, Mexico.

What is the theme of this mural?

José Clemente Orozco (1883–1949) is known for his expressive murals showing Mexican themes. He often painted frescos, which are made by applying paint to wet plaster on walls. Look for these details:

- Orozco created unity with a color scheme dominated by dark shades.
- Tints of red, yellow, and green on the highlights provide contrast.
- Most of the figures are shown from the back. Hiding their faces makes them symbols rather than individuals.

Social Realism

The hard life of Mexico's working poor was a common theme for Orozco. He often painted realistic scenes showing the struggles of the working class. For this reason, he was called a "Social Realist."

In *The Working Class,* Orozco showed a group of workers trudging through the streets. With heads bowed and backs bent, they seem to be headed home after a day of hard labor. How did Orozco make it seem as if this scene is taking place in late evening?

Technique Tip

Practice Murals

Muralists often plan their huge works of art by making smaller versions. This allows them to try different ideas before painting the design on a wall. Once the composition is complete, they sometimes use grids to enlarge their plan to wall size.

Studio 1

Create a Mural for Your School

Use what you have learned about murals to work in groups to create a mural for your school.

Materials

- ✓ sketches from your Sketchbook Journal
- ✓ drawing pencils, rulers
- ✓ 12" × 18" drawing paper
- ✓ 48" × 120" craft paper
- ✓ acrylic paints, paintbrushes

1 **Work with your group to design a section of the mural. Make several sketches of activities at your school. Draw scenes from class, sports events, and daily life.**

2 **Redraw parts from each group member's design onto the craft paper. Use grids to transfer the designs.**

3 **Choose a color scheme that fits your group's theme and paint your section of the mural.**

Review and Reflect

- What activities did your group show in your mural?
- What is the theme of the mural? How does each section of the mural relate visually to the others?
- What does the mural say about you, your classmates, and your school?
- In what location in your city would you like to see your mural painted? Why?

Lesson 2

Mosaic Expression

You may recall the Roman mosaic you studied on page 175. A mosaic is made by fitting together small pieces of colored glass, stone, tile, and other materials called tesserae. These objects are glued to a surface, such as a wall, a sidewalk, or furniture. The space around the tesserae is filled with a plaster called grout. As a medium, mosaic is timeless. Many modern artists create mosaics.

A Modern Mosaic

A mosaic can also be a mural when it appears on a wall. To make this work of art, Isaiah Zagar glued small bits of found objects to an exterior wall. He used broken mirror pieces, brightly colored clay shards, and pieces of glass and tile. Zagar's works of art add to the beauty of their surroundings in Philadelphia.

In *Pemberton Street Mosaic*, Zagar created patterns of swirling rhythms with hundreds of tesserae. Different colors of grout help guide your eye around the composition. Near the center of the mural, Zagar placed two portraits. The portraits hint at the creative energy that occurs in the home of two writers. What message might a mural on the side of your house suggest about the people who live there?

Isaiah Zagar. (Detail) *Pemberton Street Mosaic*, 1997. Mixed-media mosaic, 12 by 25 feet. Philadelphia, PA. Courtesy of Snyderman Gallery. Photo by Barry Halkin.

What kinds of tesserae can you identify in this mural?

Isaiah Zagar. *Sculptured Roof Garden,* 1997. Mixed-media mosaic, 10 by 15 feet. Philadelphia, PA. Courtesy of Snyderman Gallery. Photo by Barry Halkin.

Zagar created this mural atop his Philadelphia art studio.

An Artist's Mission

Zagar decorated his Philadelphia art gallery with a mosaic in 1969. He enjoyed it so much that he glued swirling rhythms of tesserae to a wall in his studio.

Neighbors liked his mosaics, so they asked him to make one for a neighborhood church. Soon, he was an artist with a mission to turn the walls of condemned and rundown buildings into concrete canvases.

Zagar has decorated more than two dozen local structures. This mosaic is on the roof of his studio. What is one difference between the work of art on this page and Zagar's other one on the previous page?

Research

Use your library or the Internet to learn how the ancient Romans created mosaics. Find out what materials they used to fill the negative space around the tesserae. Then discover how modern artists make mosaics. Make notes about how the methods the Romans used are the same and different from those today.

Studio 2 Setup

Neighborhood *Mosaic Mural*

John Yancey. *East Austin Mural,* 2003. Austin, TX. © John Yancy.

How does this mosaic mural show space?

The artist used linear perspective and overlapping to show space in this mosaic mural. Notice these details:

- The buildings get smaller as they approach the vanishing point on the horizon.
- The lines on the road lead to the vanishing point.
- The figures in the foreground overlap the road in the middle ground and the buildings in the background.

Outside Art

Artists consider the location of murals as they design them. This mosaic mural adorns the wall of a neighborhood in Austin, Texas. It shows a well-dressed couple in old-fashioned clothes strolling past buildings and houses.

This mosaic is actually half of a larger work of art. The other half shows scenes of children fixing a bicycle and musicians playing. Both halves pay tribute to the neighborhood's rich history. What types of scenes could you show in a mural of your neighborhood?

Technique Tip

Tesserae on Demand

Artists who make mosaics of tile often create their own tesserae. They do this by breaking clay tiles into smaller shapes. You can do the same thing with paper tesserae. Tear different colors of construction paper or old magazine photos into pieces of more or less the same size.

Studio 2

Design a Mosaic Mural

Use what you have learned about mosaics to design a mosaic mural.

Materials

- ✓ 12" × 18" black construction paper
- ✓ pencil
- ✓ scraps of colored construction paper and old magazines
- ✓ glue or glue stick

1 **On a sheet of black construction paper, lightly draw an animal from your imagination in its environment.**

2 **Cut and tear scraps of colored paper or magazine pages to create tesserae. Arrange them on the drawing.**

3 **Glue the tesserae in place, working from the center of the design outward. Leave black spaces around the tesserae.**

Review and Reflect

- Describe the lines, shapes, and colors you included in your mosaic.
- How did your use of color help you create value and depth?
- How does the mood of your mosaic reflect the animal and its environment?
- What did you learn about using tesserae that may help you create an actual mosaic mural?

Lesson 3

The Art of Assemblage

"That's a heap of junk!" Artists sometimes hear such words about the materials they plan to assemble into a work of art. To the imaginative eye, a "heap of junk" may become an enchanting robot. It may become a dazzling wall of wooden shapes and forms. Artists rearrange and piece together old and new items into works of art called **assemblages.** That heap of used objects can transform a space into a place of beauty or humor.

Unity in Assemblage

Artists often use found objects in assemblages. A **found object** is any item that an artist finds and uses in an artwork. Found objects can be things made by humans, such as car parts. They can also be natural objects, such as pieces of tree bark.

Louise Nevelson built *Dawn* of a variety of found objects. What objects can you identify in Nevelson's assemblage?

One challenge assemblage artists face is providing unity to objects that have a variety of colors and shapes. Nevelson solved this problem by painting her entire assemblage gold. This gives a sense of wholeness and completion to *Dawn.* Try to envision the assemblage before it was painted. What colors, textures, and forms do you suppose it had?

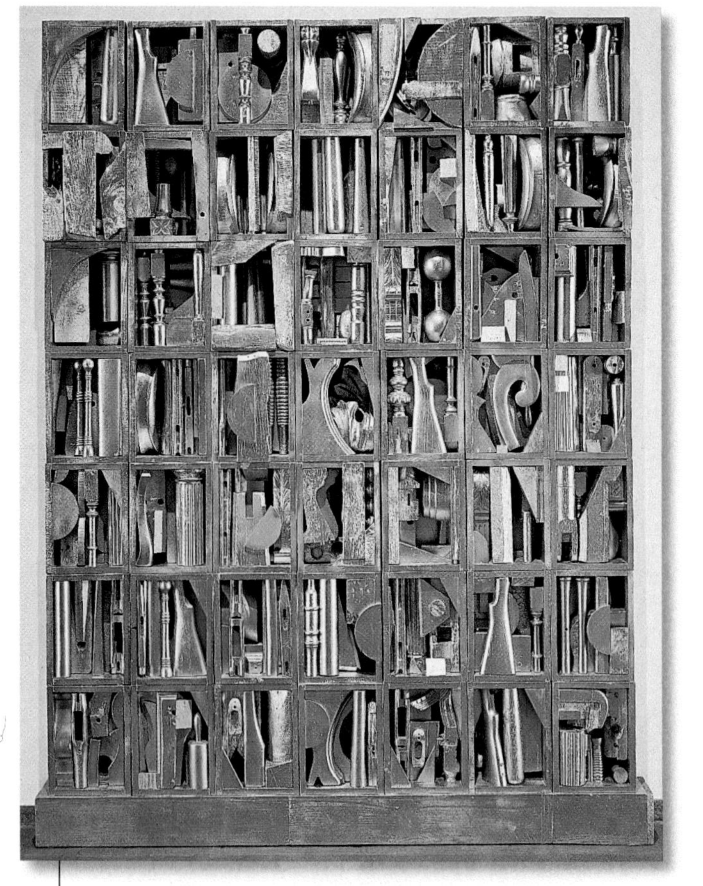

Louise Nevelson. *Dawn,* 1962. Wood painted gold, 94 1/2 by 75 1/2 by 7 3/4 inches. Private collection. © Estate of Louise Nevelson/Artists Rights Society (ARS), New York. Photograph courtesy of Pace Wildenstein.

About her attraction to gold paint, Nevelson said, "Gold . . . reflects the great sun."

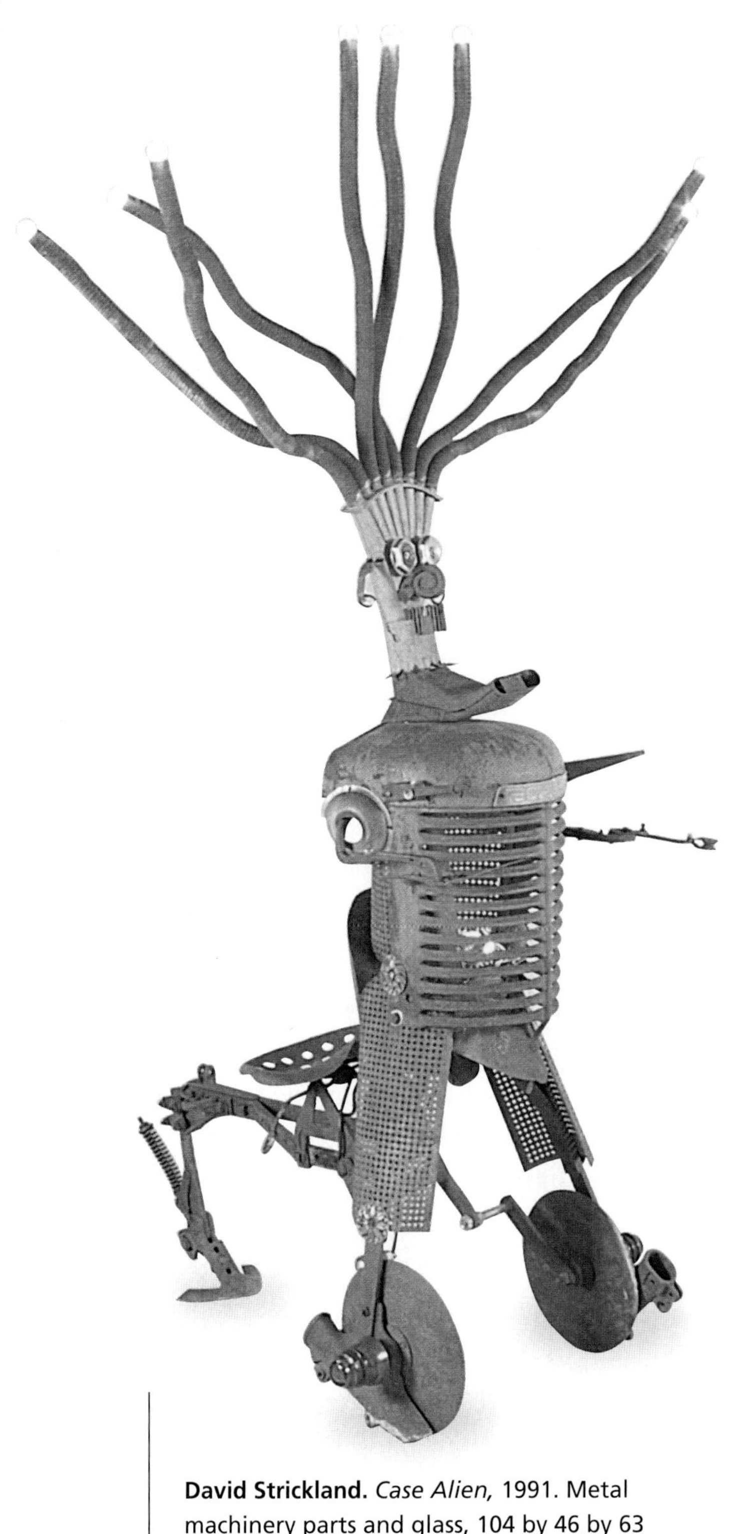

David Strickland. *Case Alien,* 1991. Metal machinery parts and glass, 104 by 46 by 63 inches. Private collection. Photograph by George Holmes. © 1998 Blanton Museum of Art, University of Texas, Austin, TX.

What provides unity in this assemblage?

Variety in Assemblage

Artists use their imagination to decide how found objects might work together in an artwork. They might arrange the objects in different ways before deciding on a plan. Think about objects that you have found or collected. How might you assemble them into a work of art?

David Strickland made *Case Alien* of tractor parts. Most of these parts were the same rusty color, so Strickland had a built-in way of showing unity. Notice the elements of art he used to provide variety. Strickland carefully chose parts with different shapes and textures to add variety. Compare the round, smooth tractor grill that makes up the robot's chest with the narrow, twisted pipes used for hair. Notice the lights at the ends of the hair and inside the robot's chest. How would you describe the mood of *Case Alien?*

Sketchbook Journal

Create several thumbnail sketches of ideas for an assemblage made from found objects. Take notes about different types of objects that might make an interesting assemblage. Where might you find objects that could be used in an assemblage?

Studio 3 Setup
Abstractly *Expressive*

Robert Rauschenberg. *Bed,* 1955. Combine painting: oil and pencil on pillow, quilt, and sheet on wooden supports, 75 1/4 by 31 1/2 inches. Museum of Modern Art. © Robert Rauschenberg/Licensed by VAGA, New York.

What objects do you recognize in this "combine painting"?

American artist Robert Rauschenberg (1925–) combined spattered and smeared paint with a pillow and a quilt in this work of art. Look for these details:

- The warm oranges and yellows of the quilt contrast with the neutral colors of most of the paint. This contrast adds variety to the artwork.
- Some of the paint smears are of a similar hue to the quilt. This gives unity to the artwork.

Combine Painting

Rauschenberg's technique shows his critique of Abstract Expressionism. In his artwork *Bed,* he combines the use of Abstract Expressionist painting with cast-off items to poke fun at the seriousness of the style. Is it any wonder that he calls his artworks **combine paintings?** Some of his compositions combine paint and materials such as comic strips or newsprint. He has also used old umbrellas, vintage photographs, and used tires, along with splashes of paint. What sorts of objects might you attach to a combine painting of your own?

Technique Tip

A Light Touch

Make your combine paintings easier to produce by using light, flat objects. Flat objects give you more surface area to glue. Light objects can be glued to drawing paper. Heavier objects require canvas board or another sturdy surface.

Studio 3

Create a Combine Painting

Use what you have learned about assemblage to create a combine painting.

Materials

- ✓ 18" × 24" white drawing paper, canvas board, or other painting surface
- ✓ glue
- ✓ used plastic toys, prize ribbons, letters, and other memorabilia
- ✓ acrylic paint or other water-soluble paint
- ✓ paintbrushes, mixing tray

1 **Plan a composition that combines painting with a memorable object that is flat and can be glued to a surface.**

2 **Select a surface for your combine painting. Place the object on the surface and lightly pencil around its shape. Remove the object.**

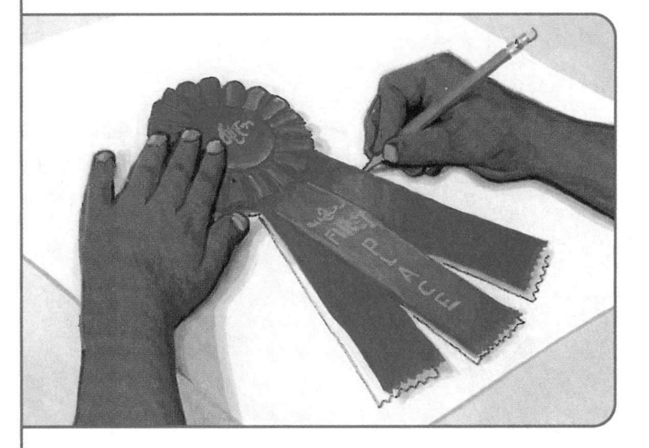

3 **Add rhythmic and colorful brushstrokes of paint to your surface. Glue your memorable object onto the surface.**

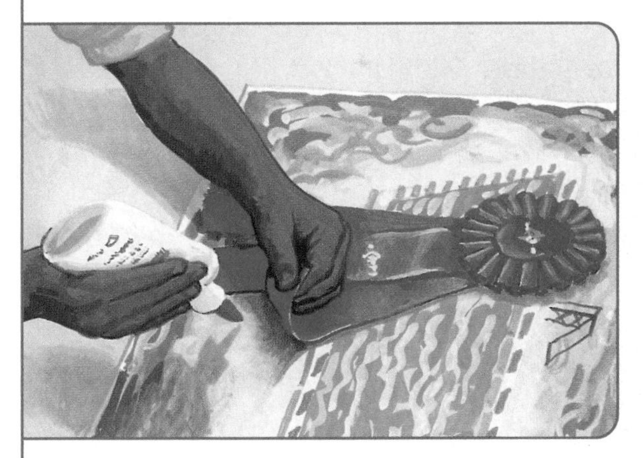

Review and Reflect

- What is happening in your combine painting?
- How do the shapes and forms work together?
- What is your intended meaning?
- To whom might you present this artwork as a gift? Explain why.

Lesson 4

Expressive Points of View

The works of art on these two pages all show the same subject: a tree. One main difference among them is the **point of view,** the angle from which a viewer sees an object or a scene. Artists can choose a point of view to express their feelings about a subject. Consider how the different points of view in these paintings change the way you think or feel about the tree.

Depends on How You Look at It

The most common point of view is a **straight-on view,** as shown by Piet Mondrian in *The Red Tree.* This image shows the tree from a familiar angle. If you look back on all the images in this book, you will see that most of them show a straight-on point of view. This view allows viewers to focus on other parts of the composition.

Artists sometimes show their subjects from more dramatic angles. Georgia O'Keeffe painted *The Lawrence Tree* from a **ground-level view,** or worm's-eye view. The tree is viewed as a worm or an ant might see it. This point of view can help artists express their feelings about the power of their subjects. How do the stars help establish the mood of this painting?

Piet Mondrian. *Avond: The Red Tree,* 1908-1910. Oil on canvas, 27 5/8 by 38 1/8 inches. Gemeentemuseum Den Haag, The Netherlands. ©2005 Mondrian/Holtzman Trust c/o HCR International, Warrenton, VA.

How would you describe the artist's point of view?

Georgia O'Keeffe. *The Lawrence Tree,* 1929. Oil on canvas, 31 by 39 1/4 inches. Wadsworth Atheneum, Hartford, CT. The Ella Gallup Sumner and Mary Catlin Sumner Collection Fund. Photo by Malcolm Varon, New York. © The Georgia O'Keeffe Foundation/Artists Rights Society (ARS), New York/ADAGP, Paris.

Georgia O'Keeffe was inspired to paint this image as she stargazed through tree branches on a friend's ranch.

Andrew Wyeth. *The Hunter,* 1943. Tempera on masonite, 33 by 33 7/8 inches. The Toledo Museum of Art, Toledo, OH. Elizabeth C. Mau Bequest Fund.

What a Bird Sees

Andrew Wyeth painted *The Hunter* from a **bird's-eye view.** This view shows what a bird might see while flying overhead. This point of view can be an effective way of making the viewer forget that the image is a flat, two-dimensional composition. In *The Hunter,* the trunk of a sycamore tree appears large at the top and recedes almost immediately to the forest floor. There, a tiny figure of a hunter appears. Notice that from this point of view, a leaf can be the same size as a human figure. What message might the artist be communicating through this point of view?

Sketchbook Journal

Filmmakers are experts at using point of view to affect how you feel about characters. As you watch movies or TV programs, notice the camera angles used to film each character. How does each view affect your opinion of a character? How can you use these views in your own works of art?

Studio 4 Setup

Abstract *Points of View*

Friedensreich Hundertwasser. *808A End of Waters on the Roof,* 1985. Woodcut in 28 colors, 20 1/2 by 25 3/8 inches. © 1998 Gruener Janura AG, Glarus, Switzerland.

How many points of view did the artist use in this artwork?

Artists are not limited to one point of view in a single composition. The artist used two points of view to show this abstract **cityscape,** or view of a city. Look for these details:

- The artist used geometric shapes and a straight-on point of view for the buildings.
- Organic shapes make up the blue water, which is shown from a bird's-eye view. This point of view is hinted at by the mention of a roof in the title.
- The artist simplified and flattened the shapes of buildings and other objects.

A Self-Portrait?

Have you ever thought of a cityscape as a self-portrait? Austrian artist Friedensreich Hundertwasser (1928–2000) intended this work of art to be an image of himself. The tightly wound blue spiral symbolizes the artist. The eye in the center is symbolic of his eye. What emotions do you think the artist wanted to express? How does the composition make you feel?

Technique Tip

Use Linear Perspective

Linear perspective can help you show how objects look from bird's-eye and worm's-eye views. For a bird's-eye view, establish a vanishing point on the ground. Pick a vanishing point in the sky for a worm's-eye view. Bring the lines of your object closer together as they fade into the distance and meet at the vanishing point.

Studio 4

Create an Abstract Cityscape

Use what you have learned about point of view to create an abstract cityscape.

Materials

- ✓ photographs of cities
- ✓ 12" × 18" white drawing paper
- ✓ ruler, pencil
- ✓ tempera paint, paintbrushes, mixing tray

1 **Examine pictures of large cities. Make a list of objects you see in the sky and near the ground.**

2 **Draw an abstract design of your favorite city. Simplify shapes of objects on your list. Show some from different points of view.**

3 **Add bright colors to your design using tempera paints.**

Review and Reflect

- Tell about the shapes you created for your abstract design.
- What points of view did you use? Explain how your selection affects the composition.
- How would you describe the mood of your abstract cityscape?
- Where do you imagine your cityscape might best be displayed?

Meet *the Artist*

Georgia O'Keeffe

Like many artists, Georgia O'Keeffe began her art career by drawing and painting in a realistic style. Soon her artworks took on an abstract style, yet her subjects remained recognizable. In this way, she abstracted, or pulled, only the key shapes from realistic subjects to show in her artworks. These abstract shapes, painted with bold colors, became the most important parts of her drawings and paintings. Her new style helped O'Keeffe express her ideas and feelings.

Georgia O'Keeffe was still an active painter at the age of ninety.

"I found I could say things with color and shapes that I couldn't say in any other way—things I had no words for."

—GEORGIA O'KEEFFE

Finding a Voice

O'Keeffe knew early that she wanted to be a painter. But after studying art in Chicago and New York, she gave up painting for four years. Then she began attending lectures by Alon Bement at the University of Virginia. Bement thought artists should not copy nature exactly. He believed artists should use color like a musician uses notes. They should use their emotions to guide them. O'Keeffe agreed. She traveled south, teaching art at a school in Amarillo, Texas. She began to draw what she called her "Specials."

Perfecting a Style

In New York, photographer Alfred Stieglitz saw one of O'Keeffe's Specials. He began to exhibit her work in his gallery. He persuaded her to move back to New York. Soon they were married.

O'Keeffe perfected her signature style. She took the world around her as her subjects. She painted the lake near her home. She painted small details from flowers and leaves, but she painted them on a huge scale. Her colors and imagery changed when she began spending summers in New Mexico. Bleached bones and searing hills came to dominate her canvases.

Talk About It

The painting on page 264 shows O'Keeffe's abstract vision of a lake in New York. Look again at *From the Lake No. I.* How did the artist use color to reinforce the stormy mood?

The Life of Georgia O'Keeffe

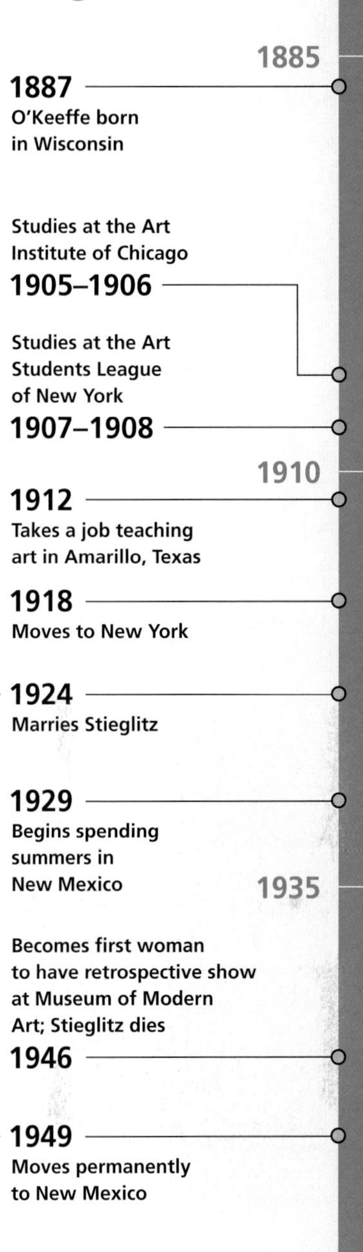

1885

1887
O'Keeffe born in Wisconsin

1905–1906
Studies at the Art Institute of Chicago

1907–1908
Studies at the Art Students League of New York

1910

1912
Takes a job teaching art in Amarillo, Texas

1918
Moves to New York

1924
Marries Stieglitz

Stieglitz and O'Keeffe

1929
Begins spending summers in New Mexico

1935

1946
Becomes first woman to have retrospective show at Museum of Modern Art; Stieglitz dies

1949
Moves permanently to New Mexico

Bisti Wilderness, New Mexico

1960

1970
Whitney Museum of American Art hosts retrospective of O'Keeffe's work

1985

1986
Dies in New Mexico

Look *and Compare*

A Change of Styles

The two paintings on page 285 are so different that they seem to be by two artists. But Georgia O'Keeffe painted both. She painted the famous American Radiator Building when she lived in New York City. Many years later, after she began spending her summers in New Mexico, O'Keeffe painted the vivid *Stump in Red Hills.*

Consider why an artist might choose to paint a night view of a cityscape.

Objects in nature were often the subject of O'Keeffe's paintings.

Radiator Building—Night, New York

O'Keeffe painted this version of the American Radiator Building not long after it was completed in 1924. Skyscrapers like this were just beginning to tower over the skyline of Manhattan. They were becoming a new symbol of urban life.

Notice how most of the shapes in this work of art are geometric. The buildings and windows create a pattern of repeated rectangles. The lighted windows and diagonal shafts of light make the building the focal point. The line of brilliant red on the left and the warm yellow window lights add variety to the cool colors of the night.

Stump in Red Hills

The twisted organic shape of a tree stump is the focal point of *Stump in Red Hills.* The stump and the creased red hills behind it are a warm contrast to the cool cityscape above it. The creases and folds in the New Mexico landscape seem almost human. Notice how the values become darker toward the bottom center of the composition. What feeling do you think O'Keeffe was trying to convey with this landscape?

Both paintings show how O'Keeffe used objects and scenes from her environment as subjects. Notice the date that each painting was made. Consider how these same scenes might be different if they were painted today.

Georgia O'Keeffe. *Radiator Building—Night, New York,* 1927. Oil on canvas, 48 by 30 inches. Alfred Stieglitz Collection of Modern Art, Fisk University, Nashville, TN. © 1997 The Georgia O'Keeffe Foundation/Artists Rights Society (ARS), New York.

Georgia O'Keeffe. *Stump in Red Hills,* 1940. Oil on canvas, 30 by 24 inches. The Georgia O'Keeffe Museum, Santa Fe, NM.

Compare & Contrast

- **What is different about the light sources in these paintings?**
- **Georgia O'Keeffe said, "Colors and shapes make a more definite statement than words." How do these paintings reflect this?**

Lesson 5

Expression Through Symbols

Does your school have a mascot? A mascot is a person, animal, or object that serves as a symbol of a school and its students. At athletic games and academic contests, the mascot is a symbol of good luck.

Totems are used in a similar way. Totems are symbols that represent clans or other subgroups of a culture. Cultures around the world use totems to symbolize their beliefs and practices.

Artist unknown, Tlingit culture. *Tlingit House Post,* date unknown. Carved and painted wood, height 89 3/4 inches. University of Pennsylvania Museum, Philadelphia, PA.

The red paint surrounding the face in the middle makes the face a focal point.

Traditional Totems

This totem pole was built by the Native American Tlingit culture from the northwest United States. The huge carved post is typical of Native American totem poles that show family histories. Such sculptures are often built to mark important events or land ownership or to honor the dead.

Notice that both sides of a centerline from top to bottom are similar. The artists used symmetrical balance. This is typical for totem poles.

A variety of symbols decorate the totem. Some stand for birds or other animals. Faces are carved into the top and center of the totem pole. The animal symbols make these faces seem to have bodies and wings. What do these symbols tell you about the Tlingit culture?

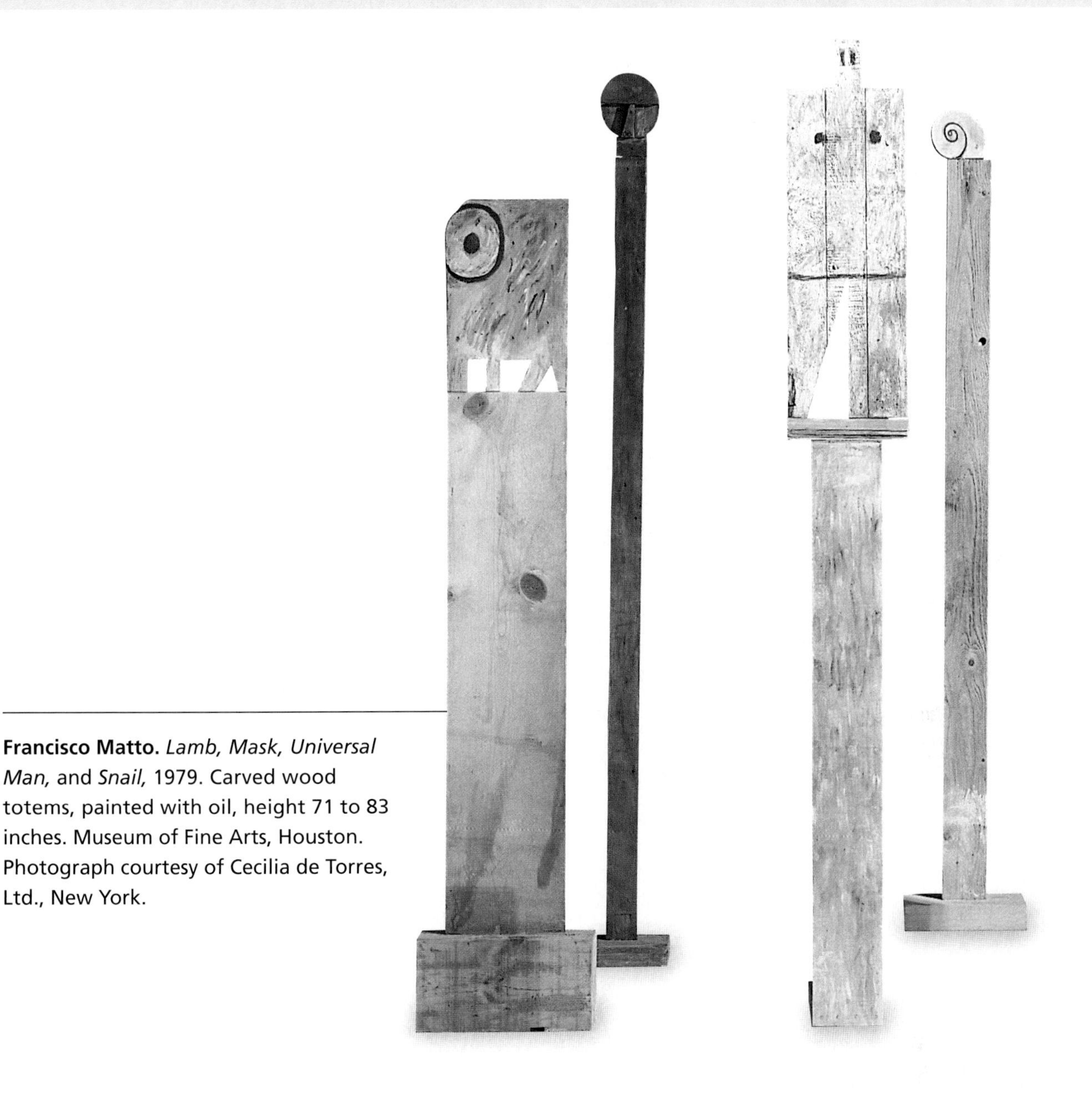

Francisco Matto. *Lamb, Mask, Universal Man,* and *Snail,* 1979. Carved wood totems, painted with oil, height 71 to 83 inches. Museum of Fine Arts, Houston. Photograph courtesy of Cecilia de Torres, Ltd., New York.

Modern Totems

Modern sculptor Francisco Matto (1911–1995) made this group of four totems. Each represents a person or thing. The artist revealed the identity of the totems in his title.

Each of Matto's four totems generally shows symmetrical balance. The totems, as a group, are positioned with asymmetrical balance in the photograph.

Matto used geometric shapes to give unity to his totems. Contrasting organic shapes create interest and emphasize figures and objects. Why do you think Matto varied the size of each totem? What cultural symbols could you use in a totem?

Research

Learn more about totem poles and their history online using keywords *totem* and *totem history.* Discover the meaning behind totems and find out how to tell fake ones from real ones. Then find out which cultures still create totems today and why.

Cultural *Carvings*

Wayne Alfred and Beau Dick. *Ga'akstalas,* 1987.

How did the artists use rhythm in this totem pole?

Native American sculptors Wayne Alfred and Beau Dick carved this totem pole. Notice these details:

- A bird sits atop a human figure, which holds an object resembling a canoe. The horizontal zigzag lines on the canoe reflect the horizontal lines of the bird's wings.
- The pattern on the wings of the bird shows regular rhythm.
- Each form has symmetrical balance.
- The complementary colors of red and green are contrasted by black and white.

Cultural Traditions

Alfred and Dick strive to understand the cultural history behind the totems and other pieces they carve. The artists learned to carve from older members of their cultural group. Now they pass the knowledge on to the next generation.

Animals are carved onto totems to evoke the qualities the animal possesses. For example, the bird at the top could be seen as noble, intelligent, and fierce. What might the human figure under the bird and the canoe represent?

Technique Tip

Sculpting with Paper

Experiment with different ways to sculpt with construction paper. You might try cutting or tearing the paper into shapes, then gluing the shapes into interesting forms. Or fold and shape the paper into forms such as cylinders, cones, or cubes. Cut paper into thin strips and roll it up to form curls. Or fold the paper into pleats and fan it out.

Studio 5

Create a Totem

Use what you have learned about expression through symbols to make your own totem.

Materials

- ✓ 12" × 18" construction paper
- ✓ tape or glue
- ✓ scissors

1 **Create a design for a totem that includes the sketches of the heads of at least three family members, friends, or animals.**

2 **Make a cylinder from a sheet of construction paper. Glue or tape it to a cardboard base.**

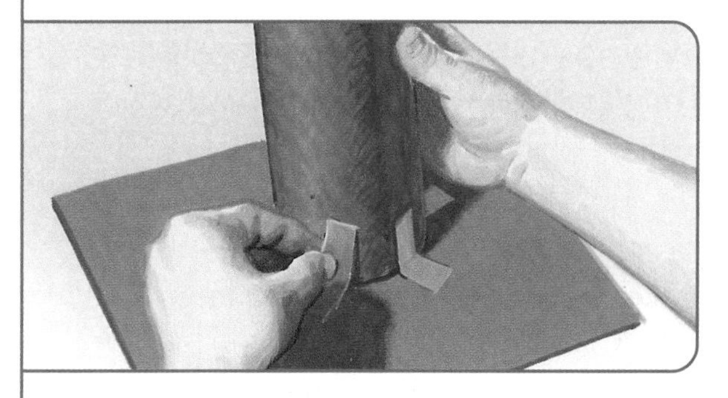

3 **Use cut construction paper and paper sculpting techniques to make the heads. Glue or tape the heads to the pole.**

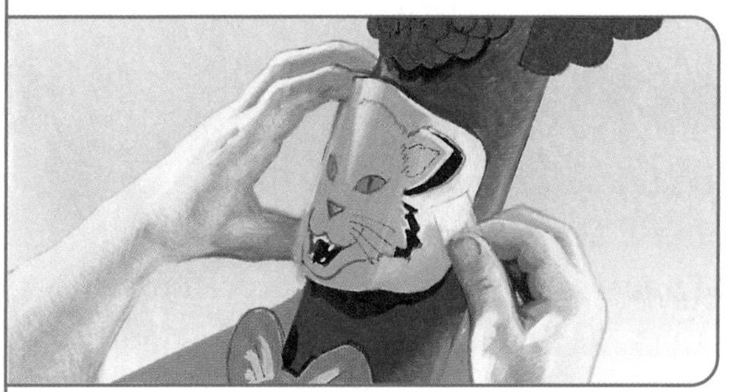

Review and Reflect

- Describe the symbols you included in your totem.
- How did you create emphasis and unity? What techniques did you use to create three-dimensional forms?
- What meaning do the symbols you included add to your totem?
- How do you think any family members or friends that you included in your totem would respond to it? Why?

Lesson 6

Masks for Expression

No one knows when people first started wearing masks and using disguises. Masks have been a part of cultures all over the world. They are often used as symbolic decorations in dances or ceremonies. They help wearers change their appearances, often to become players in a theatre of fantasy. However they are used, masks tell stories and hold special meanings about the cultures that made them.

Artist unknown, Teotihuacán culture. *Funerary Mask,* ca. A.D. 400–600. Rock and shell mosaic, 8 1/2 by 7 3/4 inches. National Museum of Anthropology, Mexico City, Mexico.

How does the use of mosaic affect the design of this mask?

The Meanings of Masks

A **mask** is a symbol that represents ideas, beliefs, or values of the artist or the culture with which it is associated. It may be used in ceremonies. It may be thought to protect a cultural group from harm.

Members of the Teotihuacán cultural group in Mexico used mosaic masks like the one above during funeral ceremonies. The artist's use of mosaic adds texture and pattern to the design. Why might a mask have been an important symbol in such a ceremony?

The gold mask on this page was made in Peru during the Inca Empire. Notice the symmetrically balanced facial proportions and the crinkly texture of the mask. The artist added more texture by creating a pattern on the edges. The choice of gold as an art medium shows the power and wealth the Inca Empire once held.

Artist unknown, Peruvian. *Inca Mask,* date unknown. Gold with paint, 21 1/4 by 12 1/8 inches. Museo Arqueológico Larco Herrera, Lima, Peru.

How would you describe the balance of this Peruvian mask?

Artist unknown. *Jaguar Mask,* 1960. Painted wood, height 9 1/2 inches. From the Girard Foundation Collection in the Museum of International Folk Art, a unit of the Museum of New Mexico, Santa Fe, NM. Photograph by Michel Monteaux.

Modern Masks

The jaguar was an important animal to ancient civilizations in Central and South America. It often stood for courage and strength.

Ancient artists carved jaguar masks and used jaguar symbols on their buildings. Some modern artists also choose the image of this fierce and powerful animal as the subject for their artworks. *Jaguar Mask* above shows a more playful interpretation by a folk artist.

Some cultures believe that the wearer of a mask takes on the qualities of the animal it represents. What qualities come to mind when you think of jaguars?

Sketchbook Journal

Make a list of your favorite animals. Take notes about the qualities that your animals possess. Are they fast? powerful? smart? protective? loyal? Make several thumbnail sketches for ideas of animal masks you would like to create.

Studio 6 Setup

Papier-Mâché *Animal Mask*

You have seen masks made of mosaic, gold, and wood. *Horned Toad Mask* is made of papier mâché. Notice these details:

- The facial proportions of the mask are about the same as those of an actual horned toad.
- The artist used colors that are similar to, but not exactly the same as, the colors of a real horned toad.

Artist unknown, North American. *Horned Toad Mask,* ca. 1996. Papier mâché, 10 by 10 by 7 inches. Private collection.

How do the facial proportions of this mask compare to a real horned toad?

Papier Mâché

Papier mâché is a sculpting medium that uses papers and liquid paste. Paper strips or torn bits of paper are pasted in five or six layers. After the paste-soaked paper has dried, the form is stiff and hard. The artist then applies paint to the form.

Artists often use an **armature,** or support, to help form their papier-mâché sculptures. The armature can be made of a variety of materials, such as clay, cardboard, or wood. For larger papier-mâché artworks, a chicken wire armature or a large balloon can be made. Artists use armatures to allow the inside of the wet paper to dry and to reduce the weight of the artwork.

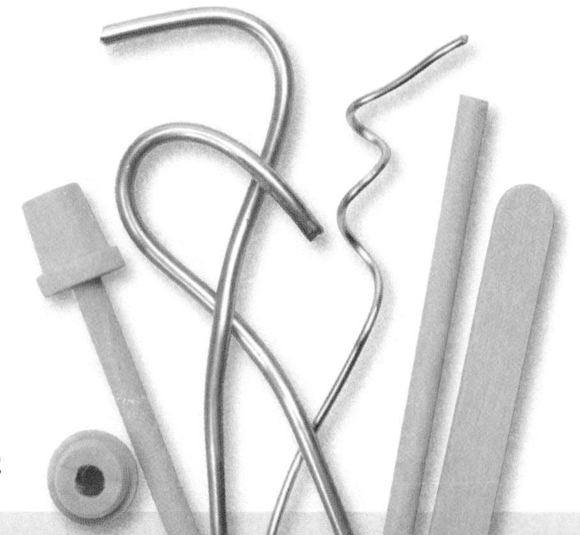

Technique Tip

Blow-Up Armature

A big, oval balloon can be the perfect armature for a mask. Blow the balloon up until it is a little bigger than your head. Build the mask on the front half of the balloon, where your face would be. Let it dry slightly, and then pop the balloon. After the inside dries, the mask should be a perfect fit for your face.

Studio 6

Create a Papier-Mâché Animal Mask

Use what you have learned about masks to make one from papier mâché.

Materials

- ✓ pencil
- ✓ 9" × 12" white drawing paper
- ✓ 12" × 18" cardboard, heavy paper
- ✓ scissors, glue, stapler ⚠
- ✓ newspaper or paper towel strips
- ✓ papier-mâché paste
- ✓ colored tissue paper
- ✓ tempera paint and paintbrush

1 **Make several thumbnail sketches of animal masks. Enlarge one onto a piece of cardboard as an armature. Carefully curve the cardboard.**

2 **Build up facial features by gluing or stapling pieces of cardboard or heavy paper to the armature. Cut slits for the eyes and nose.**

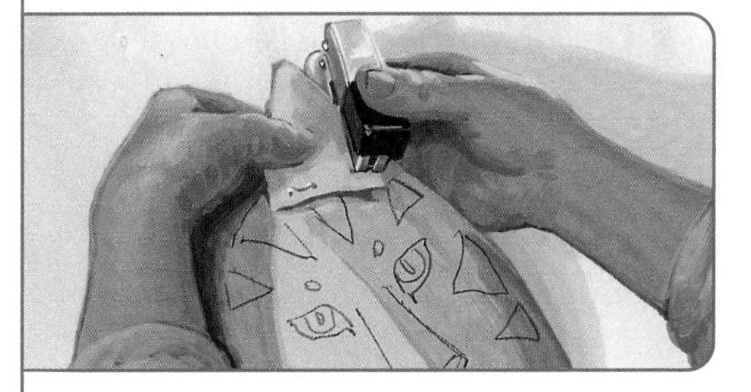

3 **Add at least three coats of papier mâché. Allow each one to dry between coats. Add color with tempera paint or glued-on colored tissue paper.**

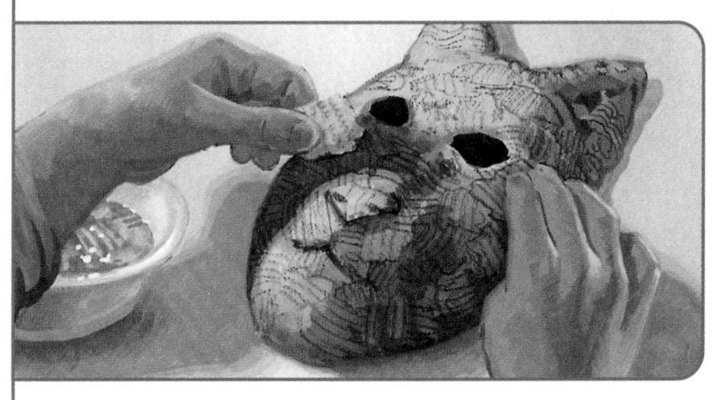

Review and Reflect

- Tell about the form you used to build your armature.
- Compare your mask's facial proportions with your own.
- Discuss the meaning of your mask. What feelings and ideas does it represent to you?
- Where will you wear your mask? How does it make you feel to wear it?

Lesson 7

Expression Through Humor

Many artists focus on serious subjects and themes. Others want to make you laugh. Think about your favorite cartoon strip or comic book, or your favorite animated movie or TV show. What about that funny birthday card you received? Artists aiming at your funny bone create these and other artworks. So if you think there is something funny going on in this picture, you are right!

Humor in Illustrations

Illustrations are pictures made for printed works, such as books and magazines. They are often meant to be funny or satirical.

Norman Rockwell, who painted this work of art, was an **illustrator** —an artist who creates pictures for printed works. Rockwell painted hundreds of covers for magazines like *The Saturday Evening Post.* His paintings were usually as realistic as the man in this painting.

Rockwell shows the man looking at an Abstract Expressionist painting. This painting style is almost the exact opposite of Rockwell's. Yet the painting on the wall looks like it could belong to almost any museum's abstract collection. What do you think the man viewing the painting is thinking about?

Norman Rockwell. *The Connoisseur,* 1962. Oil painting for *The Saturday Evening Post,* January 13, 1962. © 1962 The Normal Rockwell Family Trust.

Norman Rockwell painted many covers for *The Saturday Evening Post.*

Leo Cullum. *"It's just the architect's model, but I'm very excited."* 1997. Ink, 4 by 5 inches.

How does this illustrated cartoon express humor?

What Is So Funny?

Cartoons are drawings intended to be funny. The **cartoonists,** artists who draw cartoons, usually try to communicate a specific message. However, cartoons often mean something different to each viewer.

Read the **caption,** or the words below the drawing, to this Leo Cullum cartoon. Do you think a dog planning to build its own house is funny? How about a dog hiring an architect? Or a dog wearing a tie?

The illustrations by Cullum and Rockwell are meant to amuse. What do you think about the sense of humor of each artist? What types of illustrations do you find funny? What makes them funny to you?

Sketchbook Journal

Collect copies of some of your favorite cartoon strips. Arrange them on the pages of your Sketchbook Journal and glue or tape them in place. Write why you like them. What makes them seem funny to you? Then draw a sketch of your own cartoon strip.

Studio 7 Setup

Humor *in Caricature*

Chuck Jones. *Love Is in the Hare,* 1998. Limited edition giclée, 20 by 15 inches. © Warner Bros.

What features did the artist exaggerate in these two rabbits?

Do these figures look like real rabbits? The artist exaggerated certain features while drawing this cartoon. This technique is called **caricature.** Notice these details:

- The cartoonist exaggerated the length of the rabbits' teeth and the sizes of their eyes and cheeks.
- These rabbits have longer legs and arms and bigger feet than real rabbits.
- The title is a joke based on the phrase "Love is in the air."

What's up, Doc?

Bugs Bunny is a well-known cartoon character in many parts of the world. But do you know the name of the cartoonist who is responsible for making Bugs and his friends move frantically around the TV or movie screen?

Chuck Jones was a pioneer of cartoons that move, or **animated cartoons.** He drew Bugs and other cartoon characters. For each second of action, his teams of artists would then draw twenty-four different pictures. Each picture showed a slight movement. When shown at the rate of twenty-four frames per second, the characters seem to move.

Technique Tip

What to Exaggerate

Carefully choose what features to exaggerate. Consider your subject's character and physical features. Is your subject brainy? Make the forehead larger. Does your subject have big, beautiful eyes? Make them even bigger. Does your subject squint a lot? Exaggerate the squint.

Studio 7

Create a Caricature

Use what you have learned about expression through humor to create a caricature.

Materials

- ✓ mirror
- ✓ 9" × 12" white drawing paper
- ✓ pencil, black felt-tip pen
- ✓ colored markers, felt pens, pencils

1 **Look into a mirror and lightly draw a sketch of a self-portrait with a pencil.**

2 **Exaggerate some of your facial features with black felt-tip pen. You may wish to exaggerate the shape of your face too.**

3 **Use your favorite drawing or painting media to complete your caricature.**

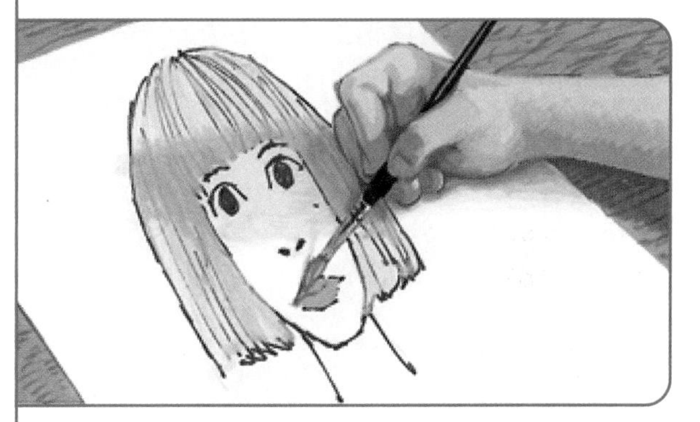

Review and Reflect

- What features did you exaggerate in your caricature?
- How does the caricature compare to the way you actually look?
- Does the caricature show something about you that you find funny? Explain.
- Do people who know you well think your caricature resembles you in a humorous way? Why or why not?

Lesson 8

The Art of Industrial Design

Many of the things you use in life are designed by an artist, to be made by a machine. This requires careful planning by the artist known as an **industrial designer.** These artists work with scientists and engineers to design products. Their goal is to create attractive, useful products that can be mass-produced in a factory. The work they do is called **industrial design.**

Form and Function

Industrial design is a type of functional art. The artworks that industrial designers create, such as a container, tool, or stove, are used by people to perform a function.

For example, find the roller skate in this work of art. Roller skates are designed to hold your feet, roll when you wear them, and look good.

Like other objects with a physical function, footwear must be designed to operate well. The job of the industrial designer is to make sure the design also looks attractive.

The designer's job does not end there, however. Once products have been bought and tested in the market, industrial designers set to work on plans to improve them.

Study the items on the greeting card poster to the right. Which items do you think were crafted by hand? Which do you think began with an industrial design? Notice any items whose design you think has changed.

Chris Pullman, art director; **Gaye Korbet and Chris Pullman,** designers. *Seasons Greetings from WGBH Design,* 1985. Courtesy of WGBH, Boston, MA.

This artwork is a large greeting card sent to friends of the designers who created it.

Planning for an Industrial Design

Industrial designers ask a lot of questions before starting a new project. Who will use the product? What products do consumers currently use? What is the product's purpose? Will a new bicycle be used to win the Tour de France or to ride to school?

The answers to these questions help designers improve their products. Some designers get answers by talking with potential customers or by conducting written surveys. A survey about a new bicycle design might ask these questions:

- Do you own a bicycle? What brand is it?
- What features do you like or dislike about your bicycle?
- What features would you like to have on a new bicycle?

What other examples of industrial design do you see in your immediate surroundings?

Sketchbook Journal

List your ideas for improving an existing product. Conduct research at the library or by talking with your friends. Make sketches of your new product design. Include notes about who would use the new product and how it will be used. How is your design an improvement over the original?

Studio 8 Setup

Prototype *Models*

Harri Koskinen, designer. *Block Lamp,* 1996. Hand-cast glass, 4 by 4 by 6 inches. The Museum of Modern Art Design Store, New York.

What uses do you think the designer intended for this light?

This lamp is a product of modern industrial design. Look for these details:

- The lamp is functional. It sends out a soft light.
- The light bulb is sandwiched between two hand-cast glass blocks. The bulb can be changed when it burns out.
- The lamp could be displayed on a table or the floor. It can also be hung from the ceiling or on a wall.

Designing Tomorrow's Products

Creating industrial designs requires a good imagination, careful planning, and a model. A **model** is an example of what a product will look like. Then a *working* model, or **prototype,** of a product is created. The prototype is then tested. If the product design passes safety and function tests, it is approved for production. Then it is mass-produced for sale to consumers.

Some designers experiment by creating several models when working on a prototype. Then they select a design for a new prototype from those models. Think of a design for a new product, or how you might improve the design of an existing product.

Technique Tip

Designing with Clay

Industrial designers use a wide range of art media to make models. Clay is especially good because you can experiment as you work. You cannot put wood back on a block after you carve it off. But you can add clay to your model. Clay is sometimes used by industrial designers to create full-size models of cars.

Studio 8

Create a Model for a Prototype

Use what you have learned about industrial design to create a model for a prototype.

Materials

- ✓ sketches of product designs from your Sketchbook Journal (optional)
- ✓ pencil
- ✓ modeling clay
- ✓ blank card for credit line

1 **Select a product design from your Sketchbook Journal or draw a new product you would enjoy designing.**

2 **Add funny or interesting features to your design. Use modeling clay to create a model for a prototype of your design.**

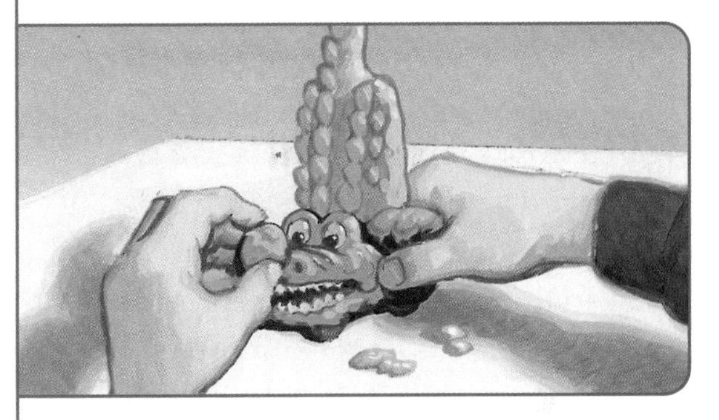

3 **Give your model an original title and display it for others to see and critique.**

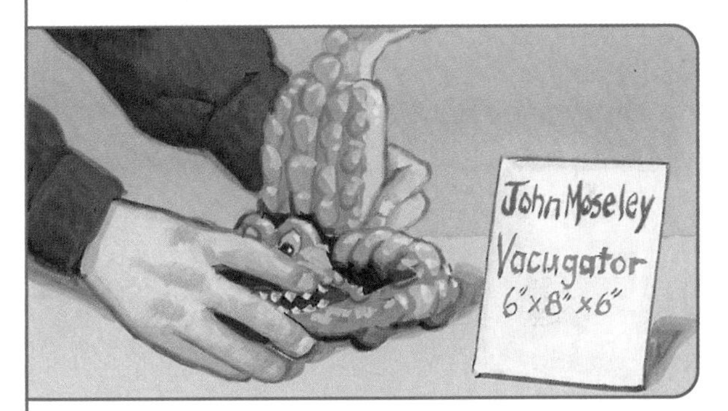

Review and Reflect

- What special features does your model have?
- How is the form and function of your model different from existing products?
- What do the lines of the form tell about the purpose of your model?
- As you made the model, what did you learn that may help you make a prototype? Do you think you improved the product? Explain.

Lesson 9

Graphic Design as Expression

Graphic design, the art of communicating with images and letters, is all around you. The work of **graphic designers** appears on billboards and book jackets. They create logos for your favorite bands and sports teams. They design everything from football jerseys to soup can labels. Their designs are also used for CD jewel cases and CD-ROM software. In fact, a team of graphic artists designed the book you are reading right now.

Posters and Logos

The vintage poster below was a gift to people who subscribed to a magazine called *Modern Art.* Artist Arthur Wesley Dow made a woodcut that was then copied using a printing process called lithograph.

Dow's interest in Japanese art shows in the poster's design. The lines and shapes of the trees reflected in the still water set a calm mood. Dow emphasized this calm mood with a muted color scheme.

Graphic designers also make logos, such as the Statue of Liberty design below. A **logo** is a visual symbol for a city, business, club, or group. Graphic designer Adrian Avram used only two colors on this logo. This simple color choice makes it easy to print the logo in a variety of sizes.

Arthur Wesley Dow. *Modern Art,* 1895. Color lithograph on paper, 20 by 15 3/4 inches. National Museum of American Art, Smithsonian Institution, Washington, D.C.

This poster was designed more than one hundred years ago.

Adrian Avram. *NYC Logo,* 2003. Digital illustration, 6 3/4 by 9 inches. Collection of the artist. © 2003 Adrian Avram.

A simple color scheme attracts attention to this logo.

Drawing with Pen and Ink

1 Select a pen and drawing paper. Technical pens have different sized tips, or nibs, which allow you to draw lines of varying width. Ballpoint pens create crisp, clean lines. Choose smooth paper when working with ink. Rough paper can absorb ink quickly and give your drawing an uneven look.

2 Draw your design in pencil first. To create circles, use a compass and a pencil, or use patterns of circles cut from posterboard. Then go over the lines with a pen. Work from one side of the paper to the other to avoid smearing ink.

3 Shade forms with one or more of the following methods:

- Use a ruler to draw a series of parallel lines that get closer together. These lines will create a light-to-dark effect.
- Try cross-hatching. Draw parallel lines. Then add a layer of lines going the other way. Space the lines out or draw them close together for light and dark areas.
- Use the stippling method. Draw points or dots with the tip of the pen. Gradually add more dots to create darker values.

Creating a Contour Drawing

1 Focus on the top of an object and draw a contour line, or outline, with your drawing tool in the air. Keep your eye on the contours of the object at all times. Continue drawing in this way, following the outside and inside contours, folds, wrinkles, and creases.

2 Place your drawing tool at the top of the paper and draw the contour lines of an object. Draw slowly to record the inside and outside folds, wrinkles, and creases as you see them. To create a continuous line, keep your hand and forearm in fluid motion and do not lift the drawing tool from the paper.

3 To create a blind contour drawing, cover your drawing paper with another sheet of paper and do not watch your progress as you observe and draw the object. To create a modified contour drawing, allow yourself to look at the drawing from time to time to correct proportions.

Creating a Gesture Drawing

1 **Practice drawing basic human shapes and forms before you begin your gesture drawing. Use geometric shapes as you quickly draw the different forms that make up the human figure, such as an oval for a head, the torso, and hips. Use cylinder shapes for the neck, arms, and legs.**

2 **Notice the movement, pose, shape, weight, and form of a figure, preferably in action. Draw the figure using quick, rhythmic, scribbling sketches for one to three minutes.**

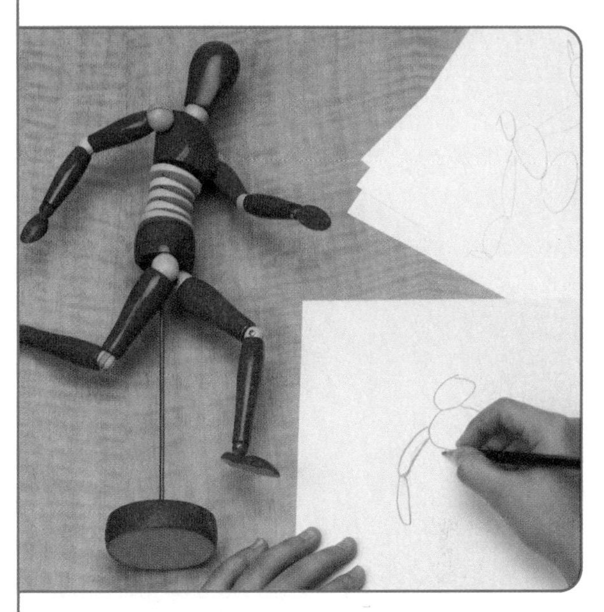

3 **As you develop your skills in gesture drawing, add more detail by showing shadows and other dark areas, light areas, gesture lines that contour around parts of a figure in action, and thick and thin lines. Try drawing on large newsprint, using charcoals, pastels, chalks, felt-tip pens, and other drawing media.**

Making a Papier-Mâché Mask

1. Create the armature, or framework, for the mask. Cut out the shape of the mask from tagboard, posterboard, or another pliable material.

2. Glue or tape pieces of scrap cardboard, newspaper, or foam core to the armature to make the facial features stand out from the surface.

3. Tear and soak newspaper strips and/or paper towels in papier-mâché paste. Apply the strips, one over the other, to build up the surface of the armature, allowing each layer to dry. Add paper towels as the final two or three layers for a smooth surface. Use soft tissue paper soaked in papier-mâché paste to form eyes, eyebrows, and other features.

4. Allow the papier mâché to dry before applying paint. For best results, use acrylic-based paint. Or apply a water-soluble sealant to the dry surface for tempera paint. Add final details with yarn, raffia, beads, metallic foils, or other found objects.

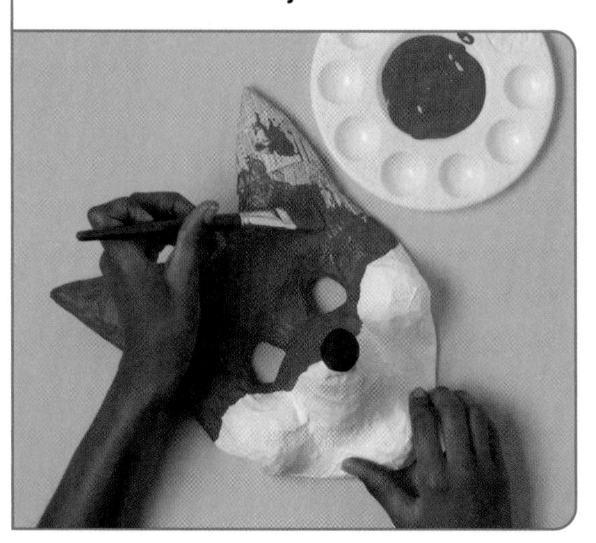

Painting with Tempera or Acrylic Paint

1 To mix a tint, begin with white paint and add a dot of colored paint. Continue adding color until you get the tint you want. To mix a shade, start with a color. Add a small amount of black paint and mix the two together. Avoid using too much black.

2 Dip the bristles of your paintbrush into the paint. Push down on the paintbrush for thick lines and use the tip for thin lines. Hold the brush at different angles to vary your lines.

3 Clean your paintbrush every time you switch colors. Dip the brush in water and wipe it on the side of the water container. Blot the brush on a paper towel before charging with the next color.

4 When finished, wash your paintbrush with warm, soapy water. Rinse the brush and blot it on a towel. Put the paintbrush into a jar, bristles up.

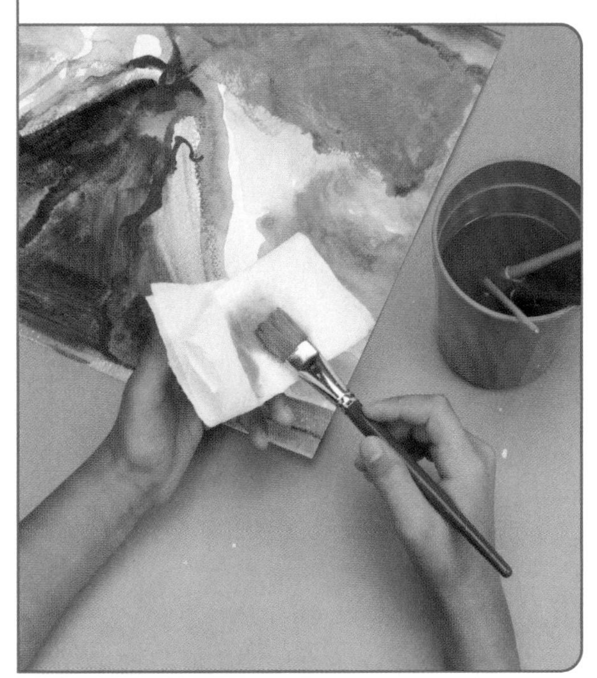

Painting with Watercolor

1 Prepare paints by brushing a large drop of water onto each color of paint. For best results, use watercolor paper for your compositions.

2 Practice mixing colors as they appear on the color wheel. Begin with a light color, such as yellow, and add a small amount of a darker color, such as blue. To create tints, add water. Water allows the white paper to show through the paint. To create shades, add a dab of black.

3 Plan a white space in your composition by creating a resist with a white crayon or a white oil pastel. Then use a wet-wash to create sky and ground areas. Wet a broad brush and paint over your paper with clear water. Charge your brush with a color and pull the brush horizontally across the top. Work your way down to the horizon line without recharging your brush. Rinse the brush and repeat with a second color. Lift your paper vertically to allow the wet wash to blend.

4 Allow your wet wash to dry before you paint details, such as boats, rafts, a dock, or birds. Use watercolor paints, crayons, or oil pastels for the details. When the painting is dry, create highlights by scraping some paint away with a scraping tool.

Making a Monoprint

1 Cover a sheet of paper or a hard, slick surface with acrylic paint. Use a pencil or pen to draw a design into the paint.

2 Place a sheet of clean paper on top of your design. Smooth it down gently with your hands. Carefully peel the paper off, known as "pulling the print," and let the paint dry.

Making a Relief Print

1 Use a pencil to draw a design on material such as a slab of clay or a clean meat tray. Cover a roller, or brayer, with water-based printers' ink or acrylic paint. Roll the ink or paint evenly over the design.

2 Place a clean sheet of paper on top of your design. Rub the paper gently with your hands. Carefully pull the print and let the ink or paint dry.

Working with Clay

Setup

When working with clay, cover your desk or work area with a plastic mat or canvas. Prepare any unwedged clay by wedging it. To wedge clay, take a large lump of it and thump it down on the work surface. Press the clay with the palms of your hands, turn it over, and press into it again. Keep pressing the clay until it has no air bubbles.

Forming a Pinch Pot

1 Make a small ball of clay and place it in the palm of your hand.

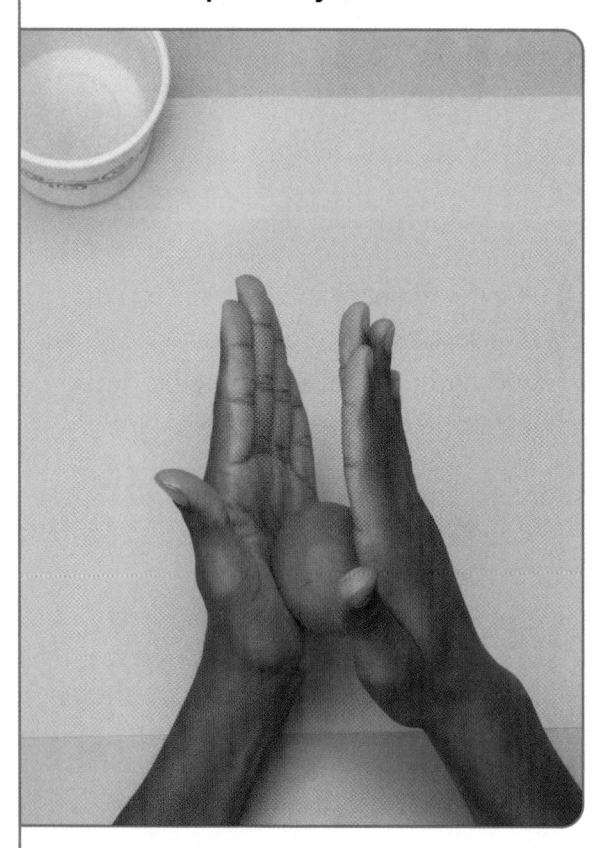

2 Press your thumb into the middle of the ball. Pinch it with your fingers.

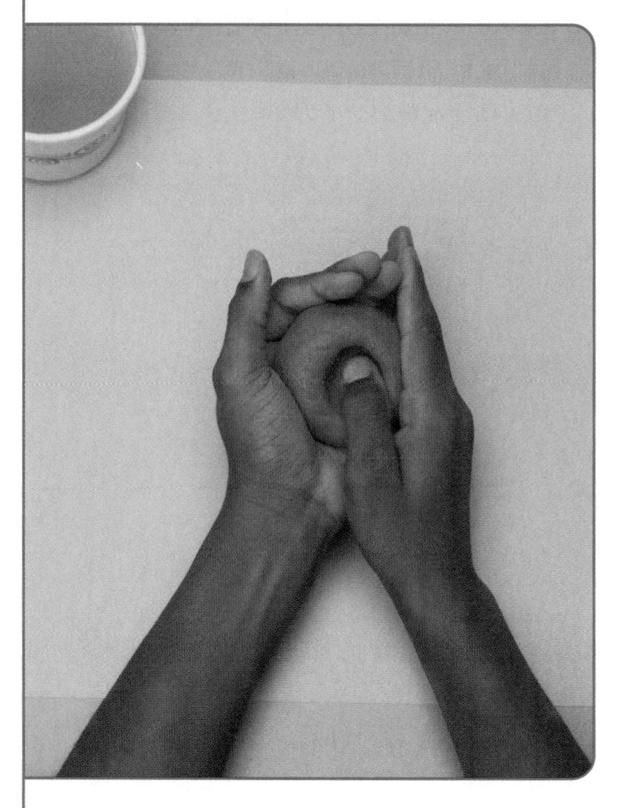

3 Start pinching at the bottom and then move up and out. Keep turning the ball as you pinch.

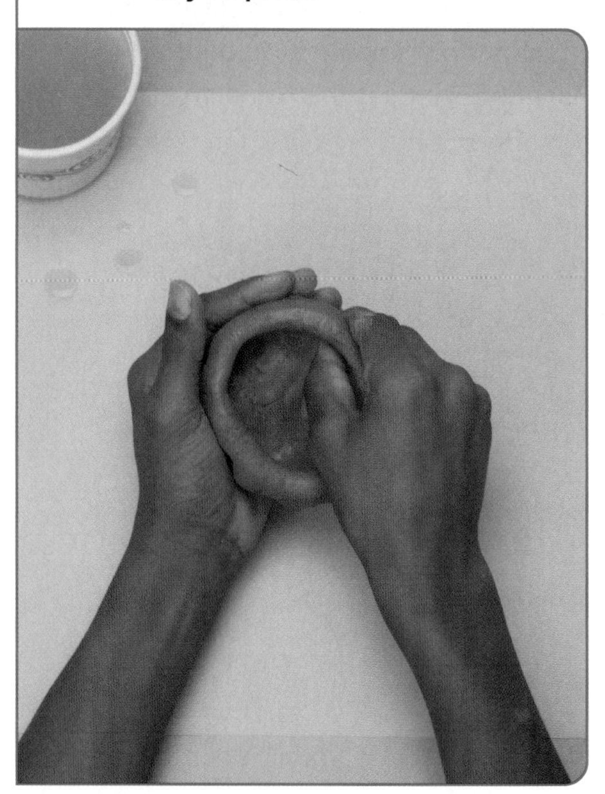

Using the Slab Method

1 Use a rolling pin to roll out a piece of wedged clay between two sticks. Roll the clay until it is approximately one-half inch thick.

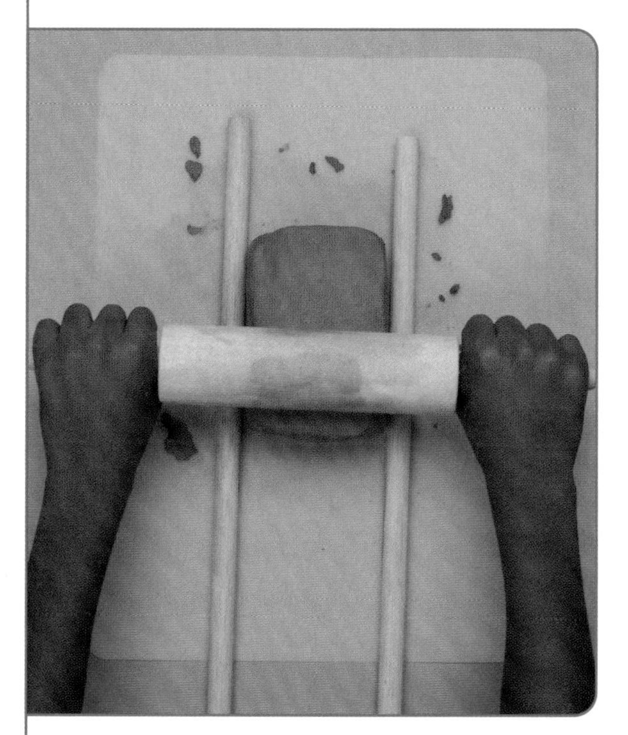

2 Cut out slabs for the bottom and sides of a container using a plastic knife.

3 Use a moist toothbrush, toothpick, or plastic fork to create score marks. These rough grooves make it easier to join one piece of clay to another.

4 Apply slip, a mixture of clay and water, to the scored edges. Then join the slab pieces together and smooth any irregular places with your fingers.

Using the Coil Method

1 **Begin with a flat and round slab as the base. Score the edges of your base.**

2 **Make a coil, or rope, of clay by rolling the clay back and forth between your hands and the work surface. Start rolling in the middle and move toward the edges.**

3 **Score each coil and apply slip to the coils and base.**

4 **Wind the coils into a form. Cut extra coils into pieces to form handles and other parts for your form. Score them and apply slip before you press them in place.**

Making a Repoussé

1 Cut a sheet of metal foil made of aluminum or copper. Place tape around the edges of the metal for safety.

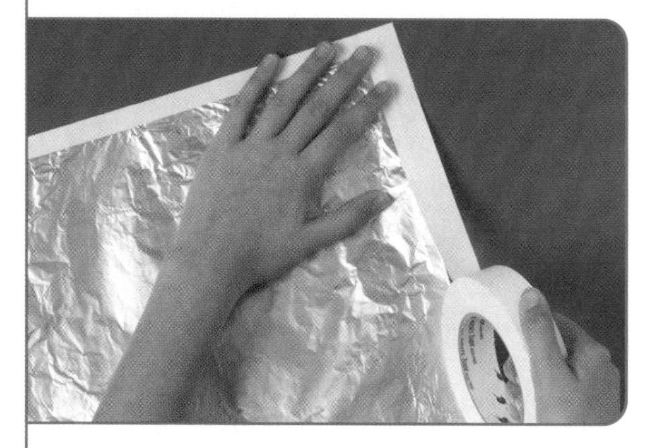

2 Draw a design on paper that will fit the size of the foil.

3 Place the foil on a soft pad, such as an old magazine or stack of newspapers. Use a blunt pencil to transfer your drawing to the foil.

4 Remove the paper design and deepen the outline in the foil using craft sticks or the eraser end of a pencil.

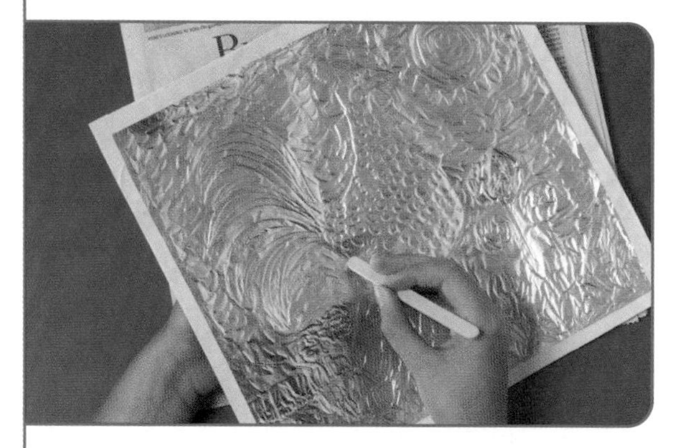

5 Turn the foil over and deepen the other shapes to make them stand out from the front side.

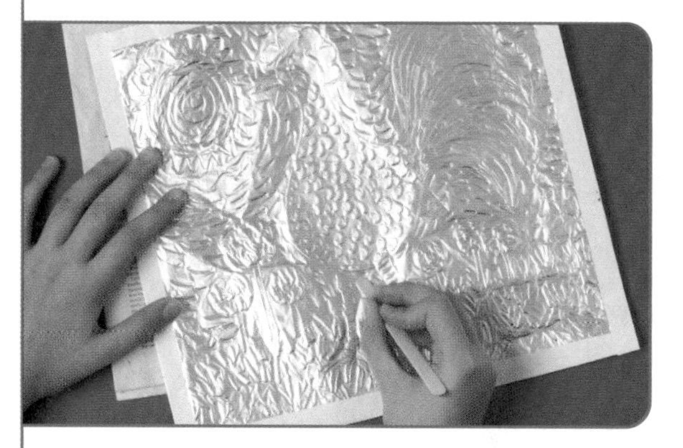

6 Brush waterproof ink or black shoe polish over the foil design. When the ink is dry, lightly buff, or rub, the raised surfaces with steel wool or a dry paper towel. Mount your repoussé on wood or heavy cardboard. Use acrylic spray to protect the artwork.

Weaving

1 Cut a piece of cardboard to make a square or rectangular loom. Use a ruler to draw lines one-half inch from the top and from the bottom. Then make a mark every one-fourth inch or so along the lines. Draw slanted lines from the edge of the cardboard to the marks. Cut along the slanted lines to make "teeth."

2 Next, create a warp. Make a loop in one end of a piece of yarn. Hook the loop around the first "tooth" at the top of the loom. Then take the yarn down to the bottom of the loom. Hook it around the first "tooth" there. Take the yarn back up to the second "tooth" at the top, hook it, and so on. Keep wrapping until the loom is filled with warp threads, or vertical lines of yarn.

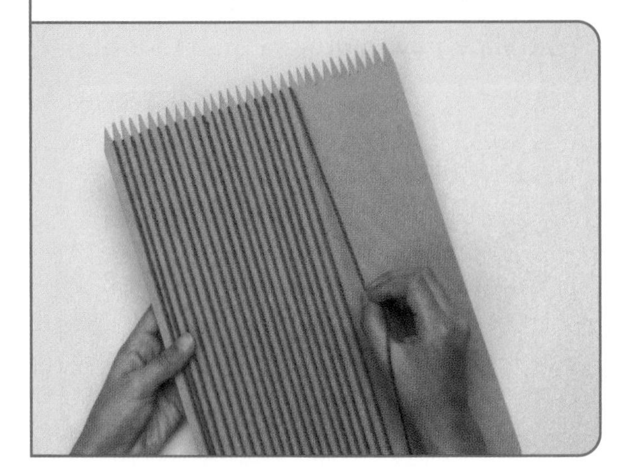

3 Finally, weave the weft. Tie yarn through a hole in a narrow craft stick. Start at the bottom center of the loom. Weave toward one edge by going over and under the warp threads. When you get to the last thread, loop the craft stick around it and start weaving back in the other direction. Keep weaving, over and under, until the loom is covered. Unhook and remove the weaving from the loom. Tie any loose end pieces.

Making Stitchery

1 Select a needle. A crewel needle, used for embroidery, is short and has a long eye. A blunt needle, used for weaving, is a big needle with a dull point. A darner is a long needle with a big eye. It is used with thick thread, such as yarn. Never use a sharp needle without the help of an adult.

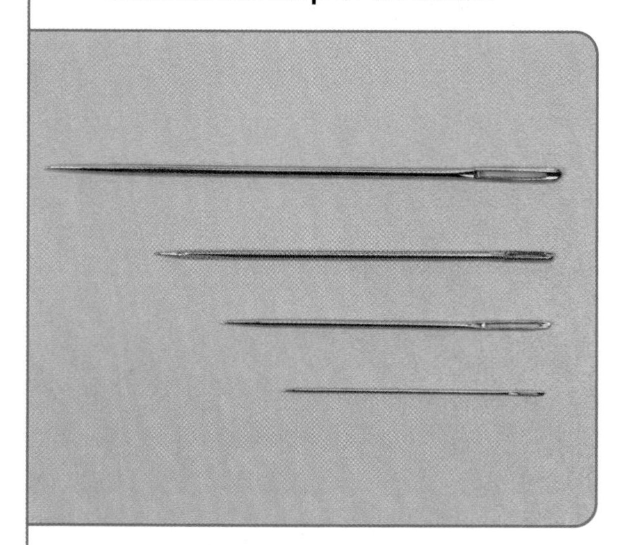

2 Thread the needle by dampening your fingers and pinching one end of the thread to flatten it. Push the flattened end through the eye of the needle and pull it through. Make a knot at the other end to keep the thread from coming through cloth.

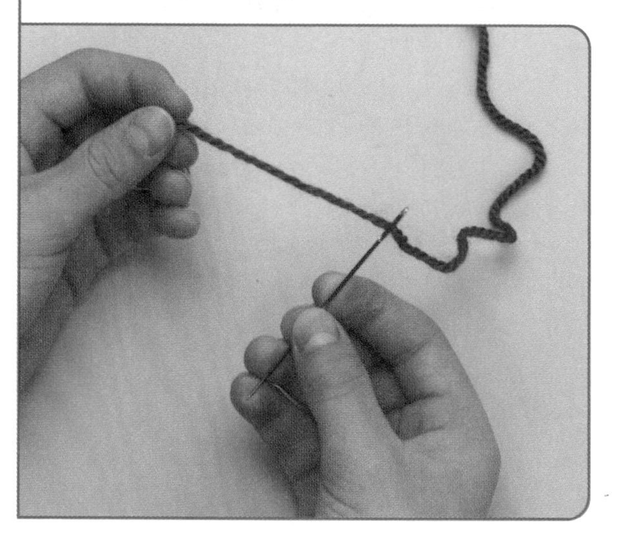

3 Start a stitch on the back of the cloth. Push the needle through and pull the thread up until the knot stops it. Continue pushing and pulling until you have finished your stitching. Finally, push the needle and thread through to the back. Make two small stitches next to each other and push the needle under these two stitches. Pull the thread through, knot it, and cut it off.

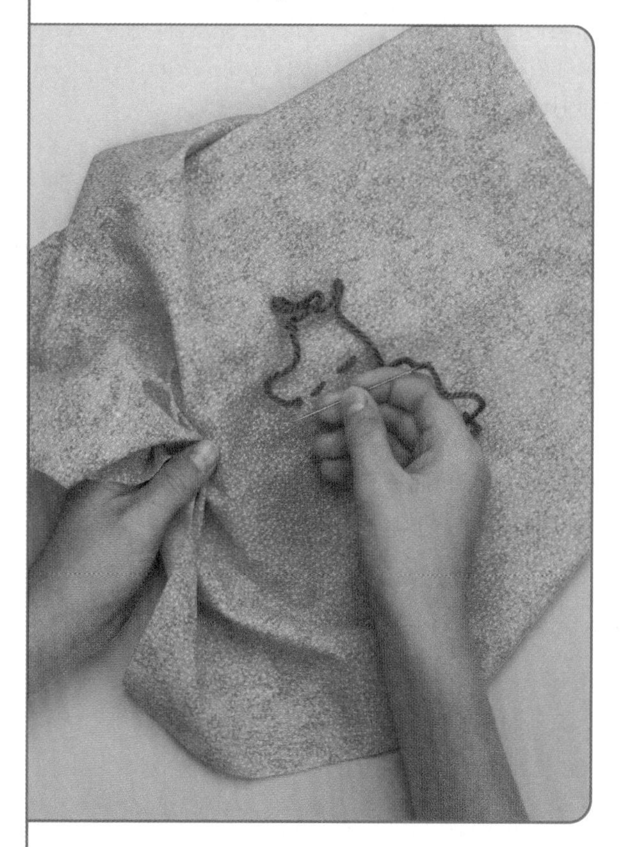

List of Artists and Artworks

Unknown Artists

Artists

Artworks

Glossary

A

abstract A style of art that does not show a realistic subject. Abstract art usually includes geometric shapes, bold colors, and lines.

Abstract Expressionism A style of artwork that developed during the two decades following World War II. The artists of this style often used bold brushstrokes or applied paint by pouring or splattering it onto huge canvases. Also known as *action painting.*

actual lines Lines that are real, not imaginary.

actual texture Textures that can be felt with the fingers. Also known as *tactile texture.*

altered proportion A technique used by an artist to change the size relationship of shapes in an artwork. See *monumental, miniature,* and *exaggerated.*

alternating rhythm Rhythm created in an artwork by repeating two or more elements on a regular, interchanging basis.

analogous [ə na′ lə gəs] Colors that appear next to each other on the color wheel. Analogous colors have one hue in common. For example, blue, blue-green, and blue-violet all contain blue. Also known as *related colors.*

Ancient Art Artworks created around the years 3500 B.C.–A.D. 400. For example, the Stonehenge monument on Salisbury Plain, England is an example of Ancient Art.

animal style Artworks, such as jewelry and other ornamentation, created during the Medieval period that show animals as the subject.

animated cartoon Motion pictures made from a series of drawings that make the characters appear as if they are moving.

applied art Artworks that are functional. Also known as *utilitarian art.*

appliqué [a plə kā′] An artwork created by sewing pieces of cloth onto a larger cloth background.

architect An artist who plans and designs buildings and other structures.

architecture The art and science of designing buildings and other structures.

armature [är′ mə chůr] A skeletal framework or support for a sculpture.

art historians Those who study art history and cultural traditions that relate to art, such as forms of government, religious beliefs, and social activities.

art history The study of art created in different times and cultures.

art media The materials used by artists to create artworks.

artwork A term that refers to any artistic object or production.

assemblage [ə sem′ blij] An additive sculpture often made of recycled objects that assume new meaning within the artwork.

assembling The technique of building a sculpture by attaching old or new objects together.

asymmetrical balance [ā sə me′ tri kal] A type of balance in which the two sides of an artwork look equally important even though they are not alike. Also known as *informal balance.*

atmospheric perspective A technique used to create the illusion of air and space in an artwork. Close-up objects are bright and consist of darker colors; faraway objects and air consist of muted colors and large portions of white. Also known as *aerial perspective.*

B

background The part of an artwork that seems the farthest away.

batik A process of creating a pattern on cloth or textile, using wax and dye.

balance The way an artwork is arranged to make different parts seem equally important. Balance is a principle of design.

base An architectural term for the bottom of a column.

binder A material, such as wax, egg, glue, resin, or oil, that binds together the coloring grains and powder in a pigment.

bird's-eye view A view shown from above. For example, a photograph of a town taken from an airplane provides a bird's-eye view.

blending A shading technique that changes the value of a color little by little.

block In printmaking, a piece of flat material, such as wood or metal, with a design on the surface, which is a mirror image of the composition that will appear as a print. The block is used to print the design. (See also *plate.*) In sculpture, a solid material, such as wood or stone, used for carving.

blueprint A photographic print used to copy the final drawing of a plan for building something.

brayer [brā′ ər] In printmaking, a rubber roller used to evenly spread ink over a surface, such as a printing block or plate.

C

capital An architectural term for the top element of a column.

caption Explanatory comment accompanying an illustration or cartoon or other image.

caricature [kar′ i kə chůr] An artwork that exaggerates the features or aspects of a person or object, usually in a humorous way.

cartoonist An artist who creates cartoons.

cartoons Drawings with humorous content.

carving A subtractive method of sculpting requiring the sculptor to cut or chip away pieces from a block of material, such as wood, stone, or other hard material.

casting A sculpting process in which a liquid, such as molten bronze or liquid plaster, is poured into a heat-proof mold to create a three-dimensional form or an impression.

ceramics The art of making objects from clay and hardening them with fire. Also, artworks made by this process.

ceremonial artworks An artistic object that is used in or displayed during certain ceremonies or formal functions.

cityscape Artwork that gives a view of a city.

collage [kə läzh′] A medium in which the artist glues bits of cut or torn paper, photographs, fabric, or other materials to a flat surface.

collagist An artist who creates collages.

color The visual quality of objects caused by the amount of light reflected by them. Color is an element of art. See *hue*.

color scheme The plan for combining colors in a work of art.

colorist An artist who uses color with great skill.

column A vertical post-like structure that carries weight in a building construction.

combine painting A technique of combining cloth and other materials with splattered and smeared paint.

complementary Colors that contrast with one another. Complementary colors are opposite one another on the color wheel.

composition Artists' plans for drawings, paintings, photographs, sculptures, and other artworks to help them communicate their ideas and feelings.

computer A programmable, electronic device that can store, retrieve, and process data.

computer-assisted art Artworks created with the help of computer software.

conservator [kən sur′ va tər] A person who works to protect artworks from damage and decay.

contours [kän′ tùrz] The edges of an object.

contrast A technique for creating emphasis in an artwork by using unlike elements, such as a light color and a dark color.

cool colors The family of colors that includes greens, blues, and violets. Cool colors bring to mind cool things, places, and feelings.

crafts Useful or decorative artworks created by hand, such as quilts, baskets, ceramics, jewelry, and furniture.

craftspeople Artists who create crafts.

creative art process The process of inventive and imaginative expression through the use of art materials and tools.

crenations Curved edges, used in architecture.

cross-hatching A shading technique using lines that cross each other.

Cubism An abstract style of art characterized by a separation of the subject into cubes and other geometric forms from multiple viewpoints. The style was developed in Paris by a group of artists during the early part of the twentieth century.

curator A person who does research for a museum. Curators recommend artworks for the museum to consider purchasing. They also select artworks for display from the museum's permanent collection.

curved line Line that changes direction gradually, expressing movement in a graceful way, such as circles and spirals.

D

design A plan for the arrangement of lines, spaces, colors, shapes, forms, and textures in an artwork. Also, the act of arranging the part of an artwork.

detail A small part of a larger artwork enlarged for closer viewing. Also, a minute or particularly interesting part of an artwork.

diagonal line A slanted edge or line.

divisionism A painting technique developed by Georges Seurat in the 1800s that uses tiny dots of color instead of lines. Also known as *pointillism.*

docent A person who gives information and conducts tours in a museum. Many docents are trained volunteers.

dome A hemispherical form.

dominance The way an artwork shows emphasis in which one element or object in the composition is visually the strongest or most important part of the work.

E

edition The total number of impressions made from one plate.

elements of art The basic parts and symbols of an artwork. The elements of art are line, color, value, shape, texture, form, and space.

elevation A drawing that shows one side of a structure.

emphasis [em(p)′ fə səs] Importance given to certain objects or areas in an artwork. Color, texture, shape, space, and size can be used to create dominance, contrast, or a focal point. Emphasis is a principle of design.

environment A person's or organism's circumstances or surroundings.

exaggerated Shown in a way that makes it seem larger or more important than it is.

expression An artist's use of symbols that holds meaning for them.

Expressionism A style of artwork developed in the twentieth century that expresses a definite or strong mood or feeling through simple designs and brilliant colors.

exterior The outside of a surface or structure.

F

facial proportions The ratio between respective parts of a face.

Fauves [fōvz] French for "wild beasts," this term was used by a French art critic viewing the works of a group of young painters exhibiting in Paris. The nickname came from the artists' use of fierce, non-realistic color and bold, apparently crude, style of painting. Also known as *Fauvists*.

Fauvism [fō′ vi zəm] A style of artwork developed by artists in France in the early 1900s, that used bold color schemes and radical color placement.

femmage Collage with women as the theme, created by Miriam Schapiro.

fiber art Artworks, such as stitchery and weaving, created from yarn, thread, or cloth.

fiber artist An artist who creates artworks by sewing, weaving, knitting, or stitching fibers together.

fibers Slender, threadlike materials that come from insects (silk), animals (wool), plants (linen, flax, cotton), and chemicals (nylon, rayon).

figure A human form in an artwork.

fine art Artworks that are created for the sole purpose of being viewed.

fired Hardened by great heat. Clay objects are sometimes fired to make ceramics.

floor plan The arrangement of rooms inside a building.

focal point A way to show emphasis in an artwork in which the artist sets an element apart from the others to create a center of interest.

folk art Art made by people who have not been formally trained in art. Folk art usually reflects the artist's culture or tradition.

foreground The part of an artwork that seems nearest.

form A three-dimensional object, such as a cube or ball, or the representation of a three-dimensional object, defined by contour, height, depth, and width. Form is an element of art.

found object Something that an artist finds and uses in an artwork. A scrap of metal or a piece of wood can be a found object.

frontal view The view of the front side of a person, animal, or object.

full figure A human form from head to toe.

G

geometric form A form such as a sphere, cube, or pyramid whose contours represent a circle, square, and triangle, respectively.

geometric shape A shape that is precise and mathematical. Circles, squares, triangles, ovals, and rectangles are geometric shapes.

German Expressionism A style of art developed in Germany in the early 1900s. The German Expressionists used simple designs and bright, bold colors to express their feelings in artworks.

gesture drawing A drawing technique in which artists move a drawing medium, such as a pencil, quickly and freely over a surface to capture the form and actions of a subject.

glaze A mixture of mostly oxides which, when applied to clay and then fired in a kiln, creates a thin, transparent, glossy coating.

graphic design The art of communicating through images and lettering, usually in commercial art, such as advertisements, signs, book jackets, Web pages, and jewel cases.

graphic designer An artist who creates commercial art.

graphics tablet A device by which pictorial information is entered into a computer, with the use of a stylus, in a manner similar to drawing.

greenware An object made from clay which, as the clay dries, becomes delicate.

ground-level view The point of view from beneath. Also known as *worm's-eye view.*

H

hatching A shading technique using thin parallel lines.

horizon line The line created in an artwork by the meeting of sky and ground, usually at the viewer's eye level.

horizontal line In an artwork, a line that runs side-to-side, parallel to the horizon. Horizontal lines can appear peaceful and calm.

hue [hyü] Another word for color.

I

illuminations Handpainted illustrations for a book.

illustration A design or picture in a book, magazine, or other print or electronic medium that visually explains the text or shows what happens in a story.

illustrator An artist who creates pictures for books, magazines, or other printed works.

impasto A technique using thick brushstrokes of paint.

implied lines Lines that are not real, but are suggested by the placement of other lines, shapes, and colors.

impression A print of an image.

Impressionism An art movement and style developed in the last 1800s by a group of French artists. Artists of the Impressionist style drew and painted their impressions of visual reality by showing the effects of light and color on everyday objects.

Impressionist An artist in the late 1800s to early 1900s who paid special attention to light and its effect on subjects in his or her paintings. Also known as *Independents.*

in the round An artwork that can be viewed from all sides. Also called *sculpture in the round.*

Independents A group of artists in France in the late 1800s and early 1900s that developed a style of artwork independent of the Realistic style.

industrial design The design of objects created and sold by industry, such as automobiles, appliances, and telephones.

industrial designer An artist who plans the appearance and form of useful objects, such as computers, telephones, cars, toys, and kitchen appliances.

intaglio [in tal′ yō] The technique of printing in which the image to be printed is cut or scratched into a surface or plate.

intensity The brightness or dullness of a hue. A hue mixed with its complement is less intense than the pure color.

interior The inside of a building or another hollow form, such as a box.

interior designer An artist who plans the layout and design of interior rooms and spaces.

intermediate color A color that is a mixture of a primary and a secondary color that are next to each other on the color wheel. Blue-green, red-orange, and red-violet are examples of intermediate colors.

L

landscape A drawing or painting that shows outdoor scenery such as trees, lakes, mountains, and fields.

landscape architect An artist who uses plants, rocks, trees, and other materials to design and create pleasing outdoor spaces.

light source A point of illumination for emphasis, contrast, unity, or dramatic effect in an artwork.

line A mark on a surface usually created by a pen, pencil, or brush. Lines vary in width, length, direction, color, and degree of curve, and can be actual or implied. Line is an element of art.

line quality The special character of any line, such as thick or thin, smooth or rough, continuous or broken.

linear perspective A technique that makes use of actual and implied lines to create the illusion of depth on a two-dimensional surface. If the lines in an artwork created with this technique are extended, they converge at a point that represents the eye level of the viewer. This point is called the vanishing point.

logo A design created by a graphic artist as a symbol to visually represent a business, club, city, or other group.

loom A frame or machine used to hold yarn, or other fibers, for weaving.

M

maquette [ma ket′] A small model made of clay that serves as a plan for a larger sculpture.

mask A cover for the face used as decoration or disguise, which can be a symbol that represents ideas, beliefs, and values of the artist or cultural group with which it is associated.

method A procedure, especially a regular and systematic way of accomplishing something, such as a studio art project.

Middle Ages The one thousand years (A.D. 400–1400) that followed the fall of the Western Roman Empire. Also known as the *Medieval period* or the *Dark Ages.*

middle ground In an artwork, the part between the foreground and the background.

miniature Artworks that are of smaller-than-life proportions.

model Someone or something an artist observes as a subject when creating an artwork. In architecture, a model is a small copy of something that represents the larger version.

modeling A technique using all types of clay, and other additive media, for building up and shaping a sculpture.

monochromatic [ma nə krō ma′ tik] A color scheme that uses different values of a single hue by showing tints and shades of the same hue.

monumental Artworks that are of larger-than-life proportions.

mood The feeling created in a work of art. For example, light values often suggest a calm, gentle mood, while dark values may seem angry, nervous, and forceful.

mosaic [mō zā′ ik] An artwork made by fitting together small pieces of paper, stone, tile, or glass. See *tesserae.*

multimedia A combination of technology-related media used to create a composition.

mural [myůr′ əl] A large artwork, usually a painting, that is created or placed on a wall or ceiling, often in a public place to convey a theme that has a political or social message.

muralist An artist who creates murals.

N

negative space The empty space around and between forms or shapes in an artwork.

neutral A word used for black, white, and tints and shades of gray. Some artists use tints and shades of brown as neutrals.

nonobjective art A type of art that usually shows color, form, and texture, but has no recognizable subject.

O

oil-based paint A paint made from a mixture of colored pigment and linseed oil.

opaque [ō pāk′] The quality of not letting light through; the opposite of transparent.

Op Art A style of art in which artists create the illusion of movement or other optical illusions. Op Art developed in the 1960s.

organic form A "free-form" which has irregular and uneven edges and is often found in nature, such as an apple, tree, or animal. See *form*.

organic shape A "free-form" shape that is irregular and uneven, such as the shape of a leaf, flower, or cloud. See *shape*.

originality An artist's own special way of showing ideas and feelings, unlike anyone else's.

overlapping Partly or completely covering one shape or form with another to show distance in an artwork.

P

palette [pa′ lət] A flat board on which a painter mixes color.

papier mâché [pā′ pər mə shā′] A process of creating forms by covering an armature or other base with strips of paper that have been soaked in watery paste, and then molding the strips. The form hardens as it dries.

patina [pə tē′ nə] Rusted surface on an armature created by natural elements (e.g., rust on iron or a greenish film on copper or bronze). Also, the finish that shows age on a wooden or other type of artifact.

pattern Repeated colors, lines, shapes, forms, or textures in an artwork. Pattern is a principle of design. Also, a plan or model to be followed when making something.

perception An artist's awareness of the elements in his or her environment derived from the use of his or her senses.

photographer A camera artist.

photomontage [fō tə män täzh′] The technique of making a two-dimensional artwork by assembling and attaching to a surface pieces of photographs, often in combination with other types of graphic material.

pigment A coloring material made from crushed minerals, plants, or chemicals, usually held together with a binder.

pixel The basic unit of the composition of an image on a television screen, computer monitor, or similar display.

plate In printmaking, a piece of flat material, such as wood or metal, with a design on the surface. The plate is used to print the design, which is a mirror image of the composition. See also *block*.

point of view Angle from which the viewer sees an object or a scene. The three points of view are the straight-on view, bird's-eye view, and ground-level or worm's-eye view.

pointillism A painting technique developed by Georges Seurat in the 1800s that uses tiny dots of color instead of lines. Also known as *divisionism*.

Pop Art A style of art developed during the 1950s. Pop artists show people, objects, or scenes from popular culture and use graphics similar to those found in advertisements or comic strips.

portrait A work of art created to show a person, animal, or group of people, usually focusing on the face.

pose The way a subject sits or stands while an artist sketches or paints a portrait.

positive space The space that a form or shape occupies in an artwork.

pottery Useful and/or decorative objects, such as vases, bowls, and dishes, that are made of clay.

pre-Columbian Existing in the Americas before Columbus.

Prehistoric Art Artworks created before written records appeared, when people were nomadic and lived mainly by hunting and gathering food. These artworks are usually found on cave walls.

primary color A color that cannot be mixed from other colors, but from which other colors are made. The primary colors are red, yellow, and blue.

principles of design Guidelines that artists use to organize the elements of art in a composition. Unity, variety, emphasis, balance, proportion, pattern, and rhythm are the principles of design.

printer A device that prints graphics or text on paper.

printing ink A type of ink that is thicker and stickier than the ink for fountain pens and that is used in the printmaking process.

printmaker An artist who uses the process of printmaking.

printmaking The process of transferring an image from an inked surface to another surface to create an artwork.

profile view The side view of a subject.

progressive rhythm Rhythm created in an artwork by showing regular changes in a repeated element, such as a series of circles that progressively increase in size from small to large. The changes may also progress from light to dark, or from bottom to top.

properties Color attributes, such as hue, value, tint, shade, and intensity.

proportion The relation of the parts of an artwork to each other and to the whole. Proportion is a principle of design.

prototype A working model of a product that will be mass-produced.

Q

quilting A type of stitchery in which the artist stitches together two layers of cloth with padding between the layers.

R

radial balance A type of balance in which lines or shapes spread out from a center point.

Realism A style of art that represents people, places, objects, or events as they are perceived by the senses rather than to idealize or interpret them.

realistic A word used to describe artworks that represent people, places, objects, or events as they are perceived by the senses.

Realistic art An artwork using Realism. See *Realism*.

regular rhythm Rhythm in an artwork created by repeating the same element, such as a shape, without variation.

relief A composition or design made so that all or part of it projects or is raised from a flat surface.

relief sculpture A type of sculpture in which forms project from a background and are meant to be seen from one side.

Renaissance [re nə sän(t)s′] The period between the 1300s and 1600s, during which new ideas and technological advances, as well as renewed interest in the classical styles of the Romans and Greeks, laid the foundation for modern art and society.

rhythm The repetition of elements, such as lines, shapes, or colors, that creates a feeling of visual motion in an artwork. Rhythm is a principle of design.

S

scale The size of an object in relation to an ideal or standard size.

scanner A device used to transfer text or graphics into a computer.

sculpting The process of taking away from a form or adding to it.

sculptor An artist who creates sculptures.

sculpture An artwork made by modeling, carving, casting, or joining materials into a three-dimensional form. Clay, wood, stone, and metal are often used to make sculptures.

sculpture in the round A sculpture that is fashioned to be viewed from all sides. Also known as *full round.*

seascape An artwork that represents the sea, ocean, or shore.

secondary color A color made by mixing two primary colors. The secondary colors are orange, violet, and green.

self-portrait An artwork that shows the likeness of the artist.

sfumato [sfü mä′ tō] A technique of painting soft, blurry, smoke-like edges in the background of a painting.

shade A color made by adding black to a hue. For example, adding black to green results in dark green. Also, the darkness of a color value. See *value.*

shading A way of showing gradual changes in lightness or darkness in a drawing or painting. Shading helps make a picture look more three-dimensional.

shading techniques The various ways an artist uses media to show gradual changes in lightness or darkness in a drawing or painting. Shading techniques include blending, stippling, hatching, and cross-hatching.

shaft An architectural term for the cylindrical pillar between the capital and base of a column.

shape A two-dimensional area created by visually connecting actual or implied lines. A shape can be geometric, such as a circle or square, or organic, having an irregular outline. Shape is an element of art.

simulated texture Texture that is suggested by the way the artist has painted or drawn certain areas of a picture. Also known as *visual texture.*

size relationships A technique that alters the proportions of compositions. The three categories are monumental, miniature, and exaggerated.

software applications Computer applications used for various functions, such as drawing, Web design, editing text, creating graphics, or altering images.

solvent A liquid, such as turpentine or water, used to control the thickness or thinness of paint.

space The open or empty area around, above, between, inside, or below objects. Shapes and forms are defined by the empty space surrounding them. Space is an element of art.

standard proportion That which appears appropriate in height, width, and depth compared to its surroundings. The human body is considered to be the standard by which the size or proportion of other objects is measured.

still life An artwork showing an arrangement of objects that cannot move on their own, such as fruit, foods, bottles, books, or cut flowers.

still photography The art and science of making a picture with a camera and film other than a motion picture or video camera.

stippling A shading technique creating dark values by applying a dot pattern.

stitchery A term for artwork created with a needle, thread or yarn, and cloth, such as a quilt.

straight-on view Point of view, usually at eye level, that encourages a viewer to focus on other aspects of a composition.

style An artist's individual way of expressing his or her ideas. Also, a technique used by a group of artists in a particular time or culture.

stylus [stī′ ləs] A pen-shaped pointing device used for entering positional information (as from a graphics tablet) into a computer.

subject A person, an animal, an object, or a scene represented in an artwork; the topic of an artwork.

Surrealism [sə rē′ ə li zəm] A style of art developed during the 1920s that emphasizes the expression of the subconscious by combining realistic images and dreamlike ideas. Many Surrealist artworks contain illusions.

symbol A letter, color, sign, or picture that represents words, messages, or ideas, such as thoughts and feelings. For example, a red heart is often used as a symbol for love.

symmetrical balance [sə me′tri kəl] A type of balance in which both sides of an artwork look the same or almost the same. Also known as *formal balance.*

T

tactile texture A texture you can feel with your hands, such as rough or smooth. Also known as *actual texture.*

tessellation A pattern created by shapes that fit together, without overlapping or leaving gaps.

tesserae [te′ sə rə] Small pieces of material, such as paper, stone, tile, or glass used to make a mosaic.

textile An artwork made from cloth or fibers, such as yarn.

texture The way something feels to the touch (actual texture) or how it may look (visual texture). Texture is an element of art.

three-quarter view The subject of an artwork that is positioned between a front view and a profile, so that you can usually see both eyes, the nose, and the mouth.

tint A light value of a color, such as pink, that is created by mixing a hue with white. Also, the lightness of a color value. See *value.*

totems Symbols that represent clans and other subgroups of a culture.

transparent The quality of letting light pass through; the opposite of opaque.

triptych [trip′ tik] A picture or carving in three panels.

U

unity The quality of seeming whole and complete, with all the parts looking right together. Unity is a principle of design.

utilitarian art Art designed for a specific purpose or function. Also known as *applied art.*

V

value The lightness or darkness of a color. Tints have a light value. Shades have a dark value. Value is an element of art.

vanishing point In linear perspective, the place on the horizon where parallel lines seem to meet or converge.

variety The use or combination of elements of art, such as line, shape, or color, to provide interest in an artwork. Variety is a principle of design.

vertical line In an artwork, a line that runs up and down, such as a flagpole or a giant redwood tree. Vertical lines usually appear strong and powerful.

visual reporter An artist who uses photographs to record and report on who, what, when, where, and how. Also known as a *photojournalist.*

visual texture The way a surface appears through the sense of vision. For example, the surface of a sculpture may appear shiny or dull. Also known as *simulated texture.*

W

warm colors The family of colors that includes reds, yellows, and oranges. Warm colors bring to mind warm things, places, and feelings.

warp In weaving, the vertical threads attached to the top and bottom of a loom through which the weft fibers are woven.

water-based paints Paints, such as tempera, watercolor, or acrylic, whose solvent is water and that use different binders and have different qualities.

weave A process of interlocking thread, yarn, or other fibers to create a fabric, usually on a loom.

weft The threads that cross over and under the warp fibers on a loom.

worm's-eye view The point of view from beneath. Also known as *ground-level view.*

Z

zigzag lines A series of diagonal lines moving in different directions (vertically, horizontally, or diagonally) that come together at sharp angles. These lines can create feelings of confusion, nervousness, or excitement.

Index

Acknowledgments

Illustrations

12, 13, 69, 73, 77, 81, 89, 93, 97, 101, 165, 169, 173, 177, 181, 189, 193, 197, 201, 205, 209, 269, 273, 277, 281, 289, 293, 237, 301, 305, 309 Tom Newsom; 19–21, 23, 27, 31, 35, 43, 47, 51, 55, 59, 111, 115, 119, 123, 127, 135, 139, 143, 147, 151, 155, 219, 223, 227, 231, 235, 243, 247, 251, 255, 259 Kyle Still; 163, 176, 218 Mike Krone

Photographs

Every effort has been made to secure permission and provide appropriate credit for photographic material. The publisher deeply regrets any omission and pledges to correct errors called to its attention in subsequent editions.

Unless otherwise acknowledged, all photographs are the property of Scott Foresman, a division of Pearson Education.

Photo locators denoted as follows: Top (T), Center (C), Bottom (B), Left (L), Right (R), Background (Bkgd).

Front Matter:

iv © Paul Conklin/PhotoEdit; 1 (T) Courtesy of Chihuly Studio, (B) 14.130.14, Greek, Attic, *Krater,* ca. 750–700 B.C.; Geometric, Attributed to the Hirschfeld Workshop, Terracotta; H.42 5/8 in. (108.25 cm), Side A: "The Metropolitan Museum of Art, Rogers Fund, 1914 (14.130.14) Photograph © 1996"/Metropolitan Museum of Art; 2 (T) © 2004 Succession H. Matisse, Paris/Artists Rights Society (ARS), NY. Photograph by Jacqueline Hyde/Phototeque, (B) Courtesy Dr. Peter T. Furst; 3 © 1990 David Hockney Studio; 4 (B) © Erich Lessing/Art Resource, NY, (T) The Tervuren Museum, Royal Museum; 5 Art Resource, NY; 6 (T) © 1998 Sally Griffiths, (B) Photo by Jonathan Kantor/Harri Koskinen/Friends of Industry, Ltd.; 7 (T) © Kent Twitchell, (B) Daemmrich Photography; 8 (T) © Archivo Iconografico, S.A./Corbis, (B) © Richard List/Corbis, (C) Digital Vision 9 © 1993 Vietnam Women's Memorial Project, Inc. Photo by Gregory Staley, Courtesy of Goodacre Studio, Santa Fe; 10 (T) © Robert Landau/Corbis, (B) © The Purcell Team/Corbis; 11 © Paul A. Souders/Corbis, Getty Images.

Units 1–6

14 SuperStock; 15 Rijks Museum Amsterdam; 16 Getty Images; 17 Courtesy of Freer Gallery of Art/Smithsonian Institution, Washington, D.C.; 18 Collection of the University of Arizona Museum of Art, Tucson; 21 Courtesy of SBC Communications Inc./Carey Ellis Company; 22 Grandma Moses Properties Co., New York.; 24 Courtesy of Chihuly Studio; 25 Courtesy of Mary-Anne Martin/Fine Art; 26 14.130.14, Greek, Attic, *Krater,* ca. 750–700 B.C.; Geometric, Attributed to the Hirschfeld Workshop, Terracotta; H.42 5/8 in. (108.25 cm), Side A: The Metropolitan Museum of Art, Rogers Fund, 1914 (14.130.14) Photograph © 1996/Metropolitan Museum of Art; 28 International Folk Art Collections at the Museum of International Folk Art, Santa Fe, NM; 29 National Museum of Women in the Arts; 30 The Museum of Modern Art, NY, Loula D. Lasker Bequest. © The Museum of Modern Art/© 2004 Artists Rights Society (ARS),NY/ADAGP, Paris/Art Resource, NY; 32 Earlie Hudnall; 33 © Musée d'Orsay, Paris/SuperStock; 34 Metropolitan Museum of Art; 36 Rijks Museum Amsterdam; 37 (C) © Musée d'Orsay, Paris/Giraudon, Paris/SuperStock, (B) © William Manning/Corbis; 38 © James Marshall/Corbis; 39 (T) The Phillips Collection, Washington, D.C. Acquired: Miss Elizabeth Hudson, 1949/Bridgeman Art Library, (C) © 2004 Andre Dérain/Artist Rights Society (ARS), NY/The Museum of Fine Arts, Houston; 40 Alfred Stieglitz Collection, 1950. (50.236.2). Photograph © 1997 The Metropolitan Museum of Art. © 2004 The Georgia O'Keeffe Foundation/Artists Rights Society (ARS), NY/Metropolitan Museum of Art; 41 © 2005 Banco de Mexico. Diego Rivera & Frida Kahlo Museums Trust. Av. Cinco de Mayo No. 2, Col. Centro, Del. Cuauhtemoc 06059, Mexico, D.F./Reproduction authorized by the Instituto Nacional de Bellas Artes y Literatura/Harvard University Art Museums, bequest of Meta and Paul J. Sachs. Photographic Services, © President and Fellows of Harvard College/The Fogg Art Museum, Harvard University; 42 © Claes Oldenburg & Coosje van Bruggen/The Art Institute of Chicago; 45 © L & M Services, Amsterdam/© CNAC/MNAM/Dist Réunion des Musées Nationaux/Art Resource, NY; 46 (T) Licensed by VAGA, New York, NY, (B) Sandy Skoglund; 48 © 2004 Paul Klee/Artist Rights Society (ARS), NY/Photo © Barnes Foundation, Merion, PA/SuperStock; 49 Courtesy Bernice Steinbaum Gallery, Miami, FL; 50 Digital Image © The Museum of Modern Art/Licensed by SCALA/Art Resource, NY. © 2004 Estate of Pablo Picasso/Artist Rights Society (ARS), NY/Art Resource, NY; 52 (T, B) Courtesy of Holly Hughes; 53 Courtesy of Louis K. Meisel Gallery; 54 Brandywine River Museum; 56 Firesign Studios; 57 (Bkgd, C) © Robyn Montana Turner; 58 © Nimatallah/Art Resource, NY. © 2004 Maurice de Vlaminck/Artists Rights Society (ARS), NY; 61 © Giraudon/Bridgeman Art Library. © 2004 Paul Klee/Artists Rights Society (ARS), NY/Bridgeman Art Library; 63 (TL) National Gallery of Art, Washington, DC. Collection of Mr. and Mrs. Paul Mellon. © 1998 Board of Trustees, National Gallery of Art, Washington, DC./Image © 2003 Board of Trustees, National Gallery of Art, Washington, (BR) SuperStock; 64 © 2004 Succession H. Matisse, Paris/Artists Rights Society (ARS), NY/The Phillips Collection, Washington, D.C.; 65 © 2004 Succession H. Matisse, Paris/Artists Rights Society (ARS), NY/Photograph by Jacqueline Hyde/Phototeque; 66 Courtesy Dr. Peter T. Furst; 66 Girard Foundation Collection at the Museum of International Folk Art, a unit of the Museum of New Mexico, Santa Fe. Photo by Michel Monteaux/International Folk Art Collections at the Museum of International Folk Art, Santa Fe, NM; 67 National Gallery of Art, Washington, D.C. Gift of the W. L. and May T. Mellon Foundation. Photograph by Bob Grove, © 1998 Board of Trustees, National Gallery of Art, Washington D.C./Image © 2003 Board of Trustees, National Gallery of Art, Washington D.C.; 68 Smithsonian American Art Museum, Washington, DC/Art Resource, NY; 70 Courtesy Brewster Arts Ltd. © 1999 Leonora Carrington/Artists Rights Society (ARS), NY/Brewster Arts Ltd.; 71 © 2004 Artists Rights Society

(ARS), New York/VG Bild-Kunst, Bonn/Milwaukee Art Museum; 72 © Christie's Images/SuperStock; 74 DDB Stock Photography; 75 © 2005 Banco de Mexico. Deigo Rivera & Frida Kahlo Museums Trust. Av. Cinco de Mayo No. 2, Col. Centro, Del. Cuauhtemoc 06059, Mexico, D.F./Reproduction authorized by the Instituto Nacional de Bellas Artes y Literatura/©Don Beatty Photography; 76 The Metropolitan Museum of Art. Anonymous gift, 1983 (1983.251). Photograph © 1983 The Metropolitan Museum of Art. © Fernando Botero, courtesy Marlborough Gallery, NY; 78 © George Grall/National Geographic/Getty Images, © Lawrence Lawry/Getty Images; 79 M. C. Escher's *Symmetry Drawing E66*/©The M. C. Escher Company, Baarn, Holland. All rights reserved.; 80 Harvard University, Photo # T1698/ Peabody Museum of Archaeology and Ethnology; 82 © 2004 Succession H. Matisse, Paris/Artists Rights Society (ARS), NY/Photograph by Jacqueline Hyde/Phototeque; 83 (B) © Bettmann/Corbis, (T) © Hulton-Deutsch Collection/ Corbis; 84 © ThinkStock/SuperStock, (BC) Corbis; 85 Image © 2003 Board of Trustees, National Gallery of Art, Washington, Acc.# MNP/FR/434/Museum Narodowe W. Poznaniu; 86 AC1999.134.1/*Two of a Kind,* 1986 by Carlos Almaraz/ © The Carlos Almaraz Estate/ Photograph © 2003 Museum Associates/Gift of Charles Anthony Seiniger/Los Angeles County Museum of Art; 87 © 1999 Andy Warhol Foundation for the Visual Arts/Artists Rights Society (ARS), NY/Carey Ellis Company; 88 Digital Vision; 90 Juane Quick-to-See Smith; 91 Courtesy New China Pictures/Byron Preiss Visual Publications; 92 Bill Kennedy/Melissa Wren Miller; 94 Digital Image © Museum of Modern Art/ Licensed by Scala/© 2004 Paul Klee/Artists Rights Society (ARS), NY/Art Resource, NY; 95 © Miriam Shapiro; 98 World Book Publishing; 99 "To the Moon and Beyond," Designer Isaiah Sheppard. World Book illustration by Steven Seymour, Bernard Thornton Artists. From THE WORLD BOOK ENCYCLOPEDIA. © 1989 World Book, Inc. By permission of the publisher.; 100 © Barnes Foundation, Merion, PA/SuperStock; 103 Courtesy of Lee Stalsworth/ © 2005 The Estate of Gwendolyn Knight Lawrence/Artists Rights Society (ARS), NY/Hirshhorn Museum and Sculpture Garden; 105 (TL) Cincinnati Art Museum, (BR) © Underwood & Underwood/Corbis; 106 M. C. Escher's *Triangle System I A3 Type I*/©The M. C. Escher Company, Baarn, Holland. All rights reserved.; 107 M.C. Escher's *Self Portrait*/©The M. C. Escher Company, Baarn, Holland. All rights reserved.; 108 The Metropolitan Museum of Art, Robert Lehman Collection, 1975 (1975.1.848). Photograph © 1985 The Metropolitan Museum of Art; 109 Courtesy of The Metropolitan Museum of Art, Harris Brisbane Dick Fund, 1928. (28.93.17); 110 (T) The Metropolitan Museum of Art, gift of Cornelius Vanderbilt, 1880 (80.3.72). Photograph © 1998 Metropolitan Museum of Art, (B) The Metropolitan Museum of Art, Rogers Fund, 1927 (27.152.2). Photograph © 1992 The Metropolitan Museum of Art; 112 © FPG International/Getty Images; 113 © Helen Frankenthaler/ Courtesy of SBC Communications Inc./Carey Ellis Company; 114 The Baltimore Museum of Art, The Cone Collection, formed by Dr. Claribel Cone and Miss Etta Cone of Baltimore, Maryland BMA 1950.196./The Baltimore Museum of Art; 116 M.C. Escher's *Rind*/©The M. C. Escher Company, Baarn, Holland. All rights reserved.; 117 © Karin Broker; 118 © Antonio Frasconi/Licensed by VAGA, NY/Gift of the Weyhe Gallery, New York, NY, 1953/Norton Simon Museum; 120 © Jacqui Hurst/Corbis; 121 Licensed by VAGA, New York, NY; 122 © 2005 Artists Rights Society (ARS), NY/ADAGP, Paris/©The Museum of Modern Art/Licensed by Scala/Art Resource, NY; 124 Barrett Kendall Publishing; 125 © The Trustees of The British Museum; 126 © Bowers Museum of Cultural Art/Corbis; 128 M.C. Escher's *Self Portrait*/©The M. C. Escher Company, Baarn, Holland. All rights reserved.; 129 (B) M. C. Escher's *Triangle System I A3 Type I*/©The M. C. Escher Company, Baarn, Holland. All rights reserved., (T) Corbis; 130 © Benjamin Shearn/Getty Images; 131 (T) M.C. Escher's *Birds and Fish*/©The M. C. Escher Company, Baarn, Holland. All rights reserved., (B) Christie's Images Ltd.; 132 (T) Courtesy of Cecilia de Torres, Ltd. NYC/©Acosta Bentos/Courtesy Museo de Arte Americano, (B) © Laurie O'Meara/Barrett Kendall Publishing; 133 Acquired through the Joyce C. Hall Estate and various Hall Family Funds/The Nelson-Atkins Museum of Art, Kansas City, MO; 134 Courtesy of Cecilia de Torres, Ltd. NYC/©Acosta Bentos/Courtesy Museo de Arte Americano; 136 © Alinari/Art Resource, NY; 137 (T) Photo by J. Griffis Smith, Courtesy of Texas Highways Magazine/ Barrett Kendall Publishing, (B) Photo by J. Griffis Smith, Texas Highways Magazine Courtesy of Texas Department of Transportation; 138 (L) © Erich Lessing/PhotoEdit, (R) Photograph courtesy of Royal Ontario Museum; 140 The Metropolitan Museum of Art, Purchase, Louisa Eldridge McBurney Gift, 1953 (53.11.6). Photograph © 1996 The Metropolitan Museum of Art; 141 (T, B) © Jerry Jacka; 142 Réunion des Musées Nationaux/Art Resource, NY; 144 © Bowers Museum of Cultural Art/Corbis; 145 Judy Walgren; 146 © 1990/David Hockney Studio; 148 © Seiji Kakizaki/Barbara Nessim Studio; 149 Barbara Nessim Studio; 150 Tim Stilson; 152 © Nan Coulter; 153 (T, C) © Judy Walgren; 154 M.C. Escher's *Symmetry Drawing E58*/©The M. C. Escher Company, Baarn, Holland. All rights reserved.; 157 © Miriam Shapiro; 159 (T) © Janet Fish/Licensed by VAGA, New York, NY, (B) © 1996/Stewart & Stewart; 160 © 2005 Banco de Mexico. Diego Rivera & Frida Kahlo Museums Trust. Av. Cinco de Mayo No. 2, Col. Centro, Del. Cuauhtemoc 06059, Mexico, D.F./Reproduction authorized by the Instituto Nacional de Bellas Artes y Literatura/San Francisco Art Institute; 161 © 2005 Banco de Mexico. Diego Rivera & Frida Kahlo Museums Trust. Av. Cinco de Mayo No. 2, Col. Centro, Del. Cuauhtemoc 06059, Mexico, D.F./Reproduction authorized by the Instituto Nacional de Bellas Artes y Literatura/© Seattle Art Museum/Corbis; 162 © Jean Clottes, Ministere de la Culture/Corbis, (BR) © Giraudon/Art Resource, NY; 163 © Steve Vidler/ SuperStock; 164 © Pierre Colombel/Corbis; 166 (T) © Wernher Krutein/Liaison International/Getty Images, (B) Metropolitan Museum of Art; 167 Art Resource, NY; 168 © Boltin Picture Library; 170 (B) © The Trustees of The British Museum, (T) © Erich Lessing/Art Resource, NY; 171 © Scala/Art Resource, NY; 172 © David Hockney; 174 © Alinari/Art Resource, NY; 175 Metropolitan Museum of Art; 176 © Scala/Art Resource, NY; 178 © Werner Forman/Art Resource, NY; 179 © Ray Manley/SuperStock; 180 (T) The J. Paul Getty Museum, (B) © Adam Woolfitt/ Robert Harding Picture Library Ltd.; 182 © 2005 Banco de Mexico. Diego Rivera & Frida Kahlo Museums Trust. Av. Cinco de Mayo No. 2, Col. Centro, Del. Cuauhtemoc 06059, Mexico, D.F./Reproduction authorized by the Instituto Nacional de Bellas Artes y Literatura/© Seattle Art Museum/ Corbis; 183 (T) © David Ball/Corbis, (C) © Bettmann/ Corbis, (B) © Francis G. Mayer/Corbis; 184 © Phillip Bailey/Corbis; 185 (T) © 2005 Banco de Mexico. Diego Rivera & Frida Kahlo Museums Trust. Av. Cinco de Mayo No.2, Col. Centro, Del. Cuauhtemoc 06059, Mexico, D.F./Reproduction authorized by the Instituto Nacional de Bellas Artes y Literatura/Worcester Art Museum, Worcester, MA, (B) The Roland P. Murdock Collection/Wichita Art Musuem, Wichita, KS; 186 © Francesco Venturi/Kea Publishing Service/Corbis; 187 © D. Dietrich/SuperStock; 188 © Erich Lessing/Art Resource, NY; 190 © Gianni Dagli Orti/Corbis; 191 © Erich Lessing/Art Resource, NY;

192 Réunion des Musées Nationaux/Art Resource, NY; 194 Metropolitan Museum of Art; 195 Metropolitan Museum of Art; 196 International Folk Art Collections at the Museum of International Folk Art, Santa Fe, NM; 198 Metropolitan Museum of Art; 199 © 2004 Wassily Kandinsky/Artists Rights Society (ARS), NY/Staedtische Galerie Im Lenbachhaus, Munich; 200 © 2004 Succession H. Matisse, Paris/Artists Rights Society (ARS), NY/Dallas Museum of Art; 202 Courtesy of Museo del Barrio; 203 The Tervuren Museum/Royal Museum; 204 International Folk Art Collections at the Museum of International Folk Art, Santa Fe, NM; 207 Courtesy of Cecilia de Torres Ltd., New York City; 208 © Erich Lessing/Art Resource, NY; 211 © Scala/Art Resource, NY; 213 (TL) © 2004 Estate of Pablo Picasso/Artist Rights Society (ARS), NY/Art Resource, NY, (BR) © Hulton-Deutsch Collection/Corbis; 214 © Miriam Shapiro; 215 © Kenna Love; 216 Earlie Hudnall; 217 Metropolitan Museum of Art; 218 (Gift of Byron and Eileen Cohen) F85–17/1 A–D/The Nelson-Atkins Museum of Art, Kansas City, MO; 220 (L) Agyptisches Museum und Papyrusammlung/Art Resource, NY, (R) Courtesy/Pace Wildenstein; 221 © Fratelli Alinari/SuperStock; 222 © Ellen Page Wilson/Pace Wildenstein; 224 Metropolitan Museum of Art; 225 © William Wegman; 226 (R, L) Metropolitan Museum of Art; 228 © Musée d'Orsay, Paris/Lauros-Giraudon, Paris/SuperStock; 230 Art Resource, NY; 232 The Minneapolis Institute of Arts; 233 Courtesy of SBC Communications Inc./Courtesy of the Charles E. Burchfield Foundation/Carey Ellis Company; 234 Image © 2003 Board of Trustees, National Gallery of Art, Washington D.C.; 236 © Kenna Love; 237 (C) Donald Woodman/Through the Flower, (B) Photo by Anne Burlock Lawver; 238 Corbis, © Steve Chenn/Corbis; 239 (T) Miriam Shapiro, (B) Courtesy of Archives Niki de Saint-Phalle; 240 The Art Institute of Chicago; 241 The Art Institute of Chicago; 242 © Erich Lessing/Art Resource, NY; 244 Staedtische Galerie Im Lenbachhaus, Munich; 245 Albright-Knox Art Gallery, Buffalo, NY; 246 © 2005 Artists Rights Society (ARS), NY/John Hay Whitney Collection/Image © 2003 Board of Trustees, National Gallery of Art, Washington D.C; 248 © Christie's Images/SuperStock; 249 © Lee N. Smith III; 250 Indianapolis Museum of Art; 252 © Estate of Roy Lichtenstein; 253 Courtesy of SBC Communications Inc./James Rosenquist/Licensed by VAGA, NY/Carey Ellis Company; 254 © Claes Oldenburg & Coosje van Bruggen/Art Resource, NY; 256 © Wendy Barry/Reprinted by permission of Houghton Mifflin Company. All rights reserved.; 257 Illustration from Home of the Brave by Allen Say, © 2002/Reprinted by permission of Houghton Mifflin Company. All rights reserved.; 258 © Carlos Gomez; 260 (BL) Corbis, (BR) © Christopher Felver/Corbis; 261 Réunion des Musées Nationaux/Art Resource, NY; 263 (TL) © 2004 Marisol Escobar/Licensed by VAGA, NY/Art Resource, NY, (B) © Oscar White/Corbis; 264 Purchased with funds from the Coffin Fine Arts Trust; Nathan Emory Coffin Collection of the Des Moines Art Center, 1984.3./Photo by Michael Tropea, Chicago, © 1997 Des Moines Art Center/© 2004 The Georgia O'Keeffe Foundation/Artists Rights Society (ARS), NY; 265 Bequest of Laura Gilpin. P1979.230.4297. © 1979/Amon Carter Museum, Fort Worth, TX; 266 © Kent Twitchell; 267 Courtesy of Social and Public Art Resource Center; 268 © Schalkwijk/Art Resource, NY; 270 Courtesy of Isaiah Zagar, artist/Photo by Barry Halkin; 271 Courtesy of Isaiah Zagar, artist/Photo by Barry Halkin; 272 Daemmrich Photography; 274 PaceWildenstein; 275 © 1998/Sally Griffiths; 276 Robert Rauschenberg Studio; 278 (L) Piet Mondrian. *Avond: The Red Tree,* 1908–1910. Oil on canvas, 27 5/8 by 38 1/8 inches. © 2005 Mondrian/Holtzman Trust. c/o HCR International, Warrenton, VA/Haags Gemeentemuseum, (R) Wadsworth Atheneum, Hartford; 279 *The Hunter,* 1943 tempera, © Andrew Wyeth/The Toledo Museum of Art; 280 Joram Harel Management; 282 Bequest of Laura Gilpin.P1979.230.4297. © 1979/Amon Carter Museum, Fort Worth, TX; 283 (T) © Bettmann/Corbis, (B) © John Warden/SuperStock; 284 (B) © Richard Cummins/Corbis, (C) © Jerry Driendl/Getty Images; 285 (T) © Fisk University/© 2004 The Georgia O'Keeffe Foundation/Artists Rights Society (ARS), NY, (B) © Geogia O'Keeffe Museum, Santa Fe/Art Resource, NY. © 2004 The Georgia O'Keeffe Foundation/Artists Rights Society (ARS), NY; 286 University of Pennsylvania Museum (Neg# T4–614)/University of Pennsylvania Museum of Archaeology & Anthropology; 287 Courtesy of Cecilia de Torres Ltd., New York City; 288 © Gunter Marx/Corbis; 290 (T) © National Museum of Anthropology, Mexico City/Explorer, Paris/SuperStock, (B) © Boltin Picture Library; 291 International Folk Art Collections at the Museum of International Folk Art, Santa Fe, NM; 292 Barrett Kendall Publishing; 294 Norman Rockwell Family Trust; 295 Cartoon Bank (Division of New Yorker Magazine); 296 Courtesy of Linda Jones Enterprises/Warner Bros.; 298 WGBH in Boston; 299 (T, TC, BC, B) Getty Images; 300 Photo by Jonathan Kantor/Harri Koskinen/Friends of Industry, Ltd.; 302 (L) © National Museum of American Art, Washington, D.C/Art Resource, NY, (R) Adrian Avram; 303 Michelle Breiner; 304 School of Visual Arts; 306 Courtesy Ellen Poon; 307 *Star Wars: Episode I—The Phantom Menace* © 1999 Lucasfilm Ltd. All rights reserved. Used under authorization. Unauthorized duplication is a violation of applicable law./Courtesy of Lucasfilm, Ltd.; 308 Smithsonian American Art Museum, Washington, DC/Art Resource, NY; 310 (BR) © Alan Ginsberg/Corbis, (BC) © Richard Schulman/Corbis; 311 © Christie's Images/Corbis; 313 (TL) Wadsworth Atheneum, Hartford, (BR) Photograph by Niki Ekstrom, © Estate of Romare Bearden/Licensed by VAGA, New York, NY.

End Matter:

314 (CL) Courtesy Freer Gallery of Art/Smithsonian Institution, Washington, DC, (BR) Courtesy of SBC Communications Inc./Carey Ellis Company, (TR)14.130.14, Greek, Attic, *Krater,* ca. 750–700 B.C.; Geometric, Attributed to the Hirschfeld Workshop, Terracotta; H.42 5/8 in. (108.25 cm), Side A: The Metropolitan Museum of Art, Rogers Fund, 1914 (14.130.14) Photograph © 1996/Metropolitan Museum of Art; 315 (CL) National Museum of Women in the Arts, (BL) Alfred Stieglitz Collection, 1950. (50.236.2). Photograph © 1997 The Metropolitan Museum of Art. © 2004 The Georgia O'Keeffe Foundation/Artists Rights Society (ARS), NY, (TR) Courtesy Bernice Steinbaum Gallery, Miami, FL, (BR) Courtesy of Holly Hughes; 316 (CL) Courtesy Dr. Peter T. Furst, (T) Courtesy Brewster Arts Ltd. © 1999 Leonora Carrington/Artists Rights Society (ARS), NY/Brewster Arts Ltd., (B) DDB Stock Photography; 317 (TL) M. C. Escher's *Symmetry Drawing E66*/©The M. C. Escher Company, Baarn, Holland. All rights reserved., (BL) AC1999.134.1/*Two of a Kind,* 1986 by Carlos Almaraz/© The Carlos Almaraz Estate/Photograph © 2003 Museum Associates/Gift of Charles Anthony Seiniger/Los Angeles County Museum of Art, (TR) Juane Quick-to-See Smith.